LIFE
It's About Time

by Gary Polizzotto

Copyright © 2008 by Gary Polizzotto

ISBN 0-7414-4883-1

Published by:

INFINITY
PUBLISHING.COM

1094 New DeHaven Street, Suite 100
West Conshohocken, PA 19428-2713
Info@buybooksontheweb.com
www.buybooksontheweb.com
Toll-free (877) BUY BOOK
Local Phone (610) 941-9999
Fax (610) 941-9959

∞

Printed in the United States of America

Published September 2009

"**F**inally! A book with only a little bit of murder yet still grabs your attention! Better than a rising moon, we hoodled, howled and then chased each other around the house. It has changed our lives forever. We give it Four Pawz up!"
Hershey & Sophie ~ *The Daisy Hill Puppy Farm Gazette*

Cover Photo: While on a solo hike through the rock hoodoos of Arches National Park in 1985, I used the camera self-timer to capture this remarkably goofy picture on the 4th attempt. I fell the other 3 times.

Revised Edition 9/2009
Formerly titled: The Hands On Life ~ and ~ It's About Time
Other publications by the author: Buy a lot of these and check back next year.

The Backward

Part 1: The Boy, the Man & The Whisper

The Midward

Part 2: It's About Time

The Forward & Post Script

The Backward

~~~~~~~

"Never judge a book by it's cover." In fact, don't even think about it. Later on you'll understand a lot more about rocks, body braces and hanging on by your fingertips. OK, now that we've got that out of the way, have you ever read a book you just couldn't put down? Well, as you're actually holding two books, we're off to a remarkably good start. Now, if you think it takes a certain degree of vanity to write about one's life and expect others to be interested in it, I totally agree. I mean, how obnoxious is that? But relax, this is not another Biography. Actually, Part I is an *Experiography* - and although I just made that up, it works. It also gets us nicely to Part II.

The truth is I've been badgered for years by folks to do this. So while you can treasure it or trash it, all of what you are about to read (except for just a few tiny details) actually happened as written. Including the ghost. And if Oprah wants me to do a polygraph, wire me up.

As you know, every decision in life has a consequence. Life is also as interesting and rewarding as you make it. So, Part I covers some quite interesting cause and effects that effectively caused me to become who I am now. And as you'll see, many times good judgment is the result of previous bad judgment and while sometimes the sand in the oyster makes a pearl, other times it's just sand in your shorts. So play along and pretend you're me as we suffer profoundly absurd dilemmas and go around the next bend in search of the good fruit. In short, I'll do all the hard work and you get the benefit of the lessons.

All from the safety of your own life. How good is that?

Part I is followed by Part II, and yes I know that's not politically correct, but it's still a workable concept. Anyway, here you'll find some views on a few aspects of life that at first glance, don't seem to warrant a deeper look. But in reality, they are often *so* obvious, few stop to think about how greatly they really do affect our lives – and on an everyday basis.

These thoughts are the results of my prior experiences and focus on "Life-*Time*" and relationships, and most importantly, how we "spend" that time in relationships. Why? Because we only get to use *any* moment of time just once.

Then it's gone. Forever.

So that's where *you* get to consider the consequences of *your* decisions and the wisdom of how you spend your Life-*Time*. And I get to watch from the safety of *my* life.

How good is that...for me?

I'll also reveal my "Better Living Through Chemistry" plan – and not only between two people, but my new Basic Food Group Pyramid of Anti-inflammatories, Aspirin, Antacids and Ambien. Because of this, I've not missed a day of work from sickness and have been the same weight for over 30 years. Maybe it's also why my eyes changed color at 54?

Anyhow, this is my ode to what I believe are the 3 major phases of life: *Learning, Understanding* and *Application*. As you'll see, several times my entire life was altered by a single sentence, thought or action. Maybe you'll find one in here for you, too. If you don't, but get a grin now and then, well, that's OK too and you may even find a little reprieve from a world getting more bizarre by the moment. Either way you win.

Perhaps you'll also discover the same truth I did:

"While the mind may bend to an ultimatum, the heart never does."

So...let's get started. We've got a lot of ground to cover and a lot of strange and truly wonderful people to meet on quite a few "roads less traveled". And I discovered a "road" can be a boat, plane, river, person, elephant, rope or a dusty narrow trail on the edge of a cliff. By the way, some people will be glad (or offended) they are here and others, that they aren't. Sorry. Also, only a feeble attempt has been made to protect the innocent or be politically correct in any way.

I'd say I'm sorry about that too, but, well...maybe not. Also, if you come across a "Huh", the word inflection is important. It's not a "Huh?" or a "Huh!", but the quiet contemplative rock back on your heels I just learned something about my life sorta "Huh".

It's the next step after a "Hmmm."

And about that title: It's a diabolical double entendre. Maybe it means sometimes we need a gentle whisper It's About Time we start living our life.

Or...it can be that Life is made up of, and all about, Time.

Choose one. Or both. Just don't sit there.

Except for Iglou and Gus, this book is dedicated to no one
in particular ~ but a lot of really great folks in general
who have given me some of their Life-*Time.*
Thanks. I mean it.

To the reader, I hope you laugh and cry,
but not so hard you injure yourself ~
And more than anything…
I wish you a really fine Life!

Unless you have other plans.

Gus

Part I

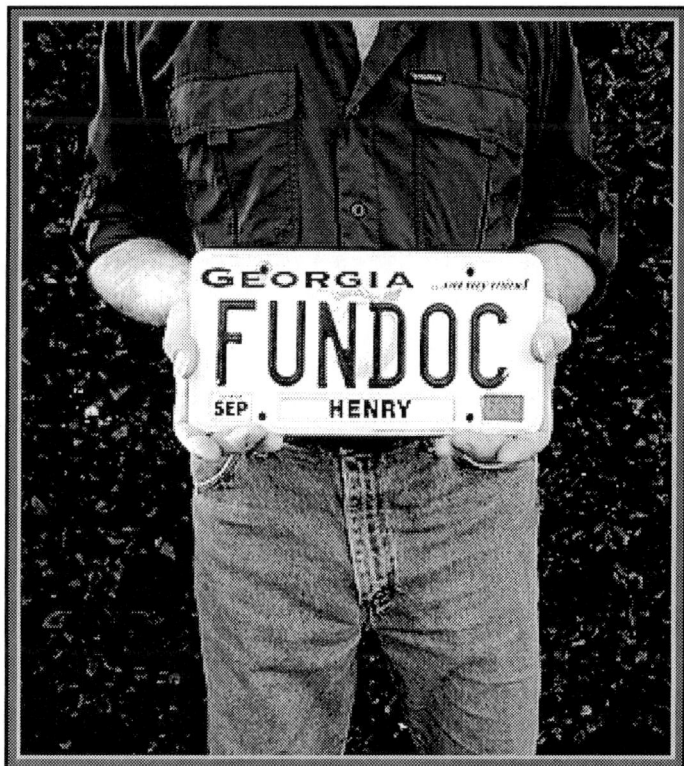

The Boy, the Man
&
The Whisper

Heart Stopping News

~~~~~~~

Emory Hospital cardiac emergency room # 3: July 2000. The doctor poised the needle before the IV port that had been jammed into the back of my hand.

Him: "This injection will stop your heart. Hopefully it will restart."

Me: "Do what? What do you mean *hopefully*?!"

~~~

Flashback: My internist once told me about being on teaching rounds with five other residents and three cardiologists. While they were examining a man who was hooked up to an EKG - and with a "crash-cart" right there in the room – the patient went into cardiac arrest. You know, Code Blue.

He died in front of all eight doctors.

And he was in a hospital.

~~~

Flashnow: "Stop my heart? But I have the *entire* rest of my life ahead of me!" (Which, considering the circumstances, I realized could just as easily be 3 minutes or 30 years.)

Oh, OK. Go ahead and stop it.

After all, I am in a hospital.

But I need to tell ya', I really wasn't *planning* on this today.

I mean, there is that.

Huh.

Big Hands, Big Feet and Ugly

~~~~~~~~~

S ee, you're already in chapter 2! Is this good or what? You're also now in suburban N.J. circa 1950's. Hi. My name is Gary and to the best of my memory, I started life as a child after giving Louise (my soon to be Mom) about 25 minutes to get to the hospital, lie down, push and scream loudly. Upon my arrival, I was a nice shade of lemon yellow due to jaundice and Iggy (my newly minted father) was certain they gave him a yellow Lab puppy to take home. The situation got significantly worse when the doctor told them prophetically

"He's going to have big hands, big feet and be ugly."

As I was also supposed to be a girl named Joanne, and in a hurried act of desperation, they named me Gary after the T.V. host, Gary Moore. At first I really hated the name but because perception is reality, I convinced myself it meant "Fearsome warrior with the big spear who slays something really bad". After that, I was fine. Besides, it's better than Horace or Dilbert. And there's also that thing about guys with big feet, which may, or may not, be true. Anyway, Gary 1.0 had been downloaded.

I can clearly remember two things about my early years: being bored and being disappointed. The doctor's solution for the boredom was a kid's tranquilizer called "mellow yellow" which turned me into a tiny zombie. Fortunately, my mother quickly discovered you don't treat boredom by making a kid catatonic, you challenge his brain instead. So at the tender age of 5 and being as fascinated with dinosaurs as any kid could get (and what little ladimus doesn't want a pet T-Rex?), she bought me a college textbook on paleontology - which I read out loud at every possible opportunity. This quickly caused them to decide the tranquilizer was actually the better choice…at least for them. I also recall being a "sensitive" little guy who was fascinated by things like the kaleidoscopic iridescence of oil on a pool of water or being soothed by the sigh of the winter night wind through pine boughs. Over time these all coalesced into the curious mind of a young boy who wanted to discover and observe "life" with a deep and often restless desire to see what's around the next bend.

For better or worse, these traits are with me to this day.

As I recall, my first foray into observing human behavior was when I locked Archie, our upstairs renter, in the basement coal bin and then went outside to make faces at him through the little window. For about 3 hours. For some odd reason, I just couldn't get him to think it was as funny as I did. After his wife noticed he was 2 hours late for dinner, my Mom, who had the ears of a bat (and could hear well too), heard him banging on the basement ceiling and finally let him out. The only way you could tell how he spent the afternoon was by the black coal dust around his nostrils. To this day I'm certain this was entirely unrelated to his later life diagnosis of Black Lung Disease.

I did other experiments in the basement too. During the phase when I had a big curiosity about spiders, I got a huge spool of really strong black thread and created a web from floor to ceiling and wall to wall. A large, dark web that lurked silently in the shadows of the basement just like any reasonably competent and malevolent spider is supposed to make. When I was finished, I turned out the lights and went to school.

For some childish reason, I forgot to tell my mother about this. Anyway, she made it about half way to the washing machine carrying her basket full of clothes when she became inextricably entangled in my novel scientific experiment which, in a moment of sudden misplaced horror, she thought *may* have actually been made by a giant spider.

If memory serves me correct, I heard the scream in my 2nd grade class clear across the street. And that was in the winter with the windows closed. From this I learned to always inform my parents of any home renovations and upgrades I performed. This was the school, by the way, that wanted to convert me from a natural left hander to a more convenient and terribly bourgeois right hander. My Mom, bless her heart, said

"He's fine just the way he is so leave him alone thank you."
Of course, that was because both she and my brother were also left handed. Dad was the only weird one.

To my Mom's credit, she instilled early in me the concept of "Don't be afraid to be an individual and think on your own." As you'll see, I had little problem taking this to heart in a big way. But she may have regretted this maxim because by the time I was 15, she began saying – or actually, pleading

"Why can't you be like everybody else?!"

3

But it was too late. I had already learned about "The Sheeple"...people acting like sheep...and had made a life long decision that pleasantly plagues me 'til today.

However, not only did my mother scream during those early years, but so did I. My next – and seriously painful - lesson occurred while attempting to study the Laws of Physics. At that time I reasoned if I stood before my hip high open dresser drawer stark naked after my bath, I could quickly grab my pajamas from the drawer while simultaneously bumping it closed with my hips.

In theory, this was doable.

In reality, a wayward near and dear body part swung in a graceful arc and came to rest over the lip of the drawer as it was closing. This ultimately prevented the drawer from *fully* closing along its forceful path, which of course, proved that two objects cannot occupy the same space at the same time. And as objects in motion also tend to stay in motion and as I was occupying a place I shouldn't have, the drawer clearly won this round.

So yes, I screamed. I also went to bed with a band-aid (large, of course) on a near decapitation and I still fear open drawers when naked. (Yes, I know someone out there is thinking "Mabel, I just don't believe I'da said that." But I did – and you're the *only* one I've told – so keep it to yourself, OK?)

Ballistics was next on my agenda to investigate because like every boy, my deepest and most heartfelt desire was for a BB gun. Well, somehow, someway and over my mother's objections (and apparently, knowledge), I procured a Daisy air rifle. I then did the original out-takes of the movie "A Christmas Story" when this little baby accidentally spit a BB straight across my bedroom and right smack into the middle of my 6 foot long dresser mirror. In doing so, it created one of the prettiest little "star" patterns I had ever seen, and one that was just the right size to nicely hide with a lovely yellow Chiquita banana sticker.

This looked completely normal and quite attractive to me. However, upon her arrival home, my Mom immediately disagreed with this aesthetic improvement and peeled it off. Unfortunately, she liked the underlying star even less. This culminated in one of those "ivory soap in the mouth standing in the corner" moments for lying to her.

I learned a lot from these two events: Actions have consequences and eating soap gives you diarrhea.

From ballistics, it was a short and happy hop into model rockets - which Mom quickly made me give up after I nearly set the neighbor's roof on fire. (Watch out Homer Hickam, Jr.)

But Louise was not entirely without her little foibles. When we would have company, she would do things like put a piece of rubber Swiss cheese in your sandwich or hide a rubber donut in amongst the others and watch you dunk it in your coffee and try to politely munch on it. Or she would use a double sided suction cup between your coffee cup and saucer. Do you think she ever got into any trouble? Uh-huh.

And nobody ever made her eat soap.

Perhaps because my Mom always wanted a daughter, she dressed me up as a little girl one Halloween. But I think the real reason may have been due to the prior year when my brother made me into a werewolf by sticking wig hair to my face with model airplane glue. All was well until the removal phase which pulled off the fake hair along with the first 11 layers of my real skin. I quickly concluded that 7 year olds really didn't need face lifts and my mother promised not to glue anything to me.

Anyway, as I was flouncing back to my house in my skirt in the dark, I neglected to see a piece of raised sidewalk, hooked my toe on it and fell forward, smashing my little hard semi-Sicilian head on a concrete wall. Fortunately, the wall remained undamaged and I had just enough wits to get up and make it two houses further to our front stairs, where I went lights out.

When I came to, I was in our brightly lit kitchen in my little red polka-dot dress, lace socks and Mary Jane shoes. I also had a headache and a misshapen head. My Mom was on the phone with the doctor who said he forgot to add "clumsy" to "big hands, big feet and ugly." Now, you gotta understand, at that moment I had a good case of amnesia but it only spanned the last hour or two. What I *did* remember was that I was a boy.

But the red fingernail polish, lipstick *and boobs* I saw in the mirror were creating a painful panic in my brain and it took a lot of motherly love and talk to convince me all was well with Gary's little world. Not to mention his recently concussed brain which warned it was not worth the risk of being a girl. Never mind some 50 years later I still barely understand them.

5

Perhaps to keep me from tripping again, and for a new perspective on life, I then took to walking on my hands almost all the time. Actually, for the next 3 years. Through the house, up stairs, down stairs, you name it. When new folks came to the house, we said hello to each other's feet.

My Mom, though somewhat perplexed by this behavior, found it a cost saving measure as she didn't have to buy me so many of the expensive but really clunky looking shoes she made me wear. I found it just as agreeable that I didn't have to wear them. But in credit to her foot foresight, to this day a tumultuous half century later, I still have aesthetically perfect feet.

Because our house sat on a hill, its long narrow driveway exited blindly amongst parked cars. Sometimes, when I needed to bike up the street, I would pedal as fast as possible down the steep driveway and shoot out into the road. Mom, as expected, frowned upon this clever use of kinetic energy and was worried someday I'd become road pizza. This was also before the law made kids wear helmets everywhere, even on the toilet.

One day, I needed to get to EC's house in a hurry so I pedaled down the driveway in a fevered frenzy and shot out into the street like a pint sized human cannon ball. As I turned uphill, something caught my attention and I glanced upward just in time to see a strafing pigeon from the nearby schoolyard launch a large liquidly load in my eye.

Calamitously, this pretty well diverted my attention from the car I immediately had a head-on with causing me to arc up over his hood and leave a fresh face poo print on his windshield.

I limped back home with my badly mangled bicycle with the square front tire thinking maybe, *just maybe*, my Mom was right about this too.

It's been rumored these head shots explains a lot about me.

Around this time, my Mom's temper began to get shorter and she was having severe headaches. Eventually she was diagnosed with EEEV (Eastern Equine Encephalitis) which was a potentially lethal virus. To this date, at 90 years old, a mosquito bite over 50 years ago continues to give her double vision. From that I learned sometimes the smallest events – even forgotten ones - can really screw things up.

And screw them up for a long, long time.

6

The Tender Years of Bonding & Evening Wear

~~~~~~~

The early disappointment I mentioned was at several levels and often with those I should have been able to look up to. Literally – such as with Larry, my 8 year older brother who was almost like family to me. When my mother would tell him to take me out to play, he'd put me in a stroller and roll me one-half block to the big 4 lane avenue…and leave me there while he went off with his friends for a couple of hours. I guess this was OK in those days as nobody really wanted to kidnap a yellow kid. Way too hard to hide. Anyway, I got to see cars. Lotsa cars at the tender age of two or so.

This, of course, explains my fascination with them today. It also explains why I know immediately if a Chevy has bad engine valve stem seals just by the smell. The next lesson of disappointment down the age road a bit, was with my peers. Little did I realize that kid's often said things they didn't mean and they didn't exactly follow through on their word. (Flash: neither do adults – or politicians.) So, I learned to depend mostly on me and I played with myself a lot. That last notion probably could have been better worded, but you know what I mean.

This all occurred whilst I sprouted in a typical post-war neighborhood of middle class homes, none of which were there before they built them. It was of mixed ethnicity and men were men who smoked and women were mostly stay-at-home moms who didn't smoke. (Note: A "stay at home mom" was a respectable job title back then.) We lived in a 3 story model where the second floor was rented to my uncle and his short term wife and the third floor to my grandparents. (We figured they needed the extra exercise.) Directly across the street was the grammar school, so I couldn't use commute time as an excuse for being late to class. That school taught me a few early lessons.

In 5th grade I had a friend who looked, dressed and acted different from the other kids. In hindsight, he may have had a learning disorder as a result of a genetic problem, but because he was so timid and looked so "delicate", the other kids made him a constant target of their taunts and physical abuse. I can clearly recall one day when I felt I was being moved outside the "accepted" social circle of the other kids because he was my friend. So, in an attempt to show them I could dish it out as good as they did, I joined the verbal cruelty knowing full well it was the wrong thing to do.

I will never forget the look of confused innocence and fear on his face at my betrayal. It was a knife in my heart and I could not believe I had let myself do this to a blameless person who did not ask for his infirmities. At that moment I went from predator to protector where I remain today.

The 'hood was very cool. It was filled with trees that were large for their size. It had nooks and crannies for kids to meet in and lots of secret shortcuts. Backyards were full of sun-soaked fresh smelling laundry swaying in the breeze. Time was slow and plentiful and Christmas was years away. We also actually had porches on the front of the house (as opposed to the fenced-decked-isolated backyard compounds we now have) and because few owned a T.V., almost every evening after dinner, folks would sit on their porch and holler out to one another across the street, next door or to people walking by and just *talk* with them.

What a concept.

In short, we all knew each other and I could walk into almost any house on the street and the people who lived there knew the people where I lived. It was like, well, having actual real neighbors. And this was good because it gave accountability to everyone, especially the kids, as there were many adult eyeballs watching our every move. Thank you folks. I mean that. You gave me many needed guardrails.

Up and down the street were my friends and they were as diverse a group as you could imagine. We had Germans, Italians, Irish, Polish, Latvians, Greeks and a lot of mutts, some of which had all four legs. You name it, they were there.

Down the street was Johnny who became one of my dearest friends and now lives thousands of miles away. He still manages to find me every few years via email, snail mail or phone just to know I am alive and well. But growing up, Johnny had it rougher than most. In a time when divorce was quite rare, Johnny's parents had taken that step primarily due, as I recall, to the father's drinking a special mix of rum and coke without the coke.

But I kinda liked his Dad because when he had a few, he'd let us peek a bit over the forbidden guardrails. His Mom was a charter member of DAM (Mothers Against Dyslexia) and while the whole situation might have been branded "dysfunctional" by today's PC standards, they still managed to keep the "fun" in the word and the friend in friendship. In doing so, his Mom always made the neighborhood teenagers feel welcome in their home and with time, it became the place to hang out for all of us as we each struggled with the angst of the painfully poignant personal problems of puberty's prickly path. (Phew!)

Around this time we also entered our own "digital" age. This meant giving someone the middle finger.

Before I ever really met Johnny, I was led to believe he was the bully of the neighborhood. One day in 1962, Teddy, the chubby and ruddy faced Greek kid, came to me in tears and said Johnny was picking on him and what was *I* going to do about it? Well, frankly, I wasn't aware I *needed* to do anything about it. But recalling my new "protector" status that thought occurred 2 hours after I had marched down the street and into Johnny's back yard where we commenced to beat the snot out of each other. (Don't worry. Kids have an endless supply of snot.) We then shook hands and our life long friendship began right then and there. And we did this with no parental intervention, no lawyers or sensitivity training about different ethnic groups. Just kids doing what kids are supposed to do. Be kids.

Here's an irony. In 1966 while in the middle of Thanksgiving Day dinner, Johnny calls me and says *he* needs help with a bully. Seems he was dating the girlfriend of the neighboring town's own bad boy who, along with 3 of his friends, discovered Johnny with her in a soda fountain store (yep - we had them back then.) They then proceeded to corner Johnny and not let him or his blonde date leave. Why he called me is unknown, but must have had something to do with all that backyard snot in 1962.

At my house, I pulled my brother aside and asked him if he'd drive me the 5 miles to the store in Glen Ridge (where Tom Cruise went to high school…whoopee) so we could extricate my bud from his dilemma. When we got there, we went in the store, past the four bad guys and ushered Johnny and the girl outside.

9

What I didn't know, is that we were followed. Out in front of the store, I was trying to get John and Kathy in the car when she, with a large degree of urgency, shouted "Gary!!"

I turned to look at her and found my face stopping a nicely placed sucker punch from the newly met bully. For him, this had an unexpected and undesired effect as I was suddenly introduced at a whole new level to the male hormone testosterone. This was then instantly mixed with about 2 quarts of adrenaline.

This handy chemical cocktail completely suppresses pain and directs you to either flee...or terminate the opponent. I chose termination. Three seconds later the score was 1 down, 3 to go and I observed the 3 backing away from the maniac who now faced them and felt no pain. Well, that was another lesson learned: The best defense really is a strong offense. And there was no parental intervention, no lawyers, no sensitivity training and no one ate lead paint off woodwork for dessert. Just kids doing what kids are supposed to do. Be kids. Eventually, I became friends with that bully too. So, I started to see a pattern here which included Sister Teresa, whom you'll meet shortly.

My next adventure with Johnny occurred one night when I was a clear thinking 18 year old and had a car. I walked down to his house and said "Hey, let's drive to the Pocono mountains in Pennsylvania. I know this river we can put my new 2 man raft on and see where it goes!" Johnny was all for that, so by 11:00 at night, we were on our way.

About 2:00 A.M. we were at the river bank and it was still snowing heavily. (Did I mention it was snowing?) This river sort of cut through the town and then carved it's way into the woods for parts unknown which is where I thought we'd go see. You know, the Huck Finn what's around the bend Moon River stuff. *(I've always wanted to know what's around the bend.)* And who needs a moon when you have snow? So, we inflated the cheap little plastic raft (2 man *only* if you were both double amputees), got in and pushed off. However, in all the excitement of the anticipated voyage, we neglected to bring any life jackets. That I didn't own any may have been a factor, but when big adventure awaits, it's important not to get hung up on extraneous details.

Anyway, we were on the river for about, oh, maybe 2 minutes when we both heard a rather loud booming looming in the densely snow splattered darkness ahead.

After going over the 12 foot waterfall - which completely shredded the raft – we then bodily got churned over and over in the recirculating outwash at the bottom. When I bobbed to the surface, I immediately mourned the loss of my new black cowboy hat, but it didn't seem worth the icy swim to retrieve it. And because the shock of the freezing water made it almost impossible to breathe, it made that a good decision. Besides, black hats are hard to find in black water in the dark. Finding Johnny was another matter as he was being quickly taken downstream and his cries were fading in the darkness. But only dead fish go with the flow and we weren't dead...yet. So before our chitlins were frozen solid, we got ourselves to the very steep bank and crawled up it in the snow, breathless and exhausted.

By now our core temperature was rapidly approaching something close to liquid nitrogen and we needed to quickly get into dry clothes. Oops. Another forgotten detail. So what were we to do? Well, after driving into town, we found an all night Laundromat brightly lit by at least 475 fluorescent lights. So in we went at about 3 A.M. Our next dilemma, since we had no extra clothes, was what to do when we put our wet stuff in the dryer besides standing there shivering stark naked?

Fortunately for us, some kind lady was considerate enough to leave her unmentionables going round and round in a dryer. And, well...*they* were almost dry. So, after I chose an ensemble of a knee length lavender teddy coordinated with pink fluffy slippers, I plunked my near frozen butt on the warm dryer while observing Johnny pick out his evening wear.

The fact the dryers faced the front glass wall of the store which was lit up like a supernova made it that much easier for us to be clearly seen in our feminine best when the local police pulled up. After spending way too long shining his headlights, flashlight and spotlights on us (like we really needed more light) and staring from the comfort - and safety - of his cruiser, I got up and went outside in the snow to meet him in my bunny slippers. After a moment, he hesitatingly came inside, hand close to his gun, to meet the new and colorful town folk. When we explained our situation, he told us to take the clothes off, return them to their rightful owner (and dryer), get dressed and get the hell out of town because "We don't need your kind."

Well, I complied and quickly dropped off my little nightie to the floor which made his jaw drop nearly the same distance.

(Not for *that* reason…although ice water does change a guy's appearance somewhat to the pitiful end of the spectrum.) No, what he saw were my legs. You see, that night I wore my brand new dark blue jeans. When they got wet for the first time, they transferred their blue-black dye to my legs, turning them a rather ghastly mottled shade of dark blue. But to his untrained eye, he thought I was going severely cyanotic and hypothermic. (Ironically, this was exactly what I was trying to prevent by being there in the first place.)

However, he was not about to hold me for warmth and I wasn't at all interested in mouth to mouth so back we went into our wet clothes. To make sure we were not a future problem for him, the cop escorted us out of town. Anyway, the adventure was over, we were still alive and we drove home in the driving snow. This event put future trip planning in a whole new light.

Folks, listen, I'm not smart enough to make this stuff up.

At the other end of my home street was ole' EC, who was also one of my best friends. EC's picture can be found in some dictionaries under "bad luck". One day, he and I were catching up on our botany studies and while trying to determine the exact odor of a slippery silver pussy willow bud, he squeezed it a bit too hard and it shot up his nose like a scalded cherry pit.

Attempts at retrieving it by smacking him on the back of his head were fruitless. It did, however, add a headache to his problem.

So, off to the emergency room we went, where they plucked it from the part of his sinuses that were in a different zip code. After returning home, we decided to move our studies from the plant to animal kingdom and see if we could capture bees in glass jars. EC went one way around the house, I another.

A few moments later I heard an "Ooof!", the sound of breaking glass and a howl in that order. When I found EC, he was laying on the ground where he tripped with the glass jar which broke and lanced open his hand which was bleeding a cheerful bright red. This was after he actually did catch a bee. The bee, now gleeful at his liberation, expressed his appreciation by stinging EC on his other hand. After leaving the emergency room for the 2nd time that day where EC was stitched and injected, his mother forbade me to be around her son anymore.

At least for the next 24 hours.

The Formative Years

~~~~~~~~

Across the street from us lived Joe, a city detective whom we all called Dick Tracy because he always seemed to "be onto something big" and knew things mere mortals didn't. Somehow Joe convinced my parents I was approaching the "coming to manhood" age (14) and should be taught to hunt - probably because he couldn't get anyone else to go with him. Amazingly, I then became the proud owner of a 12 gauge shotgun. Now this is power! Even I respect me! But as a confused kid, what's right? Bearing arms, arming bears?

Anyway, to mold, meld and mature my manhoodedness (did you catch all those m's?) Joe took me hunting at 3:00 A.M. After a long and anxious ride out to the country, we arrived at his chosen venue while it was still dark and the forest was deeply shrouded in thick fog. He walked in. I followed...tentatively.

Quite some ways into the woods with me having no idea where I was, he told me "You stay here." and he quickly disappeared into the murky darkness. Man-boy was all alone. I sat down with my back to a tree and waited. But for what? I wasn't really sure. I think we were here for deer, but could I really pull the trigger on such a beautiful and innocent creature? Well, thankfully, that's a decision I never had to make.

After about 20 minutes, the place was really starting to creep me out. The heavy silence was cloaked in a damp earth smell and I was cold and couldn't see more than 15 feet in the gloomy dense fog. Without any warning, and somewhere immediately behind and to the left of me - and *way* too close for any level of comfort, came the heart stopping piercing scream of a woman being strangled. This other worldly wail made every hair on my body stand straight up and salute while I stood up, threw the gun and ran. I also peed in my pants which I don't think was supposed to be part of the manhood thingy ritual. And I ran for I don't know how long or far, but Joe finally heard me yelling in the woods and discovered where I was.

As it was now getting light and the fog was lifting, we went back to find my gun and, I was certain, the dead woman. After finding one but not the other, we headed out. While feeling really embarrassed and very unmanly, we came across a little chipchomper sitting on a stump and Joe, believing I needed *some* display of testosterone, kept goading me to shoot it. To this day it makes me sick to my stomach that I listened to him. Fortunately, the poor creature was instantly vaporized by the 12 gauge which also deservedly knocked me on my a-double-s. I went home, immediately sold the gun and have never fired at another living creature since that day. I also will not tolerate animal abuse of any type. (I can't even watch Bambi…)

And, oh, the horrific shriek I heard? Seems a very large Bobcat had moved into that section of the woods. A very *big* cat that literally scared the pee right outta me…and taught me nature does quite fine without my involvement, thank you. You stay out of my living room, I stay out of yours and Mr. Tracy was no longer the authority I thought he was.

~~~~~~~

But perhaps my first real life lesson about "questioning authority" occurred one day while in catechism school when the kid next to me was talking behind the nun's back. She turned around and said "Gary, please stop talking." From my point of view, it wasn't even worth debating. So she went back to the board and the kid went back to talking. She turned around again, glared at me over her glasses with arms akimbo and then came over to me. While slapping the ruler in her hand, she said

"I thought I told you to stop talking?"

At this point, I needed to defend my honor so I told her,

"Sister Teresa, it wasn't me talking." She then replied

"Are you calling me a liar?" to which I said

"No, but you're calling me one and I don't appreciate it."

The next thing that happened was she slapped me with her other hand…dumb me, I hadn't seen that coming. And the very next thing after that was me slapping her back, which she *definitely* didn't see coming. I was then immediately taken by the ear to see Sister Superior Magnus Cum Laude (SSMCL) from The Church of the Sacred Heart & Swollen Prostate.

Yes, it was she, sitting behind the immense wooden desk with the triple duty starched cervical orthopedic collar. This was a woman who actually would be pretty good looking if she weren't so unattractive. When my Mom came to pick me up, the SSMCL asked me if I was sorry and would I do that again. My answer was no and yes in that order. And my Mom agreed.

As the years went by, my grandparents seemed to be getting older which apparently happens to a lot of us. My Grandmother's husband's wife, bless her heart, did her own science experiments like instead of using white vinegar on her salad, tried bleach, which gave her clear lettuce. She then used insect spray on her hair, instead of Aqua-net. This was more successful as her head was bug free for weeks. My Grandfather was a man of stern Old World dignity who I spent a lot of time with and every evening after dinner, we would walk to the candy store to get the newspaper. On the way back, we would sit on the school lawn for a spell and he would just talk to me like I was a little man and teach me things. I realized from these talks and things my Mom later told me about him, that *he believed in me.* At the time, I did not know the importance of that for a little boy.

Actually, he was quite a brilliant guy who had worked with Thomas Edison in the next town over and had made the first homebuilt radio in our area. He also built a little hothouse in the backyard and showed me how to plant and nurture living things. I still remember running home after school every day for the delicious heady scent of the warm moist earth and the thrill of seeing the little sprouts poking their heads up through the soil. Even then there was something magical about "life" to me.

And, as you'll see later on, there still is.

Eventually, Grandpa had a stroke. But he wasn't finished amazing us. When they brought him home from the hospital, he lay in bed and asked for a small chalkboard on which he drew about 12 lines. He then told us that was how many days he had left to live and proceeded to cross out one line each day. The last line was, as he predicted, his last day. I'll never know if this was an example of prophecy or a determined demonstration of the human will.

My Dad was just as amazing especially given his lack of formal education and size which was about 5' 7" and 145 lbs. (Remember those slight numbers. They're important later on.) His name was Ignazio or Iggy for short. (If you knew him well, you could call him Ig. If you knew both my parents *really* well, you could join Ig + Lou and save some time by calling them Iglou.) Anyway, it seems someone neglected to tell him about the things he couldn't or shouldn't be able to do given his minimal education. So he just went ahead and did them.

15

Of course, being 100% Sicilian helped immensely in the thick head department, but it served him well. (Apparently, these were also very stubborn genes as his grandfather was 104 and his mother over 100 when they passed away.) As he had to leave school somewhere around the 6th grade to help support his family, he found himself doing a variety of jobs including blacksmithing and working on the railroad after leaving for 12 months on a one week motorcycle trip.

After being married at 27, my father volunteered for the Navy in the middle of WW2. That generation intuitively knew freedom wasn't free and he was willing to do what he could to protect those he loved and his country. He eventually wound up on the aircraft carrier USS Cowpens where he became an aviation mechanic arriving at Pearl Harbor right after the attack. At that time, our supply of aircraft had been so decimated, we were at a distinct disadvantage. To help counter this in his own original way, he combined leftover parts from the damaged planes to create "new" fighter aircraft. This earned him a personal commendation from Fleet Admiral "Bull" Halsey.

I will always believe these folks truly were the "Greatest Generation" this country has ever seen and by fighting for the U.S., they were fighting for US.

Ignazio Polizzotto United States Navy

My brother made a like sacrifice when he joined the Navy working helicopter air-sea rescue on the most dangerous place on the planet: the deck of an aircraft carrier. He was on the nuclear carrier Enterprise during the Cuban missile blockade. It was there he watched an aircraft landing arresting cable snap in two and snake-whip its way across the deck and cut a crewman in half. It was there he saw another crewman get sucked into a jet intake as the pilot was spooling up the engine. It was there while in the middle of an attempted sea rescue of a pilot whose jet ran off the carrier, he watched him drown, trapped in the cockpit. And even though he himself swallowed far too much jet fuel attempting the rescue, he never got over "losing" that man. (In Memphis, he also got to shoot pool with Elvis at Graceland.)

Iggy and Larry - they are both my heroes.

(Quick side story: I can remember a 4th of July night when my Dad and I climbed out the 3rd story bathroom window on to the roof and him walking - me crawling behind him in complete terror - up to the very top. And there we sat straddling the peak, a little boy with his Dad's immensely strong arms wrapped safely around him thrust a zillion feet up into the heavens watching the fireworks. I felt like God Himself was protecting me. What a night. Over 50 years later and I can still feel Him holding me...)

While we're on the subject of fireworks and flammable things: One night Larry was supposed to be baby sitting me. Instead of tending to this noble and infinitely rewarding duty, he went outside and met with our neighbor, Nicky. In the furtherance of science, they both decided to see what happens if you take the gunpowder out of fireworks, empty it into a glass jar and ignite it. (Hint: It explodes.) Well, they successfully got a lot of powder in the jar and then made a clever fuse by pouring more powder in some rolled up newspaper and sticking one end of it in the jar. The jar was then placed on the brand new patio wall Nicky's father had just completed. Nicky lit the "fuse" and, in a thoughtful gesture to his father to not litter the new wall, threw the still lit match in the jar.

This, of course, made the concept of a fuse somewhat vestigial as well as entirely useless. When I saw the flash of light and heard the explosion, I knew something bad had happened. All the screaming was another solid clue.

Next, Dick Tracy from across the street, came flying out of his front door, pistol in hand. He then crouched in the middle of the street in the crepuscular light swinging his gun back and forth and saying "Where'd they go? What did they look like?!" When he saw Larry and Nicky come staggering out to the street, each covered with blood, he was convinced this was the *big* case he had waited all his life for.

Well, off to the hospital they both went for a glass picking and stitching party. Glass is an interesting thing in your body, as over time it will usually continue to work towards the surface. Years later, Larry was kissing a girl goodnight when she slapped him. When he asked her why she did that, she said

"Because you bit me!"

What had actually occurred was a piece of glass had surfaced in his lip and was sticking through his skin. Right around this time he was also suspended from high school for wearing red pants...and throwing a textbook at a teacher's head.

So these were actually the first two terrorists I knew on a personal basis. Oh, I forgot to mention the "bomb" also blew out about a 4 foot chunk of the new patio wall. A while later on, Nicky was convinced it was in his best interest to spend some time in prison for insurance fraud.

As a result of his aviation skills in the Navy and years later, my Dad decided to build an airplane at home. Remember, someone forgot to tell him he wasn't smart enough to do that and I think he passed some of that on to his kids. As a result, we had landing gear in the living room, wings on the dining room table and a pile of airplane parts in a 3 car garage behind the house that I got to help with. We also got to meet some really neat people, including dinner with Paul Poberezny who founded the EAA (Experimental Aircraft Association, which next to the FAA, is now the largest aviation organization in the world.) It was during this phase the Ig informed me that I *would* be getting my pilot's license. Starting right then at 16 years of age, because, well, *he believed in me*, something I didn't realize at the time.

But I told him I did not want to do any such thing. This conversation took place as he was strapping me into the plane with the instructor at which point he simply said

"OK. No problem."

Six flight hours later I had soloed and after another 34 hours, I had my license by which time, I was thinking this wasn't such a bad idea. Especially with the girls. Problem was I had my pilot's license before my driver's license and therefore, no way to get my dates to the airport. It was a good talking point, though. After all, I knew all about stoichiometric air/fuel ratios, density altitude, VNE and why certain clouds looked like certain clouds. On a rainy day, I even knew it was raining.

Unfortunately, I discovered this witty weather banter would almost always bring on a cold front. Good date talk? Not.

On about my 6th lesson, Ernie, my instructor, took me up in his two seat WW2 trainer, an AT-6 (SNJ to you Navy types.) We got up over the North Jersey Mountains and just after making a 225 mph pass over a lake at 25 feet (and scaring the crap out of a fisherman in a rowboat), the engine stumbled and hesitated in a power climb as we were trying to get altitude over the trees.

Ernie yelled back to me

"*Quick!* Grab that thing between your legs and pump it!!" As he was the 'pilot in command', I did just that, but thought under the circumstances, this was a bizarre request.

As the engine failed to respond to me grabbing my crotch, he looked over his shoulders at me wide-eyed and wild-eyed and yelled far more urgently,

"Not *that* thing! The red handle!" This was a manual fuel pump lever which, once I grabbed and pumped the *right* thing, the engine coughed, spit and came back to life. But in spite of this auspicious beginning, little did I know the passion for aviation that would consume me many years later.

But even with a pilot's license in hand, I never could get Judy to quite cotton to me as I hoped she would. Judy was the neighborhood blue-eyed blonde goddess who seemed to glide ethereally as she walked and always had the freshest scent to her. I never knew girls could smell so good and I was actually content to just float along behind her and sniff the air wafting away. However, in the midst of her "come closer/stay away" mixed messages to me, and given her attention by the older guys, I remained wistfully outside her social circle. I'm certain she hasn't changed a bit to this day. I bet she even still smells good. I, on the other hand, having been born in the era where parents apparently forgot to buy a BMW as their child's first car, and

19

because there was no place nearby to land an airplane, had to walk the three miles each way to school. Very uncool.

The lesson? Some could care less if you care about them. And way too many others are just plain careless.

At around this time - and thinking the pen really was mightier than the sword (unless the other guy actually *had* a sword), I invested time in myself by writing down my budding philosophical thoughts and "observations of life". This included writing a lot of poetry, most of it quite bad.

For my degree in Literature, I also read a lot of Shelley, Wordsworth, Byron, Shakespeare and for good measure, I threw in some Kierkegaard and Nietzsche stuff just to round things off.

Eventually my curious brain became fascinated with the Arthurian Legends of Camelot as told by Thomas Malory and T.H. White and J.R.R. Tolkien. To me they represented mans ongoing internal struggle between his nobler and baser sides and the *honor* of protecting another. As a keepsake, I had a replica of the sword Excalibur made. Forty years later, it is still on my fireplace. (While writing this, I had a gentle reminder of these years when I discovered all my old journals. Bad poetry and all. But best of all, my Mom found my Dad's poignant WWII diary.)

By now I had a car and one Sunday, I drove several hours into the Catskill Mountains in New York State. Upon arriving, I hiked up a rocky river bed and around the bend to Kaaterskill Falls tucked deep within a horseshoe shaped amphitheatre. After a difficult climb to the top of the 260 foot falls, I sat down on a ledge which had a breathtaking view of the valley below.

When I got up to leave, I noticed that under my right hand was a date chiseled into the rock itself. It was 1843.

The next day at college, I was late for an art class which was to meet in the library. When I got there, all the seats were taken so I stood in back off to one side. While paying attention to the teacher, my left hand was resting on a shelf of books and I absent mindedly took one out and randomly let it fall open.

When I looked down, my gasp and look of astonishment made the teacher stop talking and ask me if I was OK. I said

"I...don't know."

The page that had opened was a painting of the waterfall I had climbed the day before. The date on the painting? 1843...

Meanwhile, Back at the Ranch

~~~~~~~~

But I digress. Eventually, Dad opened up a front-end alignment shop in our home town of Bloomfield, N.J. right off "Guinea Gulch" (Bloomfield Avenue from not-so-nice Newark to upscale Caldwell.) Here he also did specialty car frame work no one else could do and as a result, we took care of all the police cars in town. In time, my brother and I joined him and it became the Iggy, Larry and Gary show. Kinda like the 3 Stooges. Oh, Joe Montana and Johnny Cadillac were there too whenever they could be. Which was about all the time.

Joe looked just like his name sounded: a guy right out of central casting for a western movie with the tanned skin, broad shoulders, square chin, bandana and cowboy boots. Actually, he looked quite a bit like Glen Campbell. Somehow he befriended my father and took him into his band "Joe Montana and the Star Rangers" where my Dad played steel guitar -which he apparently taught himself because, well, no one told him he couldn't do it.

Joe (who otherwise seemed perpetually unemployed and may have actually lived in his car) would wander around the shop playing his guitar and yodeling a lot while we were working. I think because we worked on so many Mustangs and Pintos, he thought he was back on the ranch somewhere. The customers loved this side show and because he wore sunglasses inside all the time, they also thought he was blind and would put change in our coffee cups for him. Unfortunately, this was usually before we finished the coffee. In time Larry decided to help Joe out and play his onsite drum set while he yodeled. (Joe, not Larry.) This, of course, left more work for me and my father to do and, for some reason, less change in our cups.

Even though Joe was a really friendly guy, I always felt I saw a far away trace of melancholy and loneliness in his eyes. Maybe he did miss a ranch somewhere. Or someone.

Johnny Cadillac, a natural walk-on for the *Goodfellas* movie, was a leftover mob guy old enough to be carbon dated. (As the shop was on the borderline of Bloomfield and Newark, N.J. and in a mainly Italian neighborhood, we had plenty of these visitors.) He was about 5' 2", drove only Cadillac's, was obsessed with cleanliness and was constantly washing his hands.

(Actually, he reminded me of Macbeth's line "Out damn spot!" Maybe he had his own murderies he wanted to erase.) He also thought quite highly of himself. Certainly more than his actual height would support. But he was an OK guy once you got used to him which took some effort. The truth was, Johnny made me sad as all I could see was someone who was trying desperately to perpetuate a bygone image of "power" in a present time of impotence. It was like watching a 90 year old woman dye her hair black and believing she had recaptured her youth. Even so, eventually he took to expressing his inner self by spending untold thousands to buy a full dress Harley Davidson hog on which he spent more untold thousands tarting up even more.

At the time, I had stopped racing motorcycles (somewhat illegally in the middle of the night. But I continued to race cars, legally, during the day) and took to dirt bikes and owned a tiny red 125cc Honda which could climb a wall and go across the ceiling. With - or without - me on it. Johnny's dilemma was he had no one to ride with him and he was embarrassed for me to go on my little mosquito bike next to his Hogzilla nut-cracker. So, in a flash of misguided inspiration, he went out and bought *another* full dress hog for *me* to ride. But first he had to tart that up too, which resulted in *me* being too embarrassed to be seen with him on this chrome bedazzled lit-up-like Vegas behemoth that weighed as much as a VW.

We didn't ride much.

However, as Dad, Larry and I had to test our completed repair work, I did get to drive a lot of police cars. And they had both horsepower...and psychological power. It was amazing what people would do (or stop doing) when you hovered in their rear view mirror for more than a few seconds. I called it the "halo effect" as they all became little angels.

Especially if you turned on the lights. With the siren. Which of course I never did. And as these were pursuit vehicles, it was only appropriate to determine if they were accelerating correctly. I think I got one up to about Warp 9 one day at which time the hood latch failed (only a single latch back then) and the hood flew open and wrapped itself around the windshield and over the roof. I would have thought being in a school zone would have prevented anything like that from happening.

Go figure.

I did get a lot of practical use out of the shop, as it was where I did custom paint jobs on cars and choppers and worked on my "drive it like ya' stole it" Shelby GT350 and 390 AMX I used to race. One day, for a change of pace, I showed up with a brand new Dodge stretch van straight from the showroom.

I immediately pulled it into an empty bay, pulled out an air chisel and pulled the entire roof off the van. My father watched this with a look of astonishment that said "My son's an idiot." Over the next few days I welded up a frame and covered it with fiberglass which then gave me a 30 inch higher roof.

I then installed a kitchenette, shower and folding bed inside. I had trouble figuring out the paneled basement, so I left it out. For that entire week, when a customer came in, my father would bring them over to me and with a prideful wink say

"Let me introduce you to my son the idiot."

Well anyway, the shop was an interesting place, especially given the colorful local clientele…many of who were, well, just like on the Soprano's and had the same depth and interest of a layer of rust. But my Dad, in spite of all his strengths (literally and figuratively) had a flaw: He lived to work instead of working to live and would give many services away or fail to charge customers a fair rate. (I was about 30 when my Mom finally explained to me why we had so many "dinners" of rice and potatoes. She simply didn't have the money many times to go buy food but could make a meal from old newspaper if she had to. So, under the circumstances, she did an amazing job of holding things together and I never heard her complaining except when she would complain like when she'd tell me to eat all my food because there were 1 million starving kids in China. That all came to an abrupt halt when I asked her to "Name one.")

As I recall, it was Larry who brought a bit of business acumen to the shop and started keeping the books after which we actually began to charge for our services. But work my Dad did in spite of whatever circumstance befell him. One day, he was trying to install a coil spring in a police car (mind you, a spring is strong enough to hold up a car and we were the only shop that would do this dangerous task) when a jack under the car slipped out of position. The partially compressed spring flew out and struck him in the head so hard it picked him up and slammed him against the concrete wall, knocking him unconscious.

23

After returning from the emergency room, he went back and finished the job. That's what living to work does to you. For better or worse, I picked up on this mindset and it still haunts and hurts me today. And I've had the 12 surgeries to prove it.

But I will always be grateful for his "teaching" method in the shop. Instead of telling me how to do something, he taught me how to *figure out* how to do it, which was quite different and has helped me immensely in life. And I'll always remember two things he adjured me before he died:

1. Don't buy anything you can't pay for.
2. Don't do anything during the day that will keep you up thinking at night – always treat others fairly.

How did I do? Well, I've paid for everything I have and I've kept things up at night that I thought about the next day.

Oh, he also made it clear to me your word was your contract and, therefore, your reputation - which can take a lifetime to build and can be lost in one day. Even so, character was more important because it is what you *truly* are, while your reputation is only what other people *think* you are.

~~~~~~~~~

But Dad did some cool things too. In his earlier years, he got into weightlifting. However, being dirt poor he had to invent different kinds of "weights". (How poor you ask? His parents couldn't afford clothes for him so they would sit him in front of a window with only a hat on so he could wave to his friends.) These homemade weights went from buckets of concrete with pipes in them to steel wheels off of freight trains.

Eventually, he went on to specialize in a one arm Military Press. This is different from today's style, (which is called "the snatch") where one can bring the bar up to their chest, then "jerk" it up by dropping their body down below it. In his day, it was a "straight press", meaning, you brought the bar to your chest, stopped it, and then while standing completely still, just pushed it straight up. This is much more difficult as you didn't get the upward assist of dropping your body downward.

Well, here's what this little guy seen on the next page with a great big heart did: At a body weight of 147 lbs., he pressed 219 lbs. over his head. *With one arm.* And long before steroids, set a world's record that apparently has never been broken.

In the shop he would demonstrate this gorillability by taking a 75 lb. anvil, (which was more than 50% of his body weight) and in some magical way, grasp it in one hand and hoist it over his head. For a $5.00 bet which he always won. I, on the other hand at 180 lbs., could barely pick the damn thing up with two hands, it was so awkward.

Never did figure out how he did that. But at least that part of the gene pool seemed like it was holding up its end. Literally.

Late 1930's picture of "The Ig"

Long Before the Sopranos

~~~~~~~~

If you watch the Soprano's and listen closely, you will hear Grove Street mentioned. That's where our shop was and, as I said, it was frequently blessed by many macho mafia wannabes. But it wasn't long before I had more than adequate exposure to these character's egos, coarse mannerisms and lifestyles to consider how "Neuticles" might benefit them, or more specifically, those around them. In hindsight, I find myself fascinated by the attraction some have to the Soprano show. For me, sometimes it is too well done to enjoy its portrayal of their moody insouciance.

I must say, however, the show accurately depicts the perfidious and arrogant mindset I saw so much of. It also seems full of folks with BPD (Borderline Personality Disorder) who while smiling and patting you on the back "Wit all doo respect" are evaluating you as a potential threat to their money, pride or girlfriend. They trust no one and no one trusts them.

Linda, an old patient, was a serious fan of the show and sees "Tony as a thug with a heart". I disagree. I believe his "heart" is simply the perverted sense of guilt of a self created pariah. How a person with a heart specializes in creating misery – directly and indirectly - by exploiting others, takes no responsibility for the carnage they create, thinks everyone has a price and taking by force what is not theirs, is something quite outside my frame of reference. Maybe it's the "sincerity" of his charming screen smile. But there was simply no way for me to share with her my experience of like folks who were entirely wrapped up in ego barely controlled by an emotionally unbalanced trigger.

All of whom wore a gold Cross…thank you Jesus. Amen.

In real life, my brother is friends with the show's star, James Gandolfini and says he's a really great guy who gives much unnoticed help to charities and things off screen. Allegedly, James says my brother is also a good guy as well. (So, like, I wonder how much it costs Larry to have him say that? My guess is 15% of his yearly gross. In small unmarked bills…in a paper bag.)

Now, please don't think I am picking on Italians. I'm not. I have reservations about *any* race, group or individual who "thinks more highly of themselves than they ought to" and especially those who confuse familial pride with self-worth. (Unless it's "Ferrari".) Or, who base important decisions on an emotionally impulsive basis while choosing not to be inconvenienced with the facts. Granted all families, folks and cultures have problems and we're all walking soap operas – including you and me. It's just I've seen an unspeakable amount of hurt result when people failed to invest the time to talk and reason out a problem and instead, make bad decisions based on perceived slights to their ego or pride.

This is especially frustrating when the conclusions they arrive at become more important than the actual experience itself. And you'll hear me say this more than once.

And this can be "based" on the simplest of misunderstandings. Sometimes, and even worse, they go into such complete denial that there is even a problem while they fester from the inside out and grow a tumor just for fun. (We'll visit this principle of denial again later in much more detail.)

The truth is, I have seen some of the smallest things split families and deep friendships apart for life. This, of course, elevates assigning wedding guest seats to an art form. And you know what the absolutely stupidest part about it is? After years of separation, they usually can't even remember what caused it.

Yeah, that's just a way stupid way to *spend* one's time. And I didn't understand then why people would hurt one another like that...and 35 years later, I still don't.

Although my family was half Sicilian, they had no "mafia" ties known to me. However, EC's father apparently had a few "acquaintances". As a result, I had the pleasure of having breakfast several times at the "Godfather's" house. The real one. Ruggiero Boiardo, nick named "Ritchie the Boot", lived on a private estate in the country. The gated driveway to the houses (which as I recall was actually a replica of an Italian villa where his children and spouses all lived in separate homes in this protected enclave) was lined with busts and statues of his family with Ritchie being mounted on a white horse. (You'll find pictures of these in the book "Weird N.J", p. 152-155.) Ritchie was reportedly involved with "Lucky" Luciano and other like folks during the Prohibition in Newark and was, to my understanding, the inspiration for the Godfather movies.

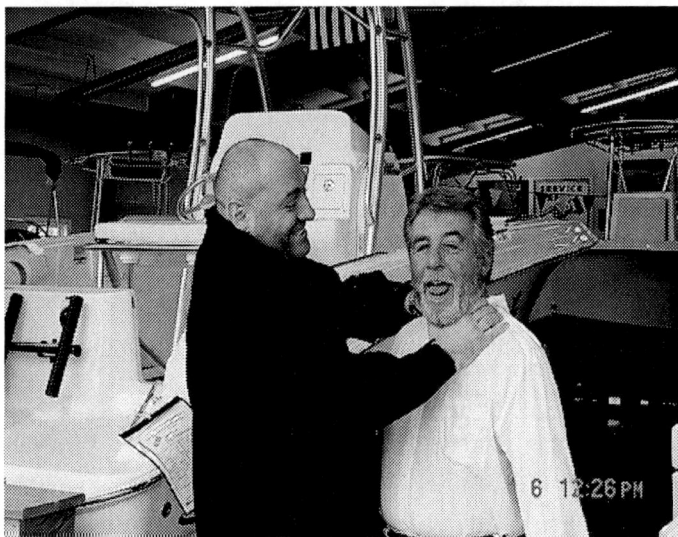

Larry is late with a payment to Tony (James Gandolfini)

In spite of the pussy willow up the nose and glass-jar-bee sting debacle, EC's father thought I was a great influence on his son and wanted him to take flying lessons with me. As such, he offered to drive both of us to the airport for my Sunday morning flying lessons. However, as we passed Boiardo's place on the way to the airport, Joe thought it a great idea to stop in for breakfast and see what the "guys" were up to.

Well, it turns out, quite a bit.

When one arrived at the top of the long driveway, there was a sort of "plaza" surrounded by individual homes in an Italian old world stone style with huge and very thick wooden doors that were, well, let's just say it: probably bulletproof. The largest home was Ritchie's.

One day after breakfast, someone gave me a tour of the compound. As we crossed the plaza, brilliantly colored peacocks roamed around freely and we came to a garden with towering 6 foot tomato plants. And there, just like in the movie, puttering around was a little hunched back old man, Ritchie himself. He smiled and waved to me and then bent over to pick up his teeth. (No, not really. I'm not even sure he even had any.)

I was then showed the in-ground swimming pool and taken to a little utility building nearby. Inside this building, it was obliquely inferred were the controls would send electrical current to the pool. And apparently not to heat it. More like accidentally on purpose dropping a toaster in your bathtub, only a *really* big toaster, if you get my drift. This to me seemed, well, simply shocking.

Up towards the back of the property, was what looked like a large stone bee hive which I was told this was a bread oven. However, it seems the FBI type folks had a different interpretation when they later discovered teeth in it and it was determined to be a personal sized crematorium. Apparently this is where the dis-invited guests spent some time after being pre-heated in the pool. (The "beehive" may have been an attempt to be ecologically "green" as it was environmentally friendlier and probably easier to clean up than the new woodchipper.)

At the breakfast table, they'd make the sign of the Cross before eating (families that pray together, stay together) at which point the conversation might turn to why so and so hadn't been seen for a few days with the questioning inference being are they spending time in the trunk of a car somewhere in Secaucus?

(Families that prey together, slay together.)

I also recall the grandson, who was maybe 8 or 9, coming up to me and asking me if I wanted to see his birthday present. I asked what it was and he told me a machine gun, which I had no reason to disbelieve. So overall, just your average Sunday morning family small talk over buttered rolls and coffee.

But in spite of all the "family" talk and warm fuzzies, one did not get the impression they were overly understanding people, especially concerning the subject of *omerta*. In fact, it was rumored EC's father mentioned something that really pissed someone off and as an object lesson for him, they took it out on EC who, one night, had more than the snot beat out of him.

It was almost his liver.

He was found badly beaten in Newark, spent a long time in the hospital and never seemed the same afterward. The last I heard from him was after a hiatus of almost 20 years when he called me at my clinic in Atlanta and immediately asked me

"What's new?"

~~~~~~~~~

But, I stray again and should return to the shop where many things with an Italian flavor were brewing. As you can see in the picture on the next page, the shop was located along a busy street and had three car bays set back about 20 feet off the street. This was handy as one could pull right into the shop onto a car alignment rack which was two parallel steel girders that spanned a 4 foot deep concrete pit. As each girder was only 15 inches wide, we did not allow a customer to drive on them as it required an "experienced professional" to not drive the car off the rails and into the pit. So we did it.

And, well…most of the time we were successful.

On both sides of the shop were stores typical of an Italian neighborhood like a barber and coffee shop and of course, the butcher, whose store was a front for the Witness Relocation Program. (I think some witnesses got "relocated" to his freezer.) But as we were constantly pulling cars in and out of the shop, we could not have cars parked in front of the bays and blocking us. This became a constant ordeal as someone would pull up, get out of their car and walk away to one of the stores. We'd then have to guess who they were and which store they were in along the block, which, frankly, was a pain in the butt and a huge time waster. This also did nothing good for Larry's infamous temper from which I learned a great deal from by simple observation.

One day, a well dressed young black couple walked away after locking their car which they left blocking two of our three driveways. Larry found them next door and nicely asked

"Could you please more your car?"

The classy girlfriend's response was for my brother to

"Go f*** yourself. We'll move it when we're ready."

Larry calmly replied "Go f*** myself? OK, I'll go f*** myself! In fact, I'll do it right now." And then he left.

Now, this was a response that should make you immediately suspicious. Upon returning to the shop, he located his favorite ice pick and proceeded to adroitly endow this fellow's car with four partially (only on the bottom) flat tires.

When the guy saw what happened, he called the police, which made things worse - for him - because we knew all the cops. And most of them were Italian – or Irish - which was just as bad.

When Junior the cop showed up and heard the story, he strongly "suggested" the owner of the car get in and immediately relocate himself, his girlfriend and the four flat tires.

Eventually the same store got another owner who took great pride in his new hairpiece. That it looked like a muskrat sock puppet with no eyes didn't appear to concern him. He also developed a habit of putting coke bottles behind Larry's tires who then went to discuss this strange behavior with him. The fur frocked fellow, feeling just a wee bit vituperative, responded by taking a swing at him. Larry, wanting to resolve this peacefully and diplomatically, put him in a headlock and dragged him into the street which is where his toupee finally popped off.

By this time, the man's wife had already called the police and Junior, who was on beat a few blocks away, came zipping up in the cruiser. Unfortunately, exactly where he hit the efficient new brakes we just installed was exactly where the muskrat lay in the street. This caused that tire to lock up solid right on top of the prized item and when the car finally skidded to a stop, the eyeless furball was a smoking hairy black smudge in the road.

Who said God doesn't have a sense of humor?

At this point, we involuntarily enrolled a truculent Larry in the Attila the Hun School for Social Graces...where, red pants and all, he was promptly expelled for threatening the teacher.

Larry on guard duty outside the shop - aggravated by a car blocking 2 bays. My converted van is far right.

Later that year, we discovered a dead man in the parking lot across the street with what appeared to be an ice pick hole in his heart. As far as we knew, it was not Larry's.

On another auspicious occasion, a fellow of the "family" (who is still in jail as of today) brought us his newly painted and finely detailed Lincoln Continental which was to be delivered the next day to an expectant buyer.

The gentleman asked us to put on new tires, brakes and shocks as he wanted the car to be "perfect" for the new owner. Unfortunately, somewhere along the day, Larry's hair trigger temper was triggered by a hair. This caused him to jump into the Lincoln, throw it into reverse and fly out of the shop backwards without, as we pilots say, "Adequate situational awareness".

For the only time in my memory, an 18 wheel tractor trailer truck came rumbling down Grove Street. By sheer luck, the tractor portion got past Larry. At that point the entire trunk of the Lincoln went under the open area of the trailer between the front and back wheels.

This was actually a fine place to be had the truck driver miraculously been able to stop right then. Which he couldn't and didn't. The subsequent and simultaneous elevating of the Lincoln's front wheels off the ground combining with the "whompwhompwhomp" as the rear truck tires had a meet and greet with the Lincoln's trunk was a bad omen. The Lincoln's hubcap that went spinning off down the road did little to indicate the actual damage the 8 truck tires did when they came trundling up and over the trunk of the car, completely flattening it while bending the entire rear of the car into an upward "L".

Without hesitation, I immediately knew we were in for something more comprehensive than a wax job.

About 3 hours later, the customer called and asked Larry (and I quote accurately):

"What's the damage?" Larry's response was

"A bit more than I expected."

These were just some of the great "Larry Moments". And there were so many more. But let him write his own book. I do know by the time I left the shop to come South to Georgia, I had test driven close to 10,000 cars, almost electrocuted myself using an arc welder, got pinned under a car when a jack slipped and set my clothes, eyebrows and hair on fire while welding a supposedly empty gas tank full of water.

Urban Renewal & Social Engineering

~~~~~~~

Then there were the other fights.

Unfortunately, there are some parts of the Italian gene pool that would benefit from a lot of chlorine. This can be seen in the young men who instinctively believe they have a corner on the testosterone market which, of course, must be displayed in all its associated stupidity whenever possible. And because like attracts like, these people seem to hang out together. For example, for an unknown reason my Dad was jumped by about five of these brave men while he was working one day at the shop. And they did him over pretty good using a 2x4 board. Which was really, and I mean *really* stupid of them.

Well, my Dad and his brother Sam (who could slap you so hard on the back he'd knock you into tomorrow) quickly came up with a Polizzotto sponsored, non-OSHA approved "Safety On The Job" event to which these fine men were "invited". This was important as drugs and violence were now beginning to move into the neighborhood and someone had to set some kind of precedent by taking a stand. And as "Polizzotto" means "police" in Italian, and as police are there to protect......we did.

Like I said before, the best defense is a strong offense. So while this great group of guys were still in the immediate vicinity, they found all of themselves snatched up and pulled inside the shop to attend this free learning experience. Once inside, my Dad had his turn with them and then, one by one, they were tossed into the car spray paint booth with my very insulted 'that you would do this to my little brother' Sicilian bull of an uncle. The big overhead pull down door was then closed and after a little bit of time and a lot of noise, the door rose and the new convert was unceremoniously expelled a changed man.

As I recall, one exited with a changed face from a broken jaw. After that day, these folks apparently realized what quality people the Polizzotto clan were and became much better citizens and eventually, customers. And guess what? Once again, it was solved with no parental intervention, no lawyers, and no anger management classes.

And "Wit all doo respect", *it was solved.*

Much of this took place before I was working there. However, by the time I arrived, it was more of the same, only different. One day, I heard yelling in the alley alongside the shop. I went to investigate and found two of these morons fighting each other. Having been involved in the martial arts for several years by then, I said "What the hell...let's try this stuff out" and waded in. The one with his back to me was easily dispatched with a single kick in the butt. And I mean *in*. It's just like getting kicked in the front and believe me, it hurts just as much. He left the scene which I thought the other would also do since there was now no one left to fight.

Or so I thought. He, however, was apparently upset that I interfered with his Pilates demonstration and as I raised my hand to show a gesture of peace, he raised his to show me his switchblade. "Oh, now this is getting interesting" I thought to myself. And while my nature is to sit down and talks things out, (Larry always complained I was *too* calm) this didn't seem like the time. I did recall my karate instructor saying most "altercations" are over in 30 seconds. But someone good with a knife can also make a fair amount of sushi in 30 seconds. Anyway, he lunged at me and, truthfully, while I was still *thinking* about what to do, my left foot reflexively kicked his right wrist and the knife went sailing right past his face. At that point, he too decided it was better to be somewhere else.

And my instructor was wrong. It was over in four seconds.

The funny thing, and like all the similar events, he came back about a week later – with a cast on his fractured wrist – and apologized to me for the trouble. But he also asked me "Did I *really* have to break his wrist?" I told him I had not planned to but that under the circumstances, and as he was coming at me with a knife, I had inadequate time to perform a detailed damage assessment analysis before acting. Besides, I explained to him, when you act like that, it's really "mind over matter" i.e., I don't mind and you don't matter.

Hopefully the lesson was clear: When you choose the behavior, you have automatically chosen the consequences. Or as the Good Book succinctly puts it, "A man reaps what he sows". But the outcome? He became a friend and customer as well. And the truth is, I never wanted to hurt him and felt bad over doing so. (Sadly, he eventually succumbed to a drug overdose.)

But these events taught me if you take out the biggest or the baddest first, the rest just usually go away.

Kinda like cutting the head off a snake.

Lest you get the wrong impression of my family, please understand at times it was simple survival in a worsening neighborhood with people who, if they couldn't find trouble, would create it. And sometimes they did so out of simple boredom. I can recall revisiting the area years after I had left and saw some of these same folks *still* hanging out on the street corners. There's a reason the "Soprano's" takes place there.

But in spite of all of these events, my Dad was actually an extremely gentle man and never once physically disciplined me. That said a lot to me. In fact, he had a way of implying a lot by saying a little. We were strolling along one time when I jumped as high as I could and came down on an ant, which fared poorly in the encounter. My Dad turned to me and asked "Why did you do that?" For some reason, it affected me greatly that I had no answer. And I learned just because you *can* do something, doesn't make it the right thing to do. But I also saw a gentleness in his heart which made me take a step closer to my own.

And he could not bear to see his own in pain as I discovered the day my finger got pulled into a bench grinder which instantly stripped off the flesh down to the bone. He became so distraught by all the blood flying around that Larry's wife had to drive me to the emergency room. Poor guy. I felt bad for *him*!

At the hospital, the doctor cleaned it up, wrapped it in gauze and said I could leave. As I got up to go, I asked him

"Are you sure it doesn't need a skin graft?" He unwrapped it, looked at me and asked

"I'm not sure. What do *you* think?" Huh? He then wrapped it up again and told me to see my family doc in a week. When I went to him, he started to unwrap the gauze, stopped and said

"Is that a bird over there?"

As I looked, he swiftly ripped the rest of the bandage off in one swell foop. After they peeled me off the ceiling, he explained the emergency room doc did me no favor and that the new skin had begun to grow right *through* the gauze, hence the necessary yank maneuver. Through the tears I asked him if there wasn't another of way of doing that! His answer?

"Trust me. I'm a doctor."

High Times

~~~~~~~

The next thing I knew, the hippy movement blew in like a Foehn Wind and the drugfest "Woodstock" had arrived. Actually, it was August of 1969 when everyone on the planet headed for Max Yasgur's farm in upstate N.Y. I was forbidden to go by my mother so I really shouldn't have been there by the time I arrived. Nonetheless, I had managed to stow away in my friend Bob's van and squirrel my way to the festival.

Bob tried very hard to be the quintessential hippy from the long hair to the granny glasses to the dope. Which is why I was banned from going with him. (My parents made the drug "issue" very clear for me: "Do them once and they'll kill you. If they don't, we will." Point taken. Also, my flying-climbing-caving activities fared much better without double vision and drooling.)

Needless to say, upon our rainy arrival at the "festival", I discovered I was totally out of my element as I had never (or to this date), done any drugs. Reading Carlos Castaneda's "Don Juan" series of fabrications was as close as I ever got. I knew even less about the music, which was OK as you couldn't hear or see it anyway. But, I *was* entirely astonished by the volume of mud and, coincidentally, girls with no bras. Sometimes the girls with no bras were even in the mud together and doing God knows what. I quickly discovered my young brain was not quite prepared to ponder all these puerile points of interest.

Anyway, Bob was about 6' 3" and weighed close to 93 lbs. wet, fully clothed, change in his pocket and 3 lbs. of mud on his 5 lb. hiking boots. With his body a Giacometti sculpture and his mind a Dali landscape, he made a penchant of believing he was a font of wisdom. He (long sentence here- take a deep breath) put this personal belief into immediate use when we were there, oh, maybe 15 minutes at which time he got some bad hash that was apparently laced with LSD from an unknown, but no doubt reputable FDA approved vendor. (Breathe) It took me the next two days to find him among the 450,000 or so people - all named Moonbeam - completely exhausted from trying to take his pants off over his head. It took him the next two weeks to find Earth. Yep...my folks were right on this one. Or, as we'd say back then, "Right on!" Maybe they mean the same thing.

Bob was part of another object lesson for me about human behavior. One early evening we were out riding our motorcycles in a nice suburban area. Bob had on his anti-establishment Captain America helmet like Peter Fonda wore in the movie *Easy Rider* and was riding in front of me when he started to pass a car. I was close in trail and as he pulled alongside the car, I was stunned to see the driver smile at him and then deliberately slam the car into him. Not once, but twice.

As Bob went down in a heap of blood, broken bones and tangled metal, he yelled to me "Get the bastard!"

I, like a well trained attack dummy, replied

"OK!"

Well, it turns out that was a bit easier said than done. I mean, what can a guy on a motorcycle do to a nut in a car? In any event, the next five minutes were pretty thrilling for me chasing this guy at 60 mph with him on the street and me on the sidewalk. This was because if I got too close behind, he slammed on his brakes. If I got in front, he tried to run me over. When I went to either side, he tried to do a "Bob" on me and force me into the curb, a tree or an oncoming car.

This was getting real old real fast as I pursued him into the next town of Glen Ridge. When I finally had to get off the sidewalk at a fork in the road, he forced me up a hill onto someone's lawn. Here, and much to my relief, my clutch cable broke forcing me to end the chase and quite possibly and prematurely, my life. Fortunately, I had plenty of time to peruse his car tag during this vehicular version of "tag - you're it" and called the cops who were waiting for him when he got home.

So here's "the rest of the story": The driver was a construction worker who after work, met his buddies for a few too many drinks and then afterward, met Bob. I discovered then that liberal hippies and conservative construction workers did not fast friends make and though this guy may have been right judging the book by its cover, you really shouldn't drive your car over it. All of which leads me to:

The more you know the more you forget.
The more you forget, the less you know.
The less you know the less you forget.
The less you forget...the more you know.
No?

Weird Encounters of the Close Kind

~~~~~~~~

They say a good ice breaker with new folks is to share your most embarrassing moment. Well, as y'all are new to me, here're a few from the vast repertoire of my callow years when puberty and embarrassment seemed to collide on a regular and galactic basis. I'm sure after this we'll be real close friends.

Ellen was an adorable little Jewish gal from a rather well-to-do neighborhood and, thinking we should go on a date first before we broke up, I asked her out.

While I was bringing her home from our first outing, I inadvertently, accidentally and completely unknowingly got involved in a drag race and during the course of a 1-2 shift, I lost the clutch. Now when I say I "lost it", I mean as in gone. It and the metal casing around it had literally exploded into large chunks which came tearing up through the console, hood and dashboard. That Ellen's feet were right next to where these large clumps of hot steel came through the floor seemed to get her attention. That she had short legs naturally and not as a result of this event was a blessing. When the trooper came by to see why I was on the side of the road, he looked over my car, asked what happened and then with a little smile, tied a rope to my front frame and towed me home 17 miles! He then graciously drove Ellen home to another town. Must've been a slow night.

Somehow I convinced her a second date was in order and would have a much better ending. When we did get together, we had a really good evening with dinner and what passed as conversation in those days. On the way home, she jokingly said

"Don't be surprised if my father comes to the door with a shotgun. Especially since the police brought me home after our last date." Ha-ha. Cute.

When we got to her house, I politely opened her car door (that's a good thing to do guys) and walked her up the stairs to the darkened front door where I gave her a hug goodnight.

As I began to leave, she asked me

"Would you like to kiss me goodnight?"

Would I?! Is a frog's butt watertight? So I gingerly kissed her and quite to my delight, I discovered it was quite delightful. (In more ways than one, I was definitely in virgin territory.)

This quickly led to something like a bee-hive frenzy of flying lips, in the middle of which the porch light (which I think was actually a 747 landing light) came on. This was followed immediately by the door slamming open and there, on the step above me and silhouetted by an inside light, was a man so big he had his own zip code. And yes, with a shotgun. Needless to say, I went from happier than a gopher in a warm cow pie to so scared I could have squeezed a charcoal briquette into a diamond with my butt cheeks.

Now that's a shame - and I was having such a good time.

A deep voice then asserted itself by demanding

"Just *what* is going on here?!"

Now, there are a few things I need to outline for you here before I proceed. Ellen's back was towards her father and I was facing him. You must also kindly note I was at that tender age somewhere between having an actual real mustache of distinction and wishing I could grow one. (Update: I can do it now in 37 minutes.) So, to enhance what little hair I had coaxed out of my upper lip in the previous 3 months, I had used my Mom's eyebrow pencil to kinda sorta fill it in before picking up Ellen. No harm done, right? Well, as I was telling her father we were just saying goodnight and turning to leave, out of the corner of my eye I caught Ellen partially turned so that there was some light on her face.

Can you see where this is going?

Because if there's such a thing as an adolescent stroke, now was the time to have it.

It was at this precise moment I discovered the eyebrow pencil liked Ellen's fair and tender skin far more than mine and it not only transferred itself from me to her, but had grown in size and glory as well. Actually quite a bit and she had a black 4 inch ring all around her mouth and along her cheeks. None of which says much about my kissing technique. (It's rumored I'm much better now.) So, stay with me here. In a flash, I perceived her father had still not seen his daughter's Al Jolson act at which time I grabbed her neck and hair with my right hand and proceeded to try and wipe the black hole off her face with my left hand.

However, from where her father stood behind her, all he could see was what looked liked I was strangling his daughter as her head whipped around and jerked back and forth. In the midst of all of this, she was trying to gurgle out a word, which didn't help dismiss the strangling idea. (I recall it being something like "Help!") And all during this attempted cleansing, I was frantically trying to convince the two of them that she had spaghetti sauce on her face from dinner and I was simply trying to wipe it off. (The fact we had Chinese food really didn't seem important at the moment.) Unfortunately, after succeeding only in spreading the smudge around even more and failing to exculpate myself, I bid a hasty adieu and quickly drove out of sight. Forever. I never had the courage to ask her out again.

Too bad. We could have had spaghetti.

On another occasion, my high school friend Rolando (a smooth talking Latin ladies man from Cuba) and I successfully convinced two young ladies of great pulchritude to go on a double date to a movie. When we got to the theatre, I offered to go get some refreshments. After taking out an equity loan on my car to pay the bill, I headed back into the dark theater. Now, at this point, you need to know the seating arrangement we cleverly designed: Trap the two girls between us so they can't escape. With this in play, I returned and came into the row on my friend's side. As I passed in front of him with my back to the screen, he pulled me down and urgently whispered

"Your fly is open!"

"Open? What do you mean open?!"

Now as a teenager, I'm not sure I ever admitted to a girl I even had any body functions that *required* a fly. I then hurriedly passed by the girls trying to divert their attention by throwing their stuff at them. When I got to my seat, I quickly turned around to face the screen and subtly but swiftly zipped myself up. After praising myself on a difficult problem solved with much class and aplomb, I began to savor the promise of my date's heavenscent Chanel #666 and who looked like she'd be more fun than Six Flags. This would be a night to remember.

As you know, Newton's 3rd Law of Physics states that for every action, there's an equal and opposite reaction. In this case, that law expressed itself like this: After hastily zipping up my fly, I forcefully plunked *down* in my seat. Simultaneously, the girl in *front* of me screamed and shot *up* like a jack-in-the-box. I was quite confused by all these things going up and down until I noticed her head arched severely backwards over her seat and a large wad of *her* hair stuck in my zipper. Quite a feat, if I say so myself. Could this really get any worse?

You have no idea.

As my zipper was now hopelessly jammed and would not come down, the girl (whose neck I had surely broken) and I had to make our way to the aisle…she leaning backwards over the seats and me with my crotch stuck to the back of her head. I could sense her boyfriend had mixed feelings about all of this. When we reached the aisle, the manager came (have I already asked you if this could get any worse?) and took out his trusty flashlight to considerately spotlight the event for those in the theatre who may have missed out on the more edifying details.

While she kneeled on her knees in front of me, he said

"Wait here." (We were going somewhere like this?) He then left us for what seemed like a year and came back with a scissor. This remedy left her with a gaping hole in her hair and me with a badly misplaced toupee. By the time the applause faded away, my date had ascended her ivory tower from where she looked down at me with a commendable level of disdain while I hoped for a miracle – like maybe I'd spontaneously combust. A short time later I excused myself. Permanently.

Of course, all of this would have been next to impossible had we gone to the drive-in movie like I suggested.

So, like what is it with me, women, lights and those truly formative moments of life? I mean, there had to be more to romance than this. Clearly Gary 2.0 had much to learn.

Because of this, I decided to seriously investigate the foreign student exchange program at my high school. In order to determine if I qualified, I submitted a formal request for them to send me abroad.

Apparently, after a long search, they couldn't find one.

Oh, while we're enjoying ourselves at the theatre, I must pass along this cautionary tale in case you are ever using crutches. While recuperating from a surgery in 1988 to re-break my leg and after having friends slide pizzas under my door for two weeks, Janette said "We need to get you out, how about a movie?" I thought that was a great idea but said we had to get there early to get a seat where my braced right leg could hang out in the aisle.

We got there just as a line was forming down the center

aisle but got the two left side aisle seats we needed. Now, I had to figure out what to do with my crutches. Well, as she was on my left, I handed her the first crutch and was trying to help her decide how to stow it. While watching her do this, I was absent mindedly taking the other crutch and trying to swing the tip in a large arc from the floor up over my head and hand it to her.

While doing this, somewhere in the medicated haze inside my brain I heard a woman screaming. And it sounded quite close by. Actually, it was right next to me in the aisle but I was still watching Janette. In the midst of this, I realized that I continued tugging at the crutch over my head because it was caught on something. So I then tugged harder. And the screams got louder.

Now Janette has the biggest blue eyes you've ever seen and as I looked at her, they got bigger than I had ever seen them. This was combined with a look on her face that was somewhere between horror and trying to suppress an outburst of inappropriate laughter. (You know the look. It's like when someone whacks their finger with a hammer and *you* are the one trying to hold back the tears?) This was combined with her beginning to gasp for air, all of which had me pretty confused.

Because the shrieking next to me was starting to sound like a punctured turkey, I felt obblegated to investigate its source. Well, funny thing: It seems that my crutch tip got caught under this woman's dress which was now 6 feet up in the air causing her to treat all the people "behind" her to a full moon almost as big as the screen. At least we didn't have to cut anyone's hair.

So even though getting first dates were not all that problematic, the follow up to a successful second encounter was becoming somewhat more elusive. One girl, Pam, did go out with me again even though on our initial date we almost sunk a boat at midnight in the middle of a lake. On the second date, we found ourselves on a mountain top at night completely surrounded by a forest fire. There was no third date.

~~~~~~~~~

And then there are those things in life you just never seem to understand the irony of. Like Maureen. Mo was bright, energetic and had a fresh innocent beauty that just made people want to be around her. You know the type. We were both involved in gymnastics and shortly after I met her she was leaving for New Mexico to attend college where she wanted to become a physical therapist for kids with disabilities.

As we were leaving her home on a date one evening, her Dad told me to "Be careful driving."

I replied "Don't worry, I *always* leave myself options." (I still try to. Its part of a pilot's training.) As I was bringing her home, I headed off the curving highway ramp but unknown to me, the engine in the car in front of us had just exploded and covered the ramp in black oil. As it was nighttime *and* raining, I never saw the big slick and guess what?

Just like that, I ran out of options.

My brand new car skidded off the road, jumped the curb and wiped out the front suspension. Maureen smacked her head on her window but overall, we were alright.

Little did we know how that head bump was a harbinger of things to come.

A short time later she left for school and one evening while walking back to her dorm on the roadside, Maureen too, ran out of options.

Literally. And for the rest of her life.

A car plowed into her from behind and picked her up on the hood. After almost 200 feet, she rolled off unconscious with her head cracked open like a melon. And the driver fled.

Mo was in a coma for almost 6 weeks. When she had stabilized somewhat after a couple of weeks, I flew out West and spent a few days in the hospital. I would talk to and read books to her, rub her arms and brush her hair hoping some of the stimulus would "wake" her brain. By the end of the week, she would flutter her eyelids, follow your finger with her eyes and move her lips, but that was about all. Still, it was something.

As you would imagine, her recovery was long, painful and difficult and she never got beyond the awareness age of a 7 year old. The jerk that hit her was never found and Mo became the *patient* of the type her heart had hoped to *treat*.

You know, the truth is, I'm not sure what I can, or was supposed to learn from that. But one thing is evident: Life is precious and *immediate*. And you never, ever know when it's going to go away, or go spinning completely out of control. But maybe the "not knowing" is exactly *what* makes it so valuable...

Hmmm.

The Universal En-Ig-ma

~~~~~~~~

At this point in my early 20's, I was slowly becoming aware of just how well known and respected my Dad actually was. I also found myself known not as Gary, but as "Iggy's Kid." And in the weirdest places such as a little roadside car dealer 150 miles away in upstate NY, where I pulled over to check out a Mustang for sale. After talking to the owner for about 5 minutes, he said "Are you Iggy's kid? I used to work with him in 1935." Well, I just about fell off the chair. Another time was 700 miles away in Chattanooga, Tennessee in a Philly cheese steak shop where it turns out the owner knew my Dad. This happened so many times that *I* decided "Why waste time" and started introducing myself as "Iggy's Kid".

There were actually many practical benefits from this moniker. One was when the Belleville, N.J. police skidded to a stop and boxed me in at the curb with 3 cars in front of a bank. Seems they had been "given a tip" I was going to rob said institution. I'll save that story for another time but I will mention the black water pistol on the front seat and machete in the trunk didn't help to initially explain things on my behalf. But my now familiar sobriquet of Iggy's Kid instantly did.

Anyway, one evening at dinner, I noticed a beautiful sunset forming. As I had started a small photography business, I wanted to get this on film so I gathered up my longest lens and raced over to Troy Towers. (Now that's spooky...I just realized they have the same initials and were set up just like miniature Twin Towers in NYC and, as you'll see, I was almost a budding terrorist in my brother's footsteps.)

Troy Towers were upscale apartments in the center of Bloomfield and were the tallest buildings around. And just great for sunset viewing. The only detail was it required a key card to get in them so my plan was to hang around the front door and go in with someone, which I did. After taking the elevator as high as it would go, I ran up the remaining stairs and popped out of the little shed door on the roof. I then went to the edge of the building and began taking pictures of an incredible sunset using a very long telephoto lens.

After a few minutes of this, I heard a police siren, which I ignored. Then there was another and yet another all from different directions. Eventually I could hear them all over town and could not imagine what was going on, but I knew it was big!

Within a few minutes, about nine police cars converged to a screeching halt (just like in the movies!) in the parking lot ten stories below me. So I leaned over, pointed the camera down and started taking pictures of them. When they saw me doing this, the cops scattered and took cover all over the place. This made me think I was on to a really big crime story about something. Hey- I could probably *sell* these pictures! As I was furthering my photography career playing Cecil B. DeMille, I heard the shed door bang open about 40 feet behind me and someone yell

"Freeze!" Yup, once again, just like in the movies. I turned around and saw four cops with guns pointing my way. Well, actually, pointing *at* me. The next thing I heard was

"Drop it!" Rut-row…this can't be good.

To which I replied "Are you crazy?!"

This was not the response they really wanted, but I mean, I was *not* going to drop an $800.00 camera and lens, which it turns out, they thought was a very expensive sniper rifle. However, under the circumstances my attempts at melioration were useless and one of the cops quickly approached and took the camera while two others grabbed me by the arms. They then dragged me down the stairs and threw me into the elevator where the head police type guy was waiting…who I knew from the shop…who then said to the others

"Oh Jesus…this is Iggy's kid, let him go."

He then informed me that the building superintendent, in the opposite tower, was eating dinner when he got a call about a "sniper on the roof". He looked up and saw me hanging over the edge and while almost choking on his steak, called the police. All of them. Which led to my pleasant elevator chat with the chief. My sentence? I had to promise an 8"x10" sunset photo to the building super. However, after seeing my portfolio, he quickly chose a picture of my dog, Susie, in the nude.

Remember, the old adage it's not what you know, but who?

Yup.

More High and Low Times

~~~~~~~~~

Around this time, I started getting more involved with "technical" (vertical) rock climbing and Troy Towers was not the only high place I visited. I found this new climbing thing somewhat odd because I am pretty much afraid of heights. I also really didn't know what I was doing when climbing other than being relatively certain I wasn't supposed to fall. But there was no one to around to teach me, so like my Dad, I attempted to teach myself. Now, while this can be good or bad, sometimes one will find themselves in a climbing situation where it's clearly bad and with few options.

Since I was not really progressing well on the learning curve, and as failing usually occurred by falling, I hooked up with John (yes, another John) the prototype Spiderman who was a little wisp of a guy with sticky fingers and toes. Or so it seemed. Spiderboy felt it would be best to drive me to upstate New York on a cold and damp windy winter day to a long line of 300 foot high sheer cliffs called the Shawangunks, or, simply, The Gunks. This was known as THE place to climb and where the experts went to become heroes and legends in their own minds and to be viewed. It's also where the newbies died and were seen at the viewing. Usually in a Glad zip lock baggie.

Anyhow, he introduced me to a new concept in rock climbing: Rope. Now this I could like as it was supposed to stop you from hitting something hard like the ground with something soft like your body. Of course, this was providing that as you fell, you didn't pluck your rope safety man off the rock above you and send him on a screamer as well.

Now, I was confident of John's climbing abilities as he was wearing all the right color clothes and all, but at about half my weight, I figured that as my safety man, the only thing that would happen if I fell is he'd follow me and I'd give him something soft to land on. Me.

Things went frightfully well until we got to a 2 inch wide ledge almost 300 feet up. Then they just got frightful. Immediately above, the rock jutted out over us a few feet in what is known as an overhang which made me shut my eyes and pretend this was a bad dream due to an even worse hangover.

But, when I opened my eyes, it was still there. So, Spiderman-John says to me, "Do exactly what I do." Right.

He was out of sight by the time he got to the "exactly" part of the instructions. I mean, he just vanished. At first I thought he took a swan dive and looked down for him. Nope. No red smudges way down there. Doing this, of course, only served to remind me exactly how much air was between me and the closest warm cheese omelet at IHOP. I then looked up and thought I could hear a voice, but the keening wind was streaming by so loudly that whatever was said just got carried away to somewhere in NJ. Probably to my mother's bat ears.

Anyway, climbers can get a condition known as "sewing machine leg". This is when you are perched on something like, oh, let's say, a 2 inch wide ledge for too long and your calf muscles start to fatigue and go into spasm. This causes your legs to tremble and your foot goes up and down like you were powering a sewing machine. Hence, sewing machine leg. Clever, no? As by now I was well into trembling, I felt like I was going to vibrate myself right off the tiny ledge. The hickey hold I had on the rock with my lips was also apparently not working as my planned back-up either. I was now getting really cold, stressed, fatigued, cramped and did I mention paralyzed with fear? I looked up at the overhang, shouted one last time the exact spot for where the rescue helicopter was to get me and got really depressed. The climbing permit, which I still have read:

"Daily Climbing Permit # 4196, $1.25. Caution: Climbing is not worth the deliberate risk of life." Great. It only cost me $1.25 to deliberately ignore putting my life at risk.

What a stupid place to end a life.

Especially mine.

Finally, I realized I was about to fall anyway and even if a copter did show up, it would only be for a body evac in the zip-lock bag. So, after distilling my options down to a total of none, I made a literal leap into space (yes, off the ledge) and grabbed the lip of the overhang with the tips of my fingers and for an eternal split second, dangled 300' off the ground. Do you remember me talking about adrenaline? I wish I could say what happened next, but I truly do not remember. The very next thing I do recall was being on the top standing next to John and slapping him on the back so hard I almost knocked him over the edge while excitedly saying something inane like

47

"That really wasn't so bad!" Fortunately, I was able to get that out before I threw up on his brand new red climbing shoes.

Last chance picture before "The Leap". Cliff face is behind legs, lake is in the valley below

I tried to get my martial arts instructor Paul to join me in this new aerial delight which I hoped would scare him as much as he did me while chasing me around the room with various sharp weapons. But he wouldn't bite. I did learn how to absorb and tolerate pain, however, in those classes which as you'll see, became quite useful later on. Now 30 years later, he and I still carry on decades long arguments every morning via email on various topics. As near as I can tell, he is usually wrong. Some kind of yin-yang Grasshopper thing I guess.

But let me tell you what came from that "leap of faith". I discovered a significant controlling element in our lives: Fear. And while it was entirely appropriate to feel fear at that time, I also learned that without it, courage and bravery cannot exist. But fear masquerades in many other subtle forms and can direct our lives mercilessly without us ever knowing it's even happening. Consider how it manifests:

> Anger - the fear of not getting what you want and the opposite of love. (Also a feeling of self importance that you have a *right* to get what you want.)
> Depression - the fear of being punished if you express your anger, so you *depress* it and turn it inwards.
> Guilt - the fear of getting caught.
> Jealousy – the fear that someone is better than you.
> Anxiety - the fear of an unknown outcome.

So, find the controlling fear attached to a negative emotion and you've gone a long way toward identifying and possibly solving your problems. Just remember "As a man thinks in his heart, so is he." In other words, good or bad, our thoughts create our emotions so eventually we become what we dwell upon. But what I learned that day is this: if my life was not immediately on the line, then what was there to fear? This took me from the most afraid I had ever been, to an internal peace I had never known. The wall I needed to climb was not in front of me, but inside of me and once again, Mark Twain was right:

"Do the thing you fear most and the death of fear is certain."

I remembered this lesson for almost 30 years until 2001. At around that time, I let fear take me to some pretty low places.

But before I got to the bad low places, I visited a lot of really neat ones while spelunking (caving) which turns out is somewhat more dangerous than climbing where people rarely get lost. Now, while climbing is stupid, doing it *in the dark* on slick slimy mud really does takes stupidity to another level. So my preference is for "horizontal" caving where one is walking or crawling, or for caves with short 50 foot drops. But even in a "vertical" cave where one needs ropes, I feel safer than exposed on the side of a cliff. Maybe it's because I can't see how far I'll fall if I mess up or, more accurately, know exactly when I'll hit bottom. You see, whether climbing or caving, most any fall over 20 feet is going to be real painful like. Or you may hit so hard, you feel no pain. This happens because you are dead.

But with climbing, the higher you are, and because you can pretty much see your downward destination, the more time you have to meditate on exactly *how* bad the sudden stop is going to hurt. (The actual *falling* part is usually quite painless.) In a cave, however, because of the darkness, you are more likely to have a surprise splat.

Caving also engendered thoughtful questions from people such as: "You go caving *underground?*" (As opposed to *above* ground?) or, "You cave at night? Isn't it dark in there?"

But the best part about caving? The thrill of discovering something *no* human eyes on the planet have *ever* seen before. Ever as in never. Which I think is pretty neat.

Even so, I must admit I've had some really *really* scary moments with caving, such as getting *really* lost. Ironically, in the long run, these bad moments were much to my advantage in learning to trust others.

On the other hand, I gave Dennis little reason to trust me.

Dennis was my best friend for a long time and we did a lot of traveling including a bit of caving together. One day, in upper NY State, we stood at the lip of a funnel shaped sinkhole that dropped into a 60 foot pit and made the decision to try and get in the cave. I rigged up a rope and was attempting to tie a crude harness to his waist as a safety line. At the time, he was facing me while standing on the down sloping entrance with his back to the pit. This put his head level a little below my miner's lamp.

As I was looking down tying the knot, I heard a buzzing crackling noise very close by that sounded like a small swarm of mosquitoes. As it was a humid summer day, I didn't pay much attention and kept working on the knot.

Then I smelled something funny.

Back then, we didn't have the benefit of electric headlamps and were still using the old carbide type, which when lit, spit out a pretty flame about an inch or two long.

For some reason I decided to look up and was greeted with the top of Dennis's head on fire. Now Dennis didn't have a lot of hair to begin with and what was there, was thin, curly and made excellent brush fire tinder. He looked like the Olympic torch.

Without thinking, I took my hand and smacked him hard on top of the head. Dennis, who still didn't have a clue what was happening, looked at me wide-eyed with a big "O" where his mouth was. But this may have been more because he was falling backwards into the pit doing a very nice flailing sort of motion. In one of those last moment gestures of friendship, my other hand grabbed the (thankfully) completed waist knot and pulled him back towards me. When I finally got him on the ground, I stomped out the remaining embers. He was grateful. Sorta.

(In yet another "irony", Dennis with whom I had lost contact for over 30 years, tracked me down while I was writing this book. Maybe the universe *does* know what's going on? He seems to think the head fire is what made him bald today.)

~~~~~~~~~

For the sake of subject context, allow me to fast forward to 2003 to a world class cave in North Georgia called Ellison's. This is considered one of "the" bad boys and it has the deepest vertical "freefall" pit in the continental USA at 586 feet. That's a lonnnng way down, folks. Actually, this cave *system* (it's about 13 miles long) is just full of mega-pits. Anyway, my close friend Ray (whose caving abilities far exceed my own which makes me much smarter than him for choosing me as a partner) wanted to "show me something" there.

After a laborious schlep up the mountain with all our gear and rope, we entered the cave and in a short bit, came to the initial 126 foot drop called (and rather facetiously so in my opinion) the "Warm-up Pit". All drops and significant features in caves are named in order to help plan what equipment you need and minimize (not prevent) you from getting lost. Sometimes. (Actually, Indian Cave in Alabama has a spot named after me called the "Gary Is Lost Room". How embarrassing.)

Ray rigged the rope and quickly rappelled down into the heavily misted chamber, which was enormous from what I could see. (Helpful hint: make sure your rope is longer than the drop. If not, then tie a big knot on the end to keep you from zipping off it and screaming all the way down until the sudden stop stops you.) I could also hear a lot of water somewhere which turned out to be a high and beautiful waterfall coming out of the wall across the room. However, the echoing roar and mist from the fall made communication and visibility almost impossible while I was on rope and I could barely see the pinpoint of Ray's headlamp far (like way too far) below when he got off the rope.

Due to the harsh and demanding environment, caving equipment is very specific to the task and for a drop over 100 feet, most folks use what's called a "rack" as a rappelling device. This allows precise speed control going down the rope. What I had instead was my beloved F-8 or, "Figure 8". (If you can visualize a six inch long "8" shape made out of a thick welded steel rod, you've basically got it. If you can't imagine it, you need to update your meds.) And it was beloved because 35 years prior, it was hand forged, hammered out and welded for me by The Ig on his personal anvil. (When he wasn't holding it over his head.) Just like Excalibur.

But the F-8 only works well on rope lengths up to 100 feet maximum. Beyond this length, it has a tendency to cause one to start spinning in circles while on rope and is difficult to control the speed of descent.

So while I was spinning around with 110 feet still to reach the floor, I began to get vertigo which is unusual for me due to my aerobatic experience in airplanes. But when you cannot see a horizon point in heavy mist and you are going downward and spinning in circles at the same time in the dark and you are not on solid ground, well, that's a different story. So I tried to slow my descent and get "my bearings" but one needs to be careful in doing that as well. The reason for this is rappel devices control your descent by using friction, which makes heat, which is bad for the rope. As such, one can actually get the device so hot as to weaken the rope. This is not recommended for the obvious reasons. Especially ten stories up in the air.

The "cure" for this is to keep moving, which of course, makes more heat and like I said, the F-8 was not good for speed control on a rope this length. But another way to help control your descent (and spinning) is to have someone below you pull down on the rope to slow or stop you. This gives you time to reorient and get things a bit more under control, but Ray couldn't hear me and I could barely see him. (As I was close to vomiting anyway, it was probably better he wasn't directly under me.) Eventually as the remaining rope length got shorter, the "8" became more effective and I slid to a very grateful stop at the bottom of the drop, a bit rattled and dizzy, but in one piece.

We then crossed this huge underground room and climbed 20 feet up a slick wall on the far side. Eventually, we came to what looked like an 8 foot high arched tunnel entrance with a small ledge about 18 inches wide running along the left side and curving around out of sight into yet more darkness. (Caves have a lot of that.) To the right of the ledge was just a void of black air which I sensed I should avoid. Yup, good idea to avoid the void.

Ray got on his belly on the ledge and scooted around the bend and told me to follow.

Without giving it much thought I did and halfway out on the ledge and while trying desperately not to slide off it, I asked him where the legendary 586 foot pit was. He told me

"About 6 inches to your right."

Now fear is a funny thing and often based on how much information you have. I had just been given too much.

Waaaay too much.

I then realized the usual cave smell of "clean damp dirt" now seemed, well, different. This snifficant finding was from an unexpected source. Me…and it had the distinct smell of fear.

From that moment on, Ray pretty much had to talk me through it. When I finally arrived at the end of the ledge, I thanked God there was a platform like area that felt much more secure. Ray then nonchalantly beckoned me to look over the edge into the monster pit and I politely declined. But then I thought, hey, I had just gone through an awful lot of effort (not to mention fear) to get to this point, so, I got down on my belly and oh ever so slowly inched and slid myself to the ledge edge. When I got to where I could poke my head over and shine my light down into the yawning gulf, my brain got goofy again because there was no visual reference point. The fact my light only shone down one fourth the almost 600 foot drop into more clouds and mist didn't help the impending vertigo at all.

Ray then pulled a rock from his pack and handed it to me. In caves, rocks are used to give one a rough estimate of pit depth if it is unknown. You simply toss the rock over the edge then count in seconds how long before you hear the clatter when it hits the bottom. Then you quickly use the effortless formula of

$$\tfrac{1}{4}\,(\text{-})\,7 \times G\ \male\ \yen\ Lx2\ \infty\ 938 \approx\ ?$$

in your head to estimate the depth of the pit. Now I am used to several seconds of silence before hearing the rock strike bottom and that's a pretty decent drop. When I threw this stone into this pit (called Fantastic Pit), I waited to hear it hit bottom. And waited. And waited. While Ray grinned. I then finished the last chapter of a book and did my hair before I heard this deep "boom" of an echo come charging up from the depths below.

I remember the hair standing up on my neck.

Now, do you know what happens to a guy when he gets into really cold water?

Well, that's exactly what my entire body did as I shrank back from the edge of the ledge and told Ray

"How about we go home? Now."

Last one out turn off the lights.

Even though I have known dozens of people who have rappelled and then climbed back out of this pit, I realized right then I'd never need to. This, I thought, was a very mature decision for someone who was only 53 years old.

Remember me saying that I was disappointed and bored? Well, caving was one way to address both of those conditions. You see, caving is definitely NOT boring. Much like doing aerobatics in an airplane, take your attention away from what you are doing and there's a good chance you won't be doing much of *anything* ever again right quick. So you learn to focus and pay attention. However, early on, I also made a deliberate effort to choose my caving partners real careful like and I chose a group of very capable people. No more Spiderman-Johns because when caving, your life may be lost or saved in a moment by the actions of another - so you want that other to be able to meet your expectations and the demand of that particular cave, as some are much harder than others.

This forced me, the self-reliant one, to depend on others to come through if needed for me, and I for them. Out of this comes trust and out of that, fast friendships you could count on.

In fact, one can almost say there's a Code of Honor as almost without exception (there's always the exception, eh?) I've found that paddlers, pilots, cavers and climbers can be depended on if things turn bad. And the reason is simple: No one ever gets hurt because a basketball lost its air or by watching a field goal on T.V. But snap a paddle in half in the middle of a vicious rapid, have a failure of a rappel device while on rope or an in-flight emergency and the consequences can quickly become dire or even deadly.

This is another reason why there is absolute respect for another's equipment and the need to "get their back" if necessary. Someday it may be you. And unlike your typical sports, I know as many excellent women in these activities as men. I've also seen – and been a part of – complete strangers risking their lives to save that of another.

In one way or another, they are all Protectors of the Realm.

54

I Looked Like I Saw a Ghost

~~~~~~~~~

Speaking of realms, I was indoctrinated into Catholicism like most Italians. However, after sitting through countless masses in undecipherable Latin, I began to drift away from the faith. So instead of going to church, I went to the diner next door which was nicknamed St. Willie's - which had nothing to do with my childhood body part jammed in the drawer rising to sainthood. At that point, and because I still struggled with mankind's perpetual three questions of "Who am I, Why am I here, Where am I going", I was fair game for anyone offering some form of believable faith. One night, I found my "answer" in a newspaper ad. And no, it was not EST or Eckankar, which sounded too much like a mouth sore to me.

The next week I showed up at a Silva Mind Control (SMC) seminar and moved into a "new age", literally and figuratively for the next 19 years of my life where I met some of the most delightfully strange people on the planet. SMC was "invented" by Jose Silva, who apparently had migrated to America – possibly by astral projection. The course was essentially divided into two parts. The first half was mostly about self-improvement and health concerns like memory, lowering blood pressure, reducing headaches, bladder control during long movies etc. all of which I found interesting.

The second half of the course was a bit more hinky and purportedly developed one's "inherent" psychic abilities by doing "readings" on another's health problems, even if they were on the moon, and then attempting to heal them. Edgar Cayce type stuff. This was all backed up with some pseudo-scientific notions about brain waves, alpha particles, nuons, freons and Hostess Twinkies.

Long story short, it was a nice group of people (most of whom I now realize would blend seamlessly into California) and after a period of time, I became an instructor for the course. I was a believer and, truthfully, did see some things that were a bit over the edge and defied my ability to explain at the time. And true or not, it made me feel I had more control over my life.

One night as my helper Joelle (who also had an unexplained frog fetish) and I were cleaning up the lecture room where we had about 30 people that day, we remarked almost simultaneously about one "weird" guy who had been in the middle of the room.

Almost as we said that, we both turned to where he had sat and somewhat to our astonishment, there was (and I really don't know how else to describe this) what appeared to be a vapor or vertical "cloud" at his seat that was sort of swaying, but stayed put. Was this really a ghost? A spirit? Did they even exist? Or did I just have bad kimchi for lunch? Who knew? Not knowing if I needed to protect her from something, I decided to go over and introduce myself. As I was walking over, Joelle said

"You *sure* you know what you're doing?"

"Of course I do."

"Well, what is it you're doing?"

"I don't know."

As I approached whatever it was I was approaching, I could feel the air temperature going down. At first, I thought I was imagining it, so I asked Joelle – who by now was hiding under a desk in the corner – to come over by me. I didn't tell her what I felt or what to look for, but as she got closer, she said

"Is it getting colder in here?"

Hmmm. I then proceeded to walk "through" the wispy cloud and to my surprise, got an immediate headache which just as quickly went away as I exited out the other side. Joelle and I then had an emergency high level psychic conference on all of this ectoplasmic stuff. In doing so, we decided the thing needed prayer so it could go get dinner with the guy who tried to leave it behind. This we did and away it went but only after we threatened to call the Psychic Hotline. Make of it what you want. In retrospect, I found it mildly interesting but of no real impact on my life other than to question things. But as you'll soon see, I had little problem doing that.

On another occasion I was working alone on my van late one night in the shop with all the building doors locked for safety. At the time, I was installing the pullout bed and had a lot of tools on the van floor by the two open rear doors.

I then heard the phone ring in the office and spent about five minutes in conversation. When I came back out, the tools in the van were all gone. I stood there puzzled then retraced my steps thinking they were in the office, on the floor or under the bed.

No dice. As I had pulled the van in along the right side of the shop, I was nearer to that wall and for some reason, my eye caught something on the window ledge. It was the screwdriver.

I thought this was odd but just figured that in a thoughtless moment, I laid it there. As I walked over to get it, I could see the next window ledge…and there was the wrench I was using.

Now the shop was a big place about 50 by 80 feet and over the next few minutes, I wound up finding all my tools spread out all over the place on the different window ledges. All the windows were locked closed and some ledges were about 8 feet above the floor in the alignment rack pits.

As you'd imagine, this was a *bit* creepy. But overall, it seemed like a harmless nuisance and once again, I simply questioned what occurred.

Questioning can be good or bad. Or at least inconvenient. Because I was requested to be my niece's Godfather, I had to be at her baptism. As we stood around the baptismal birdbath and the priest went through the ritual, he stopped periodically to ask if there were any questions. These pauses were conveniently placed at the point where I had questions. At first they were simple for the priest to answer, but as I realized the scope of the ritual and my implied future responsibilities, I got curious.

Eventually, we were talking about hell, Satan and other comfort topics. It was at this point he stopped the ceremony because he couldn't give me an answer to a question and, I recall thinking that if looks could kill, I'd be leaving the church in a body bag. And they'd be sprinkling dirt, and not water, on me. (I also think this is where Judy, my sister-in-law, almost passed out.) He then pulled out a key that was on a chain around his neck, stepped over to a wall vault, unlocked it and retrieved some musty old document written in Latin.

After a few minutes of muttering to himself in deep thought, he replaced the papers, locked the vault and put the key back inside his robe. By this time, Judy was ready to have *me* locked in the vault and the priest was ready to drown the baby. After this he wisely decided not to ask if there were any more questions. He then zipped through the remainder of the ritual, pronounced somebody "husband and wife", made the sign of the Cross and left us standing there by ourselves.

It's been said this is why my niece seems possessed.

On Into Life

~~~~~~~~

Life is a non-stop carnival of decisions and I needed to make one and figure out what to be when I grew up. I had just completed a long drawn out B.A. degree in English Literature and Art which helped me write up the shop bills using Shakespearian references. I was also getting a good case of arthritis at a very tender age of 25 from working in the shop in the drafty pits holding ice cold tools in the winter. When I could not open my hands in the morning until I ran them under hot water, it was time for a new career. And the sooner the better.

As a result of the riots in Newark in 1967, I decided being an EMT (Emergency Medical Technician) would be useful and signed up for a lengthy course at the New Jersey College of Medicine & Dentistry. Part of this training was emergency room time at Martland Hospital in Newark which was *the* trauma center there like Grady Hospital is in Atlanta. It was here I got to watch someone knock over an oxygen cylinder which tore the valve off the top. Now, when 2 million pounds of compressed air is suddenly released, something's gotta give. (Kind of like that old equal and opposite reaction hair in the zipper thingy when I sat down in the movies, remember?) In this case, the cylinder instantly went from zero to about 300 mph across the room, down the hall, through the concrete wall and came to rest in the morgue. Which I thought was appropriate. Fortunately, it didn't add any extra people to that room and the ones already there didn't seem to notice, much less care.

After getting certified as an EMT, I joined the ambulance group that worked with Anthony Imperiale (once again, Soprano watchers will know that name) to help drag wounded people off the streets and to the ER. Newark, during and after the riots, was *not* the place to go roaming, especially at night and definitely not by yourself. The reason for this was paintball had not yet been invented, so they still used the good old-fashioned lead bullets. This change of life direction for me was interesting, but seemed to go nowhere significant, so I continued to look at other health fields for almost a year.

One night, out of exasperation, I told myself "Tomorrow you *will* make a decision." The next day dawned early in the day and off to the shop I went with my new textbook on emergency surgery techniques tucked under my arm. (After many hours of self directed study, I had learned the word "micturition" which essentially means "I've got to pee." It was difficult to work into casual conversation on a date. But I tried.) As I walked into the shop a man passed by me and stole a glance at the book. He then stopped me and inquired if I was going to medical school. I said no, but that I was trying to make a decision on a future in health care. He asked me

"Have you ever considered Chiropractic?'

I replied "I can't even spell it."

He then gave me his card and told me to join him at his clinic that night after he closed. That evening he spent 2 hours explaining to me the basics of the profession and I sensed my life was about to change. After understanding chiropractic was essentially a mechanical approach to things (structure determines function) and being I *was* a mechanic, it made perfect sense to me. I also liked that it promoted health, instead of just treating sickness and considered nutrition and exercise important factors.

And really, it was a natural career move for me. I stayed in the alignment field and simply went from front ends to back ends. Nine months later, I headed off to Chiropractic College.

Truthfully, before I left, I was hesitant to commit to another three straight years of school. (The program went straight through the year back then with just a short summer and winter 10 day break.) This made me struggle with my pending decision.

As life would have it, Eloise, who I hadn't seen for almost eight years since high school, went walking by the shop one day. We chatted a bit and I mentioned I was considering going back to school but that I would be 30 before I graduated.

She looked at me with a gentle kindness one reserves only for idiots and said the simplest of things:

"Gary, in three years you're going to be 30 anyway. Why not be what and where you want to be?"

OMG. And the course of my entire life took a different turn at that very moment. In fact, almost everything in this book is the result of it. And they say women have no logic?

Thank you, Eloise.

The astronaut James Lovell said "There are people who watch things happen and there are people who make things happen and there are people who wondered what happened."

Well, there was no denying the facts: It was time for me to stop watching and wondering and to make something happen.

By this time, I had compiled a "Life-List" of things I wanted to try and accomplish - little did I know how precious and prophetic it would become. (If you don't have a list, start it now.) But most of all, I felt the current of my life start to shift...

~~~~~~~

But before I went South, I went North and lived in Vermont for three months just to have some downtime before committing to school. I got there at the peak of the fall foliage which is simply put, magnificent. One evening while watching the live local TV news, the scene cut to a furrowed field. The camera had a waist up shot of a farmer in overalls who was at least 109 years old. The background was an autumn sunset settling into a blaze of red mountains. The reporter, clearly new at the job - and dressed completely wrong with a white shirt, tie and wingtip shoes for a field assignment like this, asked him "So Mr. Greenleaf, have you lived in Vermont all your life?"

Expecting a simple answer like yes or no, the reporter quickly shoved the mike right into the farmer's face - who just stood there silently as the camera zoomed in on what looked like a giant old raisin. After an uncomfortably long silence for both TV and the reporter, the farmer scratched his chin, looked right at the camera and in a gravely slow motion drawl said

"Nottttt........yyyyet."

Perfect truth. I mean ya' gotta love it, no?

And there was wisdom in those words because if you are blessed with more time, then you still have the opportunity to steer your life in the direction you'd like to go. Your dreams do not need to taunt you if you can still move towards them.

While I was in Vermont, Dennis, whose hair had now grown back (a little...sorta) and I took a few days to go skiing in the White Mountains of New Hampshire. Upon arriving at Canon Mountain, we donned our best western ski hats and face bandanas and slid off incognito as Tex and Co-Tex. We saw few others.

Actually, it was less than a few. We saw no one. The reason, we discovered, was that we were the last folks allowed on the mountain that day because of the high winds coming up the valley. Now, you need to know Canon is very close to Mt. Washington which had the highest recorded winds on earth at 231 mph. That was *before* the gauge ripped off the chained down building and went sailing off somewhere *faster* than 231 mph.

On the day we were on Canon, they closed the lifts down as soon as we got off on top because the chairs had started to flip in circles *over* the cable. Anyway, we now needed to get back to the bottom, so off we went. Or at least tried to. I immediately ran into several problems. One was the extremely severe cold and because I didn't have any goggles on, whenever I blinked my tearing eyes, they instantly froze shut. So I advanced only about 100 feet at a time between defrostings. What I really needed though, was "hindsight" so I could see what was behind me.

This was because at one point, the wind screaming up the slope got so strong that it slowed me down, stopped me and then pushed me up the hill *backwards* on my skis. This made for one very long trip down. And a brutally cold one. At one point, I put my hand down to break a fall and in doing so, skied over my thumb, dislocating it. This confirmed my day was improving. When I tried to pull the glove off to look at it, the thumb stayed in the glove and the skin stretched back and forth like a rubber band. Finally, it popped out and I figured "What the hell", there's no one around to help me and I can't ski like this, so I worked it back into the socket.

Oooowwee!! Don't try that at home. (Years later while skiing in Switzerland, I dislocated a shoulder 4 miles from the bottom of the run. Are we thinking I should give up skiing?

When we finally stumbled frost bitten into the lodge, we were informed the temperature combined with the wind chill on the slopes was at *minus* 54 degrees. That's pretty cold. Once again I learned you just don't mess with Mother Nature. And yes, it's true that if you toss steaming hot coffee in the air at those temperatures, it will freeze and crystallize before it hits the ground.

As an object lesson, I also learned you should never, *ever* try to pee outside in anything near minus 54 degrees as something other than the pee may freeze and crystallize before it falls off and hits the ground.

Starry, Starry Night

~~~~~~~~~

Two weeks before I left New Jersey for Georgia, I met Jeanne at the shop whose personality I enjoyed. But, she was engaged and I was moving. So there ya go – she was gone and I was going. But before I left, we decided we'd drop each other a note now and then. A short while later, she wrote me saying she was now dis-engaged so on my summer break six months later, we had our first date. She lived way out in the country with her folks on a farm with lotsa land, a golden retriever and, best of all, a runway as her dad was also a pilot.

As we were entering a restaurant, I opened the door and let her in. But as I got halfway through, I stopped. She soon realized I was still standing there with a somewhat bewildered look on my face and came back asking me

"What's wrong?"

I said (and don't ask me *where* this came from) "Umm, we're going to get married and I'm going to die when I'm 33." As I was 27 at the time, that didn't seem all that far off.

She looked at me like I was from another galaxy and said

"Well, uh…that's nice. Can we eat?" Other than this little detail, the evening went well even though it was the first time she ever had dinner with an alien.

During my winter break, I again went to NJ and took Sadie with me who was my purebred albino Spartan lab rat. These are actually interesting, clean and intelligent creatures at least as smart as many of the folks I met at the shop. Sadie would sit on my shoulder when I drove and wave her little pink paw to other cars as they passed by. Anyway, by the time I got to the farm that night, it had snowed. Jeanne and I then went walking out in the wide open fields and I was in awe of the crystal clear night sky gleaming with stars that seemed to make the snow glitter like an endless sea of diamonds. Needless to say, I was deeply moved by the dreamy celestial ambivalence this all created.

As I stood there gazing at the heavens, she asked

"What are you thinking?"

Well, it *was* sort of a romantic setting, we were getting along well (mostly because we had only spent about 5 days together in one year) and it didn't seem like the time to tell her that Saturn's rings are actually made of lost airline luggage, so I replied

"I was just thinking what it would be *like* to be married to you." And although I am 100% sure this is what I said, it is not what she *heard.*

A few months later during a phone call, she asked me what the date was. I looked at my calendar and said March 3^{rd,} which was that day. She then clarified she was asking what was the date of the wedding. I asked

"Whose?"

"Ours."

Now, the fact that I was getting married – or had even asked anyone to marry me – was all news to me. I asked her if I had missed something, had blacked out or what? She then reminded me of what I said while star gazing which she had interpreted as a proposal. My subsequent explanation apparently failed to squelch the idea and I finally got to the point of saying "Oh, why not?" Now, a word to the wise here: DO NOT ever attempt to use this logic as a basis for marriage. Ever.

So she began the paper planning and I began to grow an ulcer. Within a few weeks I got to the point where I believed we didn't know each other nearly well or long enough to make this decision. I told her this and she graciously said

"I understand. Take two weeks and get back to me."

Phew! Two weeks later I got back to her and said I didn't want to get married as I really was convinced we hadn't spent sufficient time together. Her response startled me:

"Oh great, now you tell me after I've got the all the reservations made and the invitations printed up!"

Apparently, this all occurred during my 2 week time-out think-out. When I asked why she did that, she said she just thought I'd still want to do it. This did not make me happy. But even though I felt like I had just been boxed in, I also now felt guilty and after a period of time I said

"Let's do it." (Tip #2: Never marry out of guilt. But hey, I was going to die at 33, so I could hold out for that long, no?)

So we did and she moved to Georgia. Jeanne was a fine person whose abilities, intelligence and humor I enjoyed and admired, but we were not a good mix which became apparent rather quickly. About 2 years later, we had some of my fellow classmates over for dinner, during which Bob asked us how we met, got together etc. to which I related the above story. When I got to the part about her telling me about the reservations and invitations already being printed etc., she gave a short snortlaff.

Because the co-genderous humor of this topic had always eluded me, I turned to her and said

"Why did you laugh?" Her reply?

"I never did any of those things. *I just told you that.* I figured you wanted to get married and thought that would help."

We were divorced the following year. And I had yet to realize how very little I knew about relationships or how subtly we try to protect ourselves from their possible hurt. So, as there is only one thing more painful than learning from experience, and that is *not learning* from experience, here's your fair warning of the three things this taught me:

---

1.   The chances of a Long Distance Relationship going the distance are inversely proportional to the distance in the relationship. In other words, the longer the distance, the worse the odds. LDR's are nothing more than an artificially extended "good behavior" period and not much else. I mean, if you only get to see someone a little bit of time here and there and you have to go out of your way to do it, chances you are also going to justify your efforts and overlook any "real" items" you may not be particularly thrilled about. Why? Because if you did admit the shortcomings, you'd also have to admit how dumb you were to travel there to see them. Finally, no one gets to know the other under the day to day circumstances we all need to abide by. More on this later on.

2.   What people hear is not always what you intended them to hear. How they recall an experience has more effect on them than the actual experience itself. Remember that.

3.   A woman can go through an entire roll of toilet paper in under two days.

The following years of singletude and dating taught me many valuable life lessons. Some were very useful. For example, I discovered it really is possible to wash my delicates and jeans together no mater what their colors. I also learned the Zen cooking art of using a smoke alarm as a timer and after much practice, came up with my very own specialty:

Reservations.

In The Landa' Cotton

Do you remember the movie Deliverance? Would that make *you* want to go there? Me neither. I mean, visiting people who share teeth was not my idea of what the socially upward mobile did. But, I had no choice and went to Marietta, Georgia in order to attend Life Chiropractic College in January 1977. Marietta was right outside Atlanta and was known for the "Big Chicken" (Google it, you'll see!) which I lived right across the street from. Getting to Georgia was an odyssey in the making as I packed my car to the ceiling and bid a tearful good-bye to my folks in the wee hours of the morning. My Dad, not known for emotional expressiveness, surprised me by showing a moist eye at my departure. This was unexpected and made it even harder to leave.

Eighteen hours later, it was dark, cold, rainy and I was lost. And *where* was the damn 80 foot "no way you can miss it" chicken I was told about?! Anyway, I got there as soon as I arrived and found the school the next day. And as I entered "Life", my roommate's name of "Arthur" was not lost on me. As for me, my classmates quickly nicknamed me "Serpico".

Great - just what I came South to get away from!

I really liked my first teacher, Charlie, and on the first day I remember going home and saying to myself "If I ever have a partner, I'd like it to be him." (Fast forward: four years later I get a call at my clinic and it's Charlie. He got right to the point and said he'd like to come and practice with me. Wow. Talk about Vuja'-De. As a result we had a great partnership for 10 years.)

At first, school was really tough for me as I had no real established study habits and had done only moderately well as a disinterested undergrad displaying mediocre effort. And although I had saved money for tuition, I was also on a student's budget which meant a lot of whole wheat on rye sandwiches.

While at Life, I seem to recall we were carrying about 30-33 credit hours a quarter and only had off 2 weeks in the summer and the winter. But after I discovered it was exactly where I was supposed to be, I finally hit my stride and learned what study and test taking techniques worked best for me to the point I was really enjoying the stressful experience. I can also remember feeling as though I was surfing a wave that just kept moving me forward with only a little input from me. It took me a while, but part of this was the result of making a determined effort to see how much I could leave school with, as opposed to some others who tried to see how much they could get away with. In doing so, I soaked up information like a sponge. In fact, I wanted more information than they were teaching me.

At one point, I was sitting up front in Dr. C's class who was part of the administration and had the reputation of being a walking encyclopedia. After I had asked him a straightforward and valid question, he stumbled around for an answer and eventually sidestepped it. This happened 2 more times but on the third, instead of attempting to answer me, he just looked at the class, tilted his head towards me and said to them

"One of Pavlov's failed experiments" as he turned back to the board. In a moment of recalcitrance, I threw him a "friendly" Italian gesture to which the entire class said "Ooooooo....!" Later that day I put a letter in his mailbox that said I thought "I was at a professional school and did not travel 750 miles to be mocked simply because you don't know an answer. I would respect you a great deal more if you just said 'I don't know.' "

While in a different class the next day, his secretary came in and said "Is Gary Polizzotto here? Dr. C wants to see you. Now." I stood up, faced the class and said "Well, guess its goodbye folks!" and prepared myself to be expelled.

When I entered his office he came around his desk, shook my hand and asked me to have a seat while telling me "It took a lot of guts to write that letter." We then made peace based on mutual respect. He did have a request of me, however, which was could I please change my "MEDIC" car tag to something more "appropriate" to a chiropractic college? (And no, I didn't.) The outcome of all this was he put me on several committees one of which (Disciplinary) had to expel a student who went to class with a gun in his back pocket...which went off and shot him in the butt. (We had a Zero-Tolerance policy for ass-shooters.)

Eventually I became an instructor in human dissection which involved lifting a lot of dead weight. Because the school was growing so fast, we ran out of cadaver lab space and had to expand into a temporary doublewide trailer we stole from

66

somewhere in Alabama. (We told the owners we were just going to rotate the tires.) At one point, the lab teachers got down to just myself and Ron who was a really bright guy and a great lab partner. As the first cadaver class for new students was on lab protocol, respect for the dead, how to dress, handling scalpels etc., either he or I would give a short 15 minute introductory talk. To accommodate the class, we pushed the stainless steel gurneys with bodies alongside the walls, three to a side and put chairs in the middle of the room.

One day, I was bored so I told Ron to do the lecture and no matter what happened to keep talking. He looked puzzled, but said "OK." and left the room to go get a soda. While he was gone, I found a new white opaque body bag, laid it out on an empty gurney near the front of the room, climbed in and zipped it up. Shortly, the room filled up with 30 students, all a bit nervous to be around the dead and Ron launched into the talk. Have you put this together yet?

After about five minutes (and when I was almost out of air), I groaned out loud, sat bolt-upright on the table for a moment and then laid back down again with a thud…and waited. Well, it didn't take long. Within about 5 heartbeats the pandemonium peaked and the room had cleared out. And there was Ron, bless his dutiful 'lil heart, just a-droning away on how not to be squeamish around the dead.

We finally had to go outside and gather up the newly departed and bring them back in to the dearly departed.

We also had a unique way of dispensing with the used bodies in the early years. But if I tell you that, I'll have to kill you. I will tell you it's where the Soprano's got the idea.

There was one day, however, when a woman came by to make arrangements to pick up her husband's body for burial. When she came in the lab, she passed by another body we had just received and admired the subtle blue pin striped suit it was in and asked me where she could get one for her husband. I told her I could help her and to come back about an hour later. When she left, we took both bodies and switched heads.

I'm probably just kidding…..

Truth is, it's interesting – or at least ironic given the subject matter and title of this book - that over 30 years ago I chose "Life" College. I guess Life *is* where you go to learn.

Trust Me…I'm A Doctor

~~~~~~~

"The manifestations of vertebrogenic sciatic neuralgia due to foraminal stenosis are quite different than intermittent neurogenic claudication from central canal stenosis."

After a brief "Hello", these (or something equally incomprehensible) were the first words out of the mouth of my neurology professor on the first day of his class.

Dr. W, while well known for his erudition in his chosen field, had a bit of a challenge at times in coming down to our level. When our first exam was coming up, Artie, who was one quarter ahead of me, said "Here is the test he gave us, you can look it over and get an idea of what he'll be asking." Well, after reading it 12 or so times and finally learning the pronunciation of the anatomy and terms, I felt I had a feel for things and went back to my book studies.

Lo and behold - the test we got was *identical* to the test Artie gave me. Needless to say, I was shocked to get one of the highest grades in the class…but didn't know what to do with it. I felt like I had cheated, even though I hadn't intentionally done so. But before I could resolve this moral dilemma, a few students asked me to explain some of the answers to them. So I said "OK, I'll try." And faster than I could object, they began making me one of the "go to" guys which I stupidly allowed based on the following faulty logic:

"They think I know more than I do. Therefore, I need to make sure I *do* know it in order to not look really foolish."

As a result of this childish logic massaging my adult ego, I actually wound up learning a lot more than I probably would have otherwise, but I felt for the wrong reason. (A short while later I discovered Dr. W. *purposely* repeated his exams as a learning tool. That took some of the guilt away.)

Anyhow, I graduated Summa Cum Latte and thinking I knew a few things. This eventually carried into my practice where it was my turn to say "Trust me. I'm a doctor" until I had a mini-epiphany on a Wednesday. That day I had a patient in a treatment room who asked me how different electrolytes affected heart physiology. I answered as best I could, but really wasn't certain I had spoken correctly. I then made the decision the truth was more important than my appearing to be a master of the subject. Feeling a bit foolish, I turned around and pulled a reference book off the shelf and read the answer to him.

When I was done, he said

"Well now, I'm impressed." I thought he was being a bit sarcastic and replied

"What, that I was right or that I can read?"

His response was completely unexpected: "No, I'm impressed you feel secure enough with yourself to look up something in *front of me* just to be sure."

Indeed. That day I got smarter by realizing I didn't have to be nearly as smart as I thought I was. I also went from "Trust me. I'm a doctor" to "Trust me. I'll try and do the right thing."

Just before I graduated, a teacher from the college had approached me and said

"So when are you coming down to my clinic?" I asked

"Why do I want to do that?" He replied

"Well, if you are going to work there, don't you want to see it first?"

This, I thought, was a very odd job offer but after seeing his place in Atlanta, I joined his office as an independent contractor renting space. That he came from the same home town I did in New Jersey was outright weird. That he was Dr. C's brother-in-law was even weirder. About 2 weeks later as he was heading out to lunch looking troubled, I said "See ya later?"

His reply? "Maybe."

The next time I saw him was about 18 months later. It seems he went to lunch, had a personal self-discovery moment, drove to the airport and was walking on the beaches of California by dinner time. My dilemma was it took me about 4 months to find this all out. And that was after calling hospitals, local and state police, relatives etc. No one knew anything. He had just simply vanished. In the meantime, as he already had another partner before me, I approached him and said

"You need to let me know what my end of the clinic costs are until we get this figured out."

His reply was "Oh, don't worry about it, we'll get to it."

We repeated this conversation a few more times for several months until, one day, I came in and there on my desk was a note from him that said rather tersely "I no longer think it is in your best interest for you to continue practicing here." Uh, excuse me? What's that part about "in *my* best interest"?!

I did not need a blood pressure cuff to know it would be off the scale. I was livid he would do this to me after my repetitive requests being denied to meet with him and be fiscally responsible. And to leave me a *note*? And not tell me to my face?

Not.

My response note simply said "I'm not going anywhere," to which he said he would pursue a legal course. Well good for him. As he was a renter like me, he had as much, and as little, legal rights as I did.

As fate would have it, the main man missing in action called me and upon hearing what was going on, signed over his rights (as the real clinic owner) to me!

Guess who was leaving now?

But unknown to me, all was not well yet and eventually I got a default payment note from the SBA (Small Business Association). I had no idea the clinic was bought on a loan that was now in default. After meeting with them, I was told the office equipment (about $25,000 worth) was going to be auctioned off on the courthouse steps! But, hey, I could bid on it if I wanted to. So I dutifully showed up in the gray early morning rain at 7:00 A.M., looked around and saw five pigeons. None of whom had a chiropractic license, so I figured this might not be too competitive. The SBA man then emerged on the steps above, unrolled a scroll, looked around and said

"I can't believe I'm doing this: Hear ye, hear ye...we have for auction the following chiropractic equipment. What bid ye?"

I looked around – still no one there but the two of us and the five pigeons, so I asked him "What's the 'salvage value' of the equipment?" (This is what SBA would make after removing, storing and then selling it at whatever amount they could get.) He looked at me kinda funny because I had used an "insider" term and said

"How do you know about that?" So I asked him again and he said $1,950! I could not believe it would be that low. So I immediately offered $2,000, he immediately said "Sounds good to me", rolled up his wet scroll and said to the pigeons and me

"This auction is officially concluded. Let's get some coffee!" The real irony was their rush to have the auction but their delay in requesting payment, which was a full 2 years later.

70

Hmmm. This business world thing was turning out much differently that I anticipated. But so far, so good and I saw a "hands on" approach to things worked not only as a chiropractor, but in business as well. I then went out and changed my car license plate to "FUNDOC".

When Charlie finally came on board as my partner, we sat down and came up with a clinic policy. And it was stone simple: "Treat every patient as though they were a family member."

And although it was unlikely we'd usher in a personal new Gilded Age with our conservative approach and low fees, we were always busy and just as importantly, content.

Also at this time, both Charlie and I met our soon to be office manager, Kate, who hailed from a "holler" in the West Virginia mountains. On her first interview she had a hair color not found in nature and was dressed in something purple that was, uh, "unique". When asked how she was, she perkily replied "Fine as frog's hair!" A few days later she called back and requested a second meeting. So we had one…and in walked a very professionally attired and coiffed young lady. Our first question was "OK, what did you do with her?" Long story short, she became my personal angel and has stood by my side in the office and in life for almost 26 years, encouraging and believing in me through some really tough times and providing ongoing laughter through it all. We have watched each other face and grow through the various challenges of life and I have observed a courage in her that was far out of proportion to her size.

But just before Kate came on board, I had hired Sidney who was a bright and helpful recent chiropractic graduate who needed office experience, but would often speak before gathering all the facts. One day upon our return from lunch, we saw a patient waiting in the hall by the office door. Sidney and I greeted her and while I was unlocking the door, Sidney casually looked down at the girl's feet.

Now you need to know this very petite gal had polio as a child and one foot was several inches smaller than the other. Sidney, in her sweet naiveté then said

"Oh my, you have such small…..*foot*."

In attempting a quick and graceful recovery to her faux pas, she then asked the tiny 4' 10" patient

"So, whatcha' up to?" In that brief moment I learned one should really consider engaging the brain before the mouth.

One night many years later I got a call at home. The deep steady voice introduced himself as the Mayor of Atlanta.

I said "Yeah, right! Who is this really?"

He repeated his introduction and I repeated my response. Well, it turns out an orthopedic surgeon referred him to me for a neck problem. Now, I have always suspected that politicians were congenitally spineless which I consider a fundamentally insurmountable problem for a chiropractor. Also, as I got along better with the "common folk", the ego massage of working on the big brass just didn't seem worth it. So, I politely deferred and referred him to Sidney who now had a successful practice.

Not as successful was my leaving behind the NJ image. On her first clinic visit the elderly Russian woman had her daughter translate for her. When I asked if there were there any questions, the mother looked at my card, then me, and asked "Mafioso?"

Eventually, Victor, the new pediatrician, moved in down the hall and because his last name was very similar to mine, we'd get each other's calls and mail. One day I went down and said let's go for lunch and get all of this straightened out. While we were eating, we discussed some of our stranger cases. I told him of the woman who after two years and $25,000 of attempted pregnancy "fixes" (turkey baster, in vivo-vitro, frequent sex etc. – soup to nuts so to speak), decided to try chiropractic because at that point, she had nothing to lose. About six weeks later the seminal moment occurred and she was pregnant for under $70. (This is a fairly common occurrence among chiropractors and has happened to me three times that I know of.) The patient then invited me to a celebration party at her home. When I arrived, she saw me come through the door and from clear across the room she yelled out above the noise

"That's the guy who got me pregnant!" while jumping up and down and pointing at me. Her husband (who had been fined for early withdrawal at the Sperm Bank) found this, well…news.

In turn, Victor told me about a delivery he participated in where the woman had taken fertility drugs and given birth to a premature baby boy weighing only two pounds. However, it had a serious birth defect as he only had one testicle which weighed one pound alone. Eventually, after considering their options, the parents made the decision to put the child in a sanatorium because he was diagnosed as already being half nuts.

What Goes Up Must Come Down

~~~~~~~~

By 1981, it had been some time since I had last flown and it was also the advent of the "Ultralight" movement. This was not a new cigarette, but an airy one person flimsy, flexible flying "lawn chair" that by law, had to weigh less than your mother-in-law. So I built one of the very early designs, an 18 horsepower Weedhopper (which tells you all you need to know about its ability as a "flying" machine.) After completion, I got in, hopped off in the weeds and at about 300 feet up was promptly disenfranchised by my engine leaving me un-empowered. (Non-PC version: It quit.)

Now generally speaking, the one thing you don't want to hear in a plane is the noisy thing up front not making any noise. (You can't even legally log it as glider time.) At that moment, I also realized the 300 foot perspective was looking real familiar. (Getting stuck on the cliff, remember?) But because of that pesky law about gravity, it would have been better if I had a decent place to land. Which of course, I didn't. Now there's something you need to understand right up front about flying:

Taking off is optional. *Landing is not.*

The "airport" I was using was a farmer's cow pasture with the cows still in it. They weren't too much of a problem as you could see them. The real problem was what the cows were leaving in the weeds that you couldn't see. As such, cow pies became an "issue" when taking off, especially if they were still warm, soft, gooey and, most of all, sticky. When I took off this time, my nose wheel went though a fresh one and threw it up between my legs so that it splattered all over my face shield.

Looking between the splotches after the engine quit, I noticed that directly across my path and slightly below me were those real big high tension wires that I could not get over and was forced to try and dive under. (Headlines: "High-volts and Flying Crate Create Crispy Critter") But the dive increased my airspeed so that I overshot what little open area I had available to land. However, off to my right was a rather large backyard with a great big bush in the center. Remembering how jets use a cable to arrest their landings on an aircraft carrier, "Me thinks if I can smote the bush, all will be right with the world."

(I revert to Shakespeare under stress.)

So, I silently glided into the bush, flattened it and rolled out the other side pretty as you please and completely unscathed. But because this all occurred with little noise, the surprised home owner standing next to his outdoor grill, looked at me bug-eyed and speechless, with a steak hanging off his BBQ tongs. Not quite knowing the proper introduction for steak by stealth, I took off my helmet, waved and said "Medium-rare, please." I then got the plane restarted on the road, *drove* it back to the airport, fixed the problem and eventually had many enjoyable hours of flying.

The Weedhopper. Notice the massive engine.

One day, a truly wonderful memory was made during the soft twilight of an exceptionally beautiful sunset. I was puttering around right over the grass landing strip at about 3,000 feet with the sweet scent of shimmering green fields of freshly cut hay rising on the warm thermals. As I looked ahead, I could see a hawk lazing about in another thermal slightly below me. I then killed my engine and gently glided over to him and, instead of falling away, he drew up next to me about 50 feet off my left wing. He stayed there as we sailed on side by side for about one long and glorious minute into the setting sun with only the sound of the wind in our wings. Then, with a final glance and piercing cry that only a bird of prey can make, he tucked his wings and silently sheered off into the deepening nightfall.

I think he said "Bye Mama." Good job, God.

OK, let's recap just a few items over the initial 30 years. So far I've been, or have:

- Born a yellow man
- Abandoned on a street corner by my brother
- Smushed a valuable body part in a drawer
- Tranquilized as a child
- Knocked out (not up) as a girl
- Got up close and personal with a windshield
- Beat up my neighbor
- Beat up the neighbor in the next town
- Totally screwed up a baptism
- Chastised for slapping a nun
- Hoodoo'd by a Bobcat
- Assaulted by a car while on a motorcycle
- Lost Hi-Bob for a few days at Woodstock
- Watched my brother blow himself up
- Watched my brother beat up several cars
- Watched my brother beat up a toupee
- Drove fast police cars with bad hood latches
- Had breakfast with the Godfather
- Gone over a waterfall in a snowstorm at 2:00 A.M.
- Dressed in lingerie in a snowstorm
- Transferred *my* make-up to another girl's face
- Got another girl's hair stuck in my zipper
- Got stuck on a cliff 300' off the ground
- Had a Weedhopper engine failure 300' off the ground
- Set my friend's head on fire
- Got blown backwards up a mountain on skis
- Got stuck with a date on a mountain in a forest fire
- Almost arrested as a sniper
- Married as a result of a non-proposal
- Flew wing to wing with a hawk into a sunset
- Walked through a ghost
- Hid in a body bag
- Bought a $25,000 clinic for $2,000

Into The Night

~~~~~~~~

S hortly after I opened my clinic in, my Dad began to get serious headaches. As I was living 750 miles away, I didn't think I was the cause of them - at least anymore. The first diagnosis was high blood pressure and he was given medications which failed to help. The medications then were changed. This also failed to help. He then saw a dentist who said "Let me yank these teeth out. That oughta help." Which…also failed to help.

Eventually, during a routine eye exam he was told he needed to see a neurosurgeon "stat" (which means "Pronto!"). After seeing one and getting a brain MRI, the diagnostic boom we all fear was lowered and life suddenly became extremely precious. He had a glioblastoma multiforme brain tumor which had wrapped itself like an octopus around the area of the brain that controls vital life functions.

As neurologists rightly call this tumor "The Terminator", the Life-*Time* clock began ticking very loudly for him.

Now, my Dad was a guy who could absorb serious pain. (He had root canals with no injections or medication which would freak the dentist out.) So I cannot imagine the pain level this tumor put him in causing him to run down the hall slamming his head against the wall in an effort to make it go away. Yes, I know it sounds counter-productive…but it's not really.

Here's why: The brain can only process so much pain signal traveling to it from a source at one time. Don't believe me? Well, slam a door on your finger then whack your toe really good with a hammer and tell me which one hurts more. One signal will usually override the other (now you know the secret to my 10 pain free minutes a day: a really hot shower!) The fault with his logic however, was that it was *the brain itself* that was causing Dad's pain, therefore the signal did not have to travel there, it was *already* there. But intuitively, he was doing the right thing although we thought he was going crazy. What a guy.

When I heard about this in Atlanta, we did some research (no Internet back then…couldn't Google my way out of this) and found a neurosurgeon at Harvard who specialized in this form of tumor. I got the impression he was an idiot savant who couldn't open an umbrella, but could do brain surgery in the dark.

Anyway, I called him at home in Boston – interrupting his tea party it seemed - and inquired about a new experimental procedure for this tumor he was doing on beagles and could he use it on my Dad?

"Is your dad a beagle?" he asked.

"Well, no."

"Then we can't do it. But get him up here anyway - stat (see, now you know what that means) and we'll do something."

Well, that was about as hopeful a thing as I had heard so off the family went to Harvard and off the Ig went into the operating room. Many hours later he was wheeled out and Dr. Beagle Research Man came up to me and said

"I was able to get most of it out, but it will return. He has six months to live. Call me if you need me."

Twelve hours later we called because we needed him. While recovering in intensive care, Iggy threw a blood clot into the brain and had a stroke. Things were getting grimmer by the moment. So, back into the O.R. he went for another drawn out surgery where they lifted up the skull plate they had just cut out and went probing for the clot, which, amazingly, they did find.

The following months were heartbreakers for all of us as my Dad struggled to regain some level of function. I mean here was the guy who could pick up 219 lbs. with one arm or an anvil in one hand, take an automobile coil spring to the head…but now doing all he could just to hold on to a handrail and take a few steps without falling. It broke my heart to see his broken spirit.

Yes, life is precious.

But so is the quality of it. Apparently, Dr. Beagleman was not only a first class surgeon, but a psychic as well and as the six month point approached, Iggy went downhill quickly and was put into a hospital. One night, Larry called me in Atlanta at 6:45 and said "I don't think Daddy is gonna make it through the night. You need to get up here." At 7:30 the jet's wheels left the ground and I was in it. Yes, those were the pre-9/11 days at the airport.

When I got to the hospital, my father, the one and only Ig, was in a coma and I sat next to him all night, holding his hand. Larry and Mom were there as well. Did we pray? Yes we did, but for me, they were prayers of confusion and I honestly did not know to pray for healing or a quick and peaceful end.

And I remembered Jesus being in a similar situation and simply praying "…not My will, but Yours…" and that was the best I could do. Well, I don't know if it was a miracle or an answered prayer, but come early morning light, his eyes flickered open, he looked at us and he was completely lucid. The first thing out of his mouth?

"I'm starving! Someone get me a steak and a 7-UP!"

I just about fell out of my chair. But more importantly, and for an unknown reason, I recognized a moment and opportunity I would never have again and asked my Mom and brother to leave the room. Hesitatingly and with looks of confusion, they did and closed the door behind them.

Now let me stop here and say something. This next part is probably not going to mean much to you and I can understand that. But it's going to take an awful lot out of me to put it on paper because it was probably *the* forever icon moment of my life with my Dad as well as a personal revelation.

At this point I found myself "doing without thinking" and sat on the bed next to him. I took both his hands in mine and just held them. And we just looked into each other's eyes for what seemed like years and I simply said to him

"I have never *told* you I love you" followed by just that;

"I love you."

Without breaking his gaze or even blinking his gentle brown eyes, he said back to me

"I love you, too."

Simple as that.

But not so simple. I said it because at that moment I had realized I had never spoken those three words to my own father. And I said it without the need for a response from him, but just to tell him he was loved. And when he said it back to me, I was stunned to realize I had never *heard* those words from him, either.

And I finally felt good enough.

Why had we waited so long?

And the circle was completed as we lay there holding each other, while tears and time silently slipped away. He did not die then, but shortly thereafter. But I had been given my answered prayer and after 31 years, my Dad and I connected in a way we had never been able to and I could let him go when he was ready. A few minutes out of an *entire life time*…and it made all the difference.

Please hear what I just said: A *few minutes* in an entire lifetime made *all* the difference.

Is there something you need to tell someone?

Immediately after this moment, my Dad began to "cloud over" again which was perfect because I realized I had a mission. I went out into the hallway where Larry and Mom were, went up to Mom, put my hands on her shoulders, looked her in the eye and said "I love you." and she, never having any trouble saying those words, responded back. I then backed Larry against the wall and did the same thing because I had never told either of them those words. Larry, probably like me and out of disuse of the words, appeared a bit uncomfortable when I told him and he said "Me too." I am glad to say, however, with the both of us practicing saying it over the years, we can use it freely now. At that very moment, I vowed never to refrain from telling someone if I loved them. Later that day Gina, my possessed niece, folded the electric bed closed like a taco.

Iggy was still in it.

But here's what I walked away with that day: *the* stupidest word in the dictionary is "eulogy". This is where we get to say nice things to *other* people about someone dead. Here's where we get to tell others we loved the person that is gone.

Well, here's a thought: How about we tell *them* while they're alive and can hear it too? Like before I go flying again...

What Went Up Did Come Down

~~~~~~~~

After my ultralight debacle, I decided I needed a slightly more "sophisticated" ultralight and ordered a "Foxbat Trike". This was essentially a hang glider wing connected to a frame below it with a rear facing engine and rudimentary landing gear underneath. While building this kit, I saw what I felt was a significant design flaw with the control system as it seemed you needed three hands to fly the plane. This made me one hand short which meant either I or the plane was flawed. So I called the manufacturer and they assured me

"There's nothing to worry about *once you get off the ground*, it's very natural." Uh, OK. I just need to get in the air, and *then* figure it out, that's all. I guess I can do that.

Once the plane was completed, I took it to the same farmer's dirt strip where I had previously dropped in on the neighbor's BBQ. As I sat on the runway, and just before giving it full throttle to take off, a little voice in my head (or an angel on my shoulder) desperately warned

"Gary, you're going to get hurt."

In the other ear I heard "Gary, you never *ever* get hurt!"

I've always wondered whose voice *that* was.

Now, while God may have made the world in 7 days, little did I know I was about to completely undo mine in 7 seconds. Almost instantly, the overpowered flying kite was airborne and headed up. And I mean *up*. Like way too steep type up. Now most aircraft cannot maintain a 60 degree angle of climb for very long before they run out of forward momentum and "stall", meaning you get so slow the wing stops providing lift and the nose drops down steeply. And as "stalling is falling", this was not something I wanted to practice this close to the ground.

But aha! - In spite of the manufacturer's comments, the noted design flaw on the ground was just as flawed in the air. In fact, it was worse and the plane was now in a meteoric dive only 100 feet above the ground. Now 100 feet isn't high for a plane that's flying.

But it's *terribly* high for someone to be in a plane that is *not flying* and headed straight for the ground. I immediately updated my pre-takeoff comments to

"Oh this is really going to hurt!"

Even so, every pilot has one thing drilled into them for such a circumstance: FLY THE PLANE! Even if you can't, even if it's falling apart and even, as I was, you're completely terrified, you fly the plane until it stops or you're dead. Which caused me to again revise my original pre-take-off thought: I won't get hurt.

I'll die instead. Huh.

Now, do you recall my first date with Jeanne and my comment about dying when I was 33? Guess which year of my life this is all happening in? Luckily, I was only slightly killed.

At some point in the very brief long drawn out descent, I remembered to kill the engine and being able to alter the plane's direction slightly so as not to smash into the side of a barn or go into the adjacent verdant but dense woods.

Instead, I did something infinitely more clever and headed directly for the perceived soft safety of a barbed wire fence.

Before I say what happened next, picture the plane like this: Go in your backyard and find a lawn chair and sit in it. What you see in front of you is the openness I had in front of me. Now imagine a "pusher" engine behind you and a wing over you and you have it. There was no protective cockpit, windshield or any structure in front of or to the side of the hapless pilot. This was wind in the face bugs in the teeth flying. And because the pilot was right out front, he *always* arrived at the scene of the accident first. Even before the plane.

They (whoever "they" are) say in times like this your life flashes before you. Well, if it did, it must have been *really* fast because I missed all of it, even the credits. What did happen was everything seemed to transition to slow motion which I attribute to the brain processing everything while in hyperdrive. After all, it didn't have a helluva lot of time left. So by comparison to "regular time", the speeded up brain gave me the sensation of a slowed down reality.

Don't worry, I understand it.

During this phase of the fall I clearly remember the following two thoughts: "I hope those I love know I love them." And "I've always been curious to know what it's like to die, now I'm going to find out." So, as my trained body continued to struggle with flying the plane, my mind went from fear, disbelief, panic and acceptance in an eye blink.

Then came the sickening sound of snapping wood and bone.

Fortunately the ground broke my fall just as I plunged into the barbed wire at about 40 mph. However, for some reason the tough wire did not break and I slid along it into the stout fencepost. In doing so, my body got caught on the individual barbs and pushed them all together. Then my right knee hit the 4 inch thick post and snapped it in two. The post, in kind, drove my kneecap into my leg and shattered my thigh in 8 pieces. Next, the plane broke in half and threw me about 20 feet to where I lay in a grass filled gully. Which was 5 feet below the level of the runway…which meant no one could see me. As I lay there on my stomach, I realized I felt absolutely no pain. Given the circumstances I just participated in, I found this remarkable and joyful. That was until it occurred to me I had broken my neck and I would never feel *anything* ever again.

Even a Wee Willie dresser drawer closing…awww damn!

But wait! I'm an EMT *and* a doctor. As a trained professional I'm supposed to know how to check these things out! So, I started to methodically go down the list: wiggle the fingers: check; wiggle the toes: check; so now I know all the wiring to the 4 corners is OK. Any major internal organs lying outside my body? Negative. No pain, not *too much* blood. Shoot, "This is f***ing unbelievable! I was just drop kicked by Thor and didn't get hurt at all! I may just as well stand up."

At this point, I was convinced my lap belt was what saved me as I reached under my belly and unlatched it. It really didn't occur to me until much later that the belt simply came along with me for the ride when I was ejected from the wreckage and neither of its ends was even attached to anything. But it made me feel better to "take it off" anyway.

Can we say "shock"?

I then started to push myself up on my hands and knees at which point I noticed, for the first time mind you, that my right leg from mid-thigh on down, was at a 90 degree angle to the upper thigh. Immediately, my anatomical training told me this was, well, not anatomically appropriate. Oh, and the delirious blast of pain that arrived at that same moment and dropped me instantly and breathlessly to the ground confirmed this diagnosis.

The very next words I heard in my head (and in my very best doctor's bed side voice) could only have come from years of training:

"I need to re-evaluate the situation."

Honest to God. To this day I still can't believe I actually said that to myself. So I lay there quietly wondering what to do and more importantly, what would happen next.

(I've heard 6" makes a difference. Well, had the plane been 6" to the left when it hit the fence post, I'da walked away. Six to the right and I'd be a falsetto. Or worse - a castrato.)

A few minutes later I heard voices at the top of the gully and was overjoyed to know help would soon be on the way. But I don't think they knew me as they kept saying to each other "Willy Makit?" I did know enough not to budge and when *they* saw me not moving, I clearly heard them yell out to some others

"Forget it, we're too late."

Now, let me tell you how weird it is to have someone close by refer to you in the past tense. It's actually so weird, it'll cause you to *invent* profanity that never existed just to get their attention, which I did and which made them jump back about three feet. I also told them "I'm *not* dead!" Finally, the EMS arrived, they splinted my leg and dislocated fingers and bandaged where the 3 strands of barbed wire caught me across the throat, chest and foot. We then headed off to the emergency room where I only fell off the stretcher inside the ambulance once as we whipped around the exit ramp. It was at this point the situation seemed to finally broach the "FUBAR BUNDY" stage. (Feel free to Google that.)

Gratefully, I was not aware that not only was my thigh at a 90 degree angle to my body, but that my entire life was about to take a similar turn as well onto a one way street.

Overall, this was not a good day to be me.

Interestingly, my mind would not allow itself to recall the last 2-3 seconds of the accident or the actual impact and I could only "view" the accident as a spectator from far away. It wasn't until 6 months later while watching a true re-enactment of an airliner crash on T.V. that it clicked. An interviewed passenger recalled he didn't tell his wife he loved her before he left that day. Then he realized it was because he didn't. But he also said all he could see was a "bulls-eye" on the ground.

And that was the trigger. That's when I remembered and was flooded by every final detail - including the Big Splat. I also understood that's as close as I wanted to come in killing myself.

Wreckamended

~~~~~~~~

The next 16 days in the hospital were truly a comedy of errors and a book in itself so we'll peruse just a few of the character building moments.

After arriving, it was 24 hours before I was able to have emergency surgery as there was an "emergency" before me. It seems having a dark purple thigh the size of your waist with a right angle in the middle of it was not considered an emergency. So I had to get in line. At least they didn't make me stand. Did I mention I was in a one day window *between* health insurance policies when all of this happened? The immediate lesson learned? Always have health insurance *at the time* you have your accident planned for. This little oversight cost me $15,000 plus.

After a Valium they rolled me into surgery the next day and the last words the strange masked man said to me were

"I might have to amputate your leg." Drowsily I replied

"No, I like my leg! I've had it as long as I can remember!!"

I woke up with a 27 inch J-shaped incision in my right thigh and a 12" stainless steel pin sticking out of both sides of my shin bone…which was eventually removed with a hand cranked Black & Decker drill. Attached to this pin was a bracket with a rope to a weight hanging over the bed to traction the leg straight. I clearly remember hoping no one *ever* bumped into it.

An hour later after my good friend George bumped into it, I finally got the good pain meds. If it weren't for them, I would have never been able to join the yellow whitewater raft paddled by the people with purple helmets going down the hallway. My other dear friend Kara then visited me with her camera and wanted to document all of this for posterity. So she took a bunch of pictures of me writhing in compelling agony. The next day she promptly dropped her camera into the biggest lake in Georgia. Somehow she retrieved it and the film survived.

The hospital then seized upon an opportunity to experiment on me with a new device called a CPM or "Constant Passive Motion" machine. (To some degree, loaning my body has now made a CPM standard procedure for many kinds of surgery, but I experienced the first rather crude unit in Atlanta.) They placed my leg in what looked like an old gutter that was hinged under the knee. Over the knee went a horseshoe shaped bracket with a rope on the top of it. This rope went up to a pulley on the top bed frame, down the length of the bed to another pulley and then downward where it was tied to a revolving arm of a motor.

The idea was as the arm rotated slowly, the rope would alternately pull the leg up and down constantly bending it at the knee. Without this bending motion, the knee would otherwise heal with more scar tissue and less flexibility.

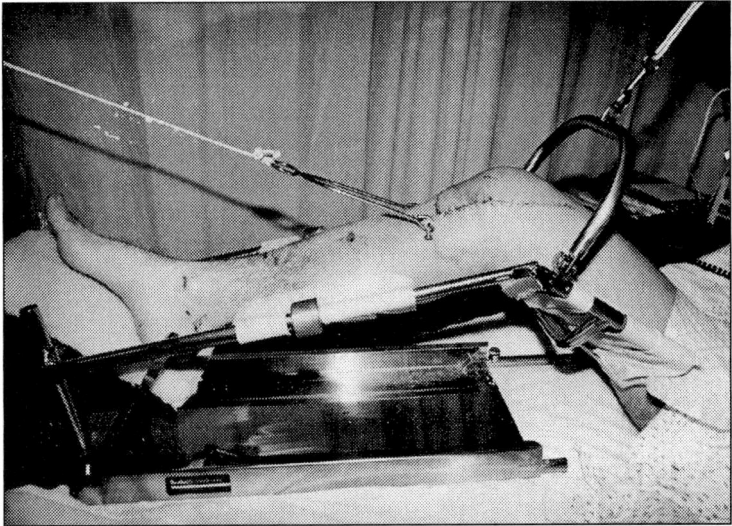

Leg traction and CPM machine

By this time I was on pretty heavy morphine and around 3:00 A.M., my consciousness bubble percolated to the surface because I sensed something was not quite right. And then I drifted off again into a somewhat tenebrous funk. This happened two or three times until I was finally jolted awake. Because the CPM unit was experimental and new to the staff, the janitor didn't quite set it up per the provided instructions and somehow managed to incorrectly connect the rope to the revolving arm. This caused the rope to shorten a small fraction with every revolution, which as you can predict given enough time, eventually left me hanging upside down from the overhead frame like a opossum two feet off the bed. In time, the staff heard my screaming and quickly responded with a professional level of bewilderment before deciding to cut me down.

The next day I awoke with a new knot on the rope, my hair looking like I had stuck my tongue in an outlet and a murderer next to me. During the night, Treeman was moved into my semi-private room. Treeman was a 34 year old 6' 3" black dude who had just had both hips replaced…and had recently been in prison for murder. Oh great. And me with no where – or way - to run. But hey, he can't run either, so I guess that makes us even.

That day he was still knocked out form the anesthesia aftereffects and in a very deep sleep when a nurse came in. She went up to him and called his name and he didn't respond. She called a bit louder and finally resorted to shaking him awake. When he finally and groggily asked her what she wanted, she said (honest to God)

"Wake up- it's time to take your *sleeping* medicine."

I couldn't believe this and thought it was something only done on T.V. comedy routines. I said to her "You have *got* to be kidding, right?! The man was in a coma!"

Her response? "Doctor's orders."

Well butter my butt and call me a biscuit.

Why didn't I know that?!

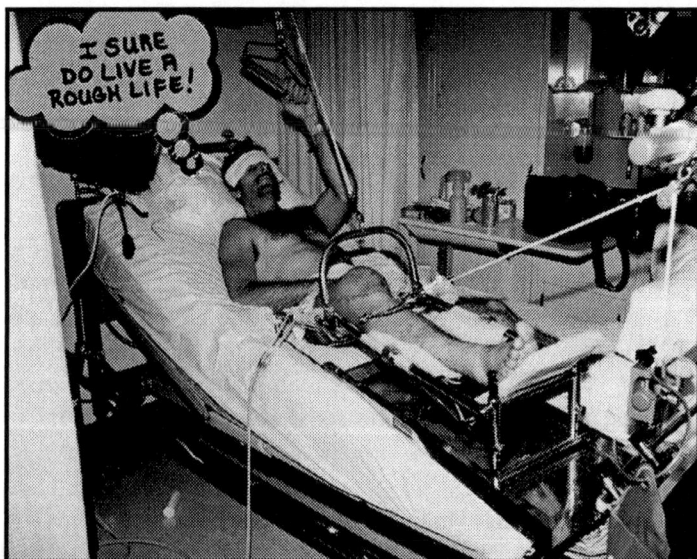

By the next day we began to know each other better and figured we could best deal with our pain by trying to make the other guy as miserable as possible through the time tested methods of ridicule and humiliation. I'd goad him by asking if he would teach me how to tap dance and spit watermelon seeds (which I thought was really funny given our respective injuries) and he'd say "I'm gonna get you white boy...you just wait." Anyhow, as the taunts deepened over the days, so did a real friendship. We were comrades in pain and it made us feel good to make fun of each other. And you know what? Laughter made the pain seem less as we lay there enjoying our nutritious and healing meals of Jell-O, apple juice and a sugary desert.

Well, eventually Treeman did get the white boy. When the time was right, he looked over at me and said

"Hey cracker, here it comes". This was said just before he asked his sister to pull the curtain closed between us.

I had no idea what he was talking about. Turns out he had a skin condition that prevented him from shaving and about once a week he smeared this indescribably foul smelling green sludge on his face that not only dissolved hair and nearby wallpaper, but absorbed all the oxygen in the room. As he slathered on this spackling compound and the green air drifted over to me, all I could hear between my gasps for air was an evil toned "heh-heh-heh" from behind his curtain.

Apparently he was able to tolerate this stuff because he either had developed immunity to it over time, or his lungs were so scarred from constant usage, there was nothing left to ruin. I'm sure somewhere today, there's a late night TV lawyer ad for a class action lawsuit for folks who were exposed to this toxic waste. Like me. But Treeman still called me every year on the anniversary of our meeting just to say "Hi" and remind me he was out there...and that he had more sludge. Maybe he was just calling to see if I died yet from the exposure.

After 16 days of lying in the hospital with my new one inch shorter leg, I was discharged and taken outside. Upon feeling the fresh warm breeze on my face and seeing the blue of the sky, I just wept in my wheelchair. Little did I know how much life was about to really change. It's also worth mentioning that while I was in the hospital, another pilot in an identical Foxbat ultralight had an identical accident. His occurred while his wife and kids were watching his test flight. Sadly, he did not kill the engine before impact. It then tore off the motor mounts and while still running, the propeller sliced through the top of his head. Mercifully, he was killed instantly.

While at home a few weeks later, I decided to try walking outside with my crutches and new leg brace which went from my hip all the way down to the attached unbelievably ugly shoe just like my mother used to buy me. As I was making my way down the street after a rain storm, a crutch slipped on a wet spot and I fell backward. The leg, which was badly atrophied, very weak and no where being fully healed, made a gross and disgusting tearing sound much like ripping the drumstick off a turkey as I went down. The pain meter in my head simply exploded and I just lay there spilling tears in a mud puddle.

But unlike Woodstock, there were no frolicking girls to make it interesting. While I lie there waiting for the stars to go away, I tried to hail several cars as they went by for help. Each and every one saw me. And each and every one kept right on driving. Ah, the warm heart of humanity beats strong. It took me almost an hour to crawl the 200 feet back to my house.

Eventually I progressed to a cane but still walked like an orangutan. The cane, however, lent an imagined air of sophistication to the monkey boy image. Even so, I remained self conscious about my appearance and was ashamed to seek female companionship. The problem was my leg had healed in a bowed out shape and could hardly bend. It was also permanently stuck in a slightly flexed position and along with the bowing, from the back I looked like a capital letter "D". This, combined with the leg being one inch shorter made me limp around in right hand circles, which was annoying and unproductive.

So I kept to myself and pondered what this event had really done to me. It had forced me kicking and screaming into a very dark corner and had done so without my permission. You see, up to that time, almost all of my confidence in myself was based on my *physical* ability to do anything I wanted and I went from a kayaking skiing flying climbing caving black belt to someone who couldn't even cross the room. Ironically, in a way I had repeated my father's legacy. Which I found depressing and if I found *myself* worthy of rejection, why would anyone else ever be interested in me? So I needed to find another strong point other than my looks because it was clear that wasn't working either.

Oh sure, I'd see ladies look and give me the "once over". But this only meant they looked once...and it was over. It was during this phase I also learned to never ask a girl how old she weighed.

Amazingly, my cane which I was so ashamed of came to my rescue. It seems that when I finally got the courage to go out and socialize, I looked so pitiful the woman's natural nurturosity had mercy on me. In other words, they approached me, which was *entirely* unexpected. Now due to flying for so many years, I have somewhat of a hearing impeachment and I don't always hear clearly what someone says. (And sometimes I hear what I want to hear.) But one of the best "hook, line and sinkers" ever happened this way: I was standing alone when this gal comes over and begins to walk in circles around me, looking me up and down and saying over and over

"I just can't believe this..."

"What can't you believe?"

"You look *exactly* like my third husband!"

"Third?! Just how *many* times *have* you been married?!"

"Twice."

Someone else equally to the point said

"You've been a bad boy. Go to *my* room!" There, she inferred, I would get divine advice on the Sermon *of* the Mount.

Yet another lady educated me in the nuances of fortune cookie wisdom with this counsel: Regardless of what the little strip of paper says, you add at the end of it "Between the sheets."

Try it. You'll like it.

Especially if you try it with someone you like.

It was also around this time that due to the stress of constant pain, my hair quickly began to go gray. At first I thought it gave me a look of distinction. Now it's more like extinction.

In any case, if you define "change" as the result of dissatisfaction and opportunity intersecting, I was ready to consider this the opportunity and accept the change! As a result, and ever so slowly, I was once again getting at ease with myself and other folks as I merged back into the social world. What happened was simple: I began to accept who I was and actually began to enjoy and develop other parts of my being other than the physical. By this time I had gone from Camelot to Limpalot – and while still in a great deal of pain, I was grateful to be alive.

And ever so slowly, the Wreck was being amended.

Timing Is Everything – Especially With a Bullet

~~~~~~~~~

This move into the "cerebral" and away from the physical did not occur overnight, nor did I let go of my adrenaline fixes easily. To help ease the transition, Larry (who was now selling boats in N.J.) had one of his friends custom make me a "Bullet 130". This was a small boat with two seats and no windshield that was originally created for a new class of 100 mph Open Ocean Racing the common man could afford. It was very sleek and strongly resembled a "Cigarette" racing boat and had a double hull which made it virtually indestructible and supposedly unsinkable. The hull was also a new design which gave it the uncanny ability to essentially ignore the basic "rules" of boat handling. In fact, it seemed the rougher the water, the more it liked it.

In Atlanta I had no ocean handy but we do have some very large man-made lakes such as Lanier which has some very large man-made cabin cruisers cruising around with people in the cabins. Well, these boats make nice wakes and the bigger the boat, the bigger the waves behind it. So, because I'm a pilot, and by trial and painful error, I learned to fly the Bullet by jumping these wakes. For a warm-up, you could drop in about 100' behind the bigger boats and slightly angle the nose of the Bullet off the top of the cresting wake which would allow you to effectively "surf" behind the boat as long as you wanted.

But the real fun was using the cruiser's wake as a liquid ramp and jumping it. To do this, you would circle around and angle up behind it at 40 mph or so and, *if* you held your upper lip just right, you'd make one helluva leap. Sometimes you'd go about 100 feet straight line and get 6-8 feet in the air while doing it - all of which could be exhausting work. Now, similar to a fall while climbing, air is relatively soft. But like rock and dirt, water can be pretty hard when you hit it all of a sudden like. So the key was to manage the landing correctly which could either be velvety soft - or turn into a brutal pounding. I think it was Elizabeth who got the spinal compression fracture.

As I recall, that was a non-velvet landing.

One day while in the midst of a prolonged, but pleasurable pounding, Julie gasped "My God! How long can you keep it up?!" I almost said "Hours!" before I realized she was asking about driving the boat, by which time a big cruiser came by and I had one of those Southern "Hey, watch this!" moments. We then jumped a huge wake, but in mid air, I knew we were in trouble and could not do a thing about it. So I told her to hold on. Here's why: waves form in parallel "trains", so when you jump one, you have to carefully factor in where the next one beyond it is.

Unfortunately, this particular jump was in the pre-factor days and I saw we were not going to land before or after the next big wave, but right *into* the side of it. Now to say we "landed" would not be technically accurate. *Submarining* would be. As the nose of the boat went straight into the wall of the wave at about 40 mph, the boat, the very shapely Julie and I were right behind it and water 5 feet above us crashed over our heads. That's a lot of forceful wetness folks.

When the boat finally popped up barely level to the surface, and completely swamped to the deck I might add, I noticed I had lost my new sunglasses. (I have subsequently learned the life expectancy of sunglasses is inversely proportionate to their cost. You will go to your grave with a $5 pair and sit on the $150 pair within 10 minutes of buying them.) I had the $150 pair on which now were 100 feet below me on the lake bottom and had cut my face as a farewell gesture. This made me mad.

Jules, however, had lost not only her t-shirt, but also her bikini top. This didn't make me mad at all - and *she* smiled, so on so many levels, things started looking remarkably good.

But two thoughts instantly occurred to me: As Julie was a competitive diver and swimmer, she was in no danger of drowning, and, it was probably not the best time for me to show her how well I do a breaststroke. Instead, I gave her a bare hug.

On yet another day, I went out on the lake solo just as a storm was arriving. It was a windy day which meant you had to carefully consider wind direction for a jump lest the wind do things to you without your permission. After driving around a while, I spotted my prey, a very large cruiser, coming down the lake and headed for it. As you can see in the picture, the Bullet was a very small boat and its performance was really affected by having only one person in. As such, it would jump higher and farther because it was lighter and could go faster. As I cranked into the good sized wave, I hit it quite nicely and off I went.

Unfortunately, in about mid-jump, the gusty storm winds got under the bow and instead of the boat moving in a nice graceful arc to touchdown, the nose went straight up. All I could see was sky. This is exactly where I looked for my Maker - whom I thought I'd be meeting shortly.

The next thing I said was so "Oh s**t." and held on. From a picture someone had taken from the cruiser, the nose of the boat had shot up beyond vertical and the tail end was about 7-8 feet out of the water. As gravity inevitably took over, the boat dropped straight down tail first, but as it was still moving forward, when the prop struck the water first, it acted like a massive anchor. What happened next was that the rest of the boat pivoted around the motor and *slammed* down flat into the water.

In fact, it slammed so hard, I disappeared.

The cruiser, seeing all this, stopped, turned around and came back to see if I needed help. Oh yeah, did I. When they got there, they couldn't see me. This concerned them as there was really nowhere to hide in a Bullet. It's like looking inside a two seat sports car. You're either there or you aren't. Well, I was there alright, but stuffed up under the stubby front deck where your legs normally go. Fortunately, and the only thing I did right, was wear a kill switch on my life jacket, so the boat at least sat dead in the water. I was grateful I was not doing the same.

So, what I later learned was that while I had herniated a disc in my back, the boat *really was* indestructible.

And Gary 3.0 really wasn't.

Flying lessons in the Bullet

Pete is the best friend I never get to see. But he's one of those folks I know is out there to get my back and would give me the shirt off his if needed. He and Joni are the best of what Southern "country folk" are made of. And it's worlds apart from being a redneck. Besides, (and Pete would argue this) they don't meet enough of Jeff Foxworthy's criteria for "You may be a redneck if..." Anyway, they live on a lake with several of their jet-skis, one of which was Blackie.

One day a bunch of us took a very long jet-ski trip that eventually led us miles up a river to some picturesque shoals. We then had lunch, regrouped and turned around.

Now Blackie was one of the very early smaller jet-skis and had a peculiar problem of "porpoising" when you tried to run it fast. This made the nose jump up and down in the water. It was uncomfortable and tiring to drive and made your hands numb from holding on. And I got to drive it.

On the way back home, the others literally left me "in their wake" and I just couldn't keep up with them. So I tried different techniques to get Blackie to settle down as they got further away.

Eventually I discovered that standing up and leaning *way* over the handlebars worked best. This went well until I hit a boat wake at about 40 mph which caused the nose to pitch up and both my feet to come flying off the deck. What happened next could only be described as "special".

You see, I forgot to simply let go of the throttle and let the kill switch cut the engine. Oh no. I had to hang on for dear life. In doing so, a lot of significant things simultaneously occurred.

First my body went horizontal in the air like a trailing streamer which caused me to slam my face on the fuel tank and cut it. Eventually, as gravity took over, I went from horizontally airborne to waterborne and smacked bodily onto the surface of the lake. This then caused three more things to happen: Because I was still holding on to the hand throttle from this new and unapproved riding position, the engine went to wide open. And, as I had now transferred so much weight backward, the boat went into full porpoise mode and looked like a salmon trying to go up a waterfall. The overall effect of this now had my body rhythmically slapping up and down on the lake surface like a rag doll being pulled by a huge black skipping stone.

And just when I thought it couldn't get any worse...

From the waist down I was put directly in the exhaust of the jet motor which instantly blasted off my bathing suit while doing a hi-speed frappe on some delicate body parts.

After enduring being dragged across the lake like this for several hundred feet, in exhaustion I finally had to let go of the handlebar and...Blackie promptly stopped in about 10 feet.

Duh.

So after a completely useless search for my bathing suit, I climbed back on the jet-ski and there I sat bleeding, naked and feeling like I had spent the day going commando in a Cuisinart.

Some time later, good ole Pete discovered I was missing from the BBQ and came on a rescue mission for me.

He neglected to bring another bathing suit.

Fact: The universe is constantly expanding. That means it's bigger today than it was yesterday. Conversely, it was smaller yesterday and each day before that. If you work this back, you'll find at about 13.7 billion years the entire universe was just one single infinitely dense molecule.

A lot like my head.

Maybe Einstein said it best: "Two things are infinite: the universe and human stupidity; and I'm not sure about the universe." And he didn't even know me.

Finally, Into Friendly Skies

In spite of all that came before, the flying bug would just not go away so I next tried helicopters, which I discovered were only slightly less mysterious then women. I then bought Tweety Bird. This was an award winning KR-2, which was a side by side low wing homebuilt airplane literally made out of Styrofoam covered with fiberglass. It was also, as its name suggests, painted bright yellow which as we all know by now, was my birthright color - meaning I had to have it.

But I could never get used to it and it was too small and difficult to get in and out of with my injured leg. Eventually, I traded it for a larger Grumman AA-1 from someone who scared me just from listening to his aviation tales. Frankly, it was hard to believe he was still alive. But he wasn't much longer. You see, "There are old pilots and there are bold pilots - but there are no old bold pilots." Unfortunately, he killed himself in Tweety on the second flight. This flight was to test his repairs from the damage he did on the first flight.

I enjoyed flying the Grumman for about a year, but being the inveterate tinkerer I am, found some of the design concepts of the plane to be limiting its performance. However, FAA law states if an airplane was produced as a *certified* plane by a factory, then it's illegal to perform any modifications to them. This was something I remembered after the modifications were done. And they worked quite well too, thank you.

At this time I met Chris at the airport. Like EC, his picture is also in the dictionary under "perpetual motion". Chris has a contagious enthusiasm and is always in motion, even when he is still, which for him is moving even when he thinks he is not. While he was moving his body, hc completed one of the first Glasair kit aircraft which was essentially the same style as the Grumman (low wing, 2 seats side by side) but at the time, it looked like it flew right out of the future. It was all snarky fiberglass, fast, had long range and was immensely strong.

After talking to him about my frustrations with the Grumman, Chris – who can sometimes motivate and inspire me beyond my intelligence - went on to not so subtly urge me to *build* my own plane. I stepped back and said

"Are you crazy? I don't know how to build an airplane! Even if I did, I don't have a place to do it or the tools."

After promising me his assistance, we walked over to his homemade hangar and he showed me where it could be built which coincidentally, was right where all the tools I needed were as well. This seemed to negate most of my objections so I made a promise to myself: If I survived an upcoming surgery, I would order the kit and build the plane.

But building an entire airplane is really something of a daunting and prodigious project that seems never ending. However, I reasoned it was very much like a human being and just a collection of systems attempting to work in harmony with each other within a basic structure.

For instance, the airframe would similar to a body with the following systems: induction (lungs); exhaust (intestines); instruments (nervous); fuel (circulatory); controls (musculo-skeletal) and on and on. So I figured if I could take a person apart in the lab, I could put a plane together in a hangar.

I wrote the check for the kit from the hospital bed about an hour after I came out of the anesthesia.

Newly arrived Glasair II kit parts on my front lawn

By this time I had become disillusioned with the social crowd I associated with, (as did Chris, but he still plucked Teresa out of it and married her. Good choice) so building the plane and rebuilding an engine became my reason for literally dropping entirely out of "society" for the next 18 months. Truthfully, it had become my obsession. During this time, Chris and I virtually lived in his hangar and became fast friends, and are to this day. While the plane was under construction, passers-by always had the same question: "When are you going to fly it?" And they always got the same answer:

"Next Tuesday at 4:00." And some actually showed up.

Chris then, and now, will do anything he can to help you. (You just have to stand on his neck and twist his arm so he will let *you help* him.) He can also take a moment at times to get to the point of something. For instance, one night I got a call and we chatted a few minutes about the stock market, politics etc. when he finally told me his wife was just put in intensive care due to a horrific car accident that almost killed her!

Well, on another night, he called just as I was walking out the door with my date and explained in a relatively *non-*circumspect manner that due to the monsoon rain we were having, the hanger roof was starting to "sag a little" and I "might want to get out there." This quasi-direct to the point manner made me take note. So, that's where she and I headed. By the time we got there, the roof had completely collapsed onto my plane. Its tail was damaged and pinned to the ground, nose wheel in the air and the interior was inundated with rainwater.

As I walked up and saw this, I stared a moment and then with a hint of smile, said "Well, let's get started!" I mean, what else you gonna do? The damage was done. My dressed up date said "OK!" and jumped right in to help. Months later, she said it was at that moment she realized she loved me. Apparently, she had known too many men who under similar circumstances would have handled this very badly. Her observation of my behavior, she said, spoke volumes to her. As did hers to me.

Lesson learned: Forget what people say about themselves. *People are what they do.* And that applies to me and to you. And that's essential to remember because someone is *always* watching. Now, *all* I had to do was learn how to love back...

After the plane was completed, I got to do my first real official test flight of my handiwork. And while the anticipation of this day was killing me, I really hoped the flight didn't.

They say the best seat for a test pilot is just a trailer hitch ball because your butt is so tight, you'll never let go. I found no reason to disagree with this and the truth is, I was scared to death to strap on this several hundred mile per hour (I could go door-to-door GA to NJ faster than Delta!) untested beast and go fly it. This, as my prior climbing career taught me, was a real and reasonable fear for the unknowns of the early test phase.

I then decided I could teach myself aerobatics (a *profoundly* stupid idea) by riding the looping, barrel rolling Mindbender coaster at Six Flags over and over. This I hoped would establish some sight and muscle memory for me. This only kinda sorta worked as my first loop in the plane pulled over 6 g's and almost gave me a hernia. Lesson learned…and practice makes perfect.

Completed flying Glasair II

Flying was also joyful as well as cathartic for me. The joy was the privilege of flying an aerobatic plane and taking someone through their first loop or roll and watching the huge grin on their face and the excitement they experienced. That was fun for both of us. The catharsis? Where climbing taught me a new perspective on fear and caving on trust, flying helped me view life's problems. You see, when I was troubled by something, I'd "leave" my problem in my car, get way on up in my 3-D playground in the sky, look down and consider how big my problem really was. Most times, I could barely see the car.

But *every* time, I could see for miles around knowing there were thousands of others who also had numerous problems of their own. So what made mine any more significant?

When I would combine this with 30 minutes of aerobatics which demanded complete attention, I would be exhausted physically, mentally and emotionally – but completely refreshed. Why? Because of the dramatic change in perspective. Inevitably, from on high I'd see each of us holding on to our little problems, in our little lives, in our little city on our little infinitesimal speck of dust planet as it went hurtling through an unimaginably immense galaxy that was totally lost in an even larger universe.

Truth is, I always had a real hard time finding myself, and my problems, in the middle of all that.

The plane also provided some great bonding moments such as when Larry came down to visit me and I flew him home. He was so excited while in the air that he videoed the flight. After 2 hours of stunning scenery, he significantly improved the picture quality by removing the lens cap.

When it came time to sell my Glasair, two gentlemen from Michigan came to Georgia to take delivery of it. My home airport of Stone Mountain was notorious for a having a short, narrow, bumpy runway with opposing crosswinds at each end (from air swirling around the mountain which made for interesting take-offs and landings.) Because of this, I decided to deliver the plane to another airport that could handle private business jets and was wide, level and best of all, very long.

I gave each pilot several hours of instruction in the plane until they both demonstrated they were comfortable with the controls. At that point, they made the classic pilot error by contracting a case of "Get-home-itis" and, in an effort to beat a weather system moving in, they decided to gas up and head home. Just before they locked the canopy, and with the engine running, I flagged them down and told them in no uncertain terms that if they felt the least bit uncomfortable, to turn around and taxi back to me at the terminal. They smiled, closed the canopy and rolled away. Think you know where this is heading?

If you don't, look at the next page.

They were about a ¼ mile down the runway and still on the ground when I could see they were getting into trouble on take-off. All I could hear was my own voice saying

"No! No! Kill the engine! Oh God, no!!"

But instead of shutting the engine down, they continued the take-off. In the next few seconds, the plane did a high-speed cartwheel off the runway and skidded to a stop after shearing off the landing gear and leaving a trail of numerous other expensive parts. I got in my car and raced out there and was relieved to see them standing next to the plane and (unlike every movie you've ever seen) no sign of gas leakage, fire or imminent explosion. After owning the plane for all of 30 minutes, they did $21,000 in damages to it. Unfortunately, after they admitted it had nothing to do with the plane and everything to do with the pilot, their insurance refused to cover the repairs.

What *was* fascinating to me was my internal response. I mean, here was a project that had consumed my life for years while I poured countless hours of loving attention to thousands of details during construction. Yet when this accident occurred, and although I felt terrible for the new owners, my heart had walked away from it when the Bill of Sale was signed.

On my way home I heard on the radio a Cessna 152 had made an emergency landing across town which brought to mind an analogy. You see, no matter how much skill a pilot displays in flight, most people will only remember his landing. This is like some folks, who after you spend years trying to give them your best, only remembering the time you let them down.

"Finished" non-flying Glasair II

100

My "15 Minutes of Fame" came 18 months after selling the Glasair when I completed a Pulsar. After making a bunch of aerobatic modifications, she (all things of beauty are a she!) was ready to go to the airport. However, before doing so, I decided to assemble the entire plane together on my front lawn in a spot surrounded by four large trees and sit on the roof of the house to watch what would happen next. It was interesting. Joggers would go by, stop, scratch their heads and look like they ran into the Twilight Zone. Other's would drive by at 45 mph, brake hard and then slowly back up the street and stop in front of the house where you could see them mouth the words

"Mabel, just how in the hell did that get there?!"

Two months later "Sun 'n Fun" opened in Florida. This is the country's second largest air show and thousands of aircraft show up for the week long affair. On my 460 mile flight down, and being curious about a nuclear power plant in Florida, I flew some tight look-see circles over the cooling tower for a few minutes. Bad idea as while monitoring the aviation radio, I heard some chatter about an F-16 being dispatched from a nearby military base to "Identify the bogey over the Hot Spot". Uh…that would be me. (Post-9/11 they might dispatch a Sidewinder missile first and ask questions later.)

I quickly bid a hasty goodbye to the smoking tower and hoped the tiny fiberglass plane dissolved into the countryside.

Upon landing at the air show, the photographer from Kitplanes Magazine quickly came over and asked me if I knew how to do formation flying. I said

"I've done a little. Why?"

"Because we've never seen a Pulsar like yours or any plane with an asymmetrical paint scheme and we want your plane on the cover of the magazine. Can you do an air-to-air shoot with us tomorrow morning?" (The paint he found so interesting was "ribbons" of teal and fuchsia wrapped over a white pearl base.)

Can I? - You must be kidding- that's the biggest selling aviation magazine around! OK - I'll be there! Now you need to know that while I had done some "formation flying", it was never for photography purposes. Next time you're in a book store, look at the aviation magazine covers and ask yourself

"Are they really *that* close?"

Well, in this case, yes.

But the real difficulty I had with the shoot was their placing the photo plane *between* me and the sun. This doesn't sound like much of a problem except when you are going 100 mph in a steep bank fifty feet away from a plane that you *can't see* because of the sun's glare behind it. To counter this, the photographer was hanging out his plane's removed door and had to "walk me in" over the radio and tell me where they were. When I got in the position seen in the photo below, he said

"Hold it rrrright there!"

Oh great. If someone looks closely at the plane's control surfaces, they'll see I'm "cross-controlling" and while it looks like I'm in a left bank (turn), I'm really not. It also means I could only "hold it there" for so long before things got real squirrelly. Well, it turned out it was long enough and as they promised, the plane showed up on the cover with a nicely done article inside.

So there you go: That was my entire 15 Minutes. And you had to be in the aviation world to know it. Or else it just flew by.

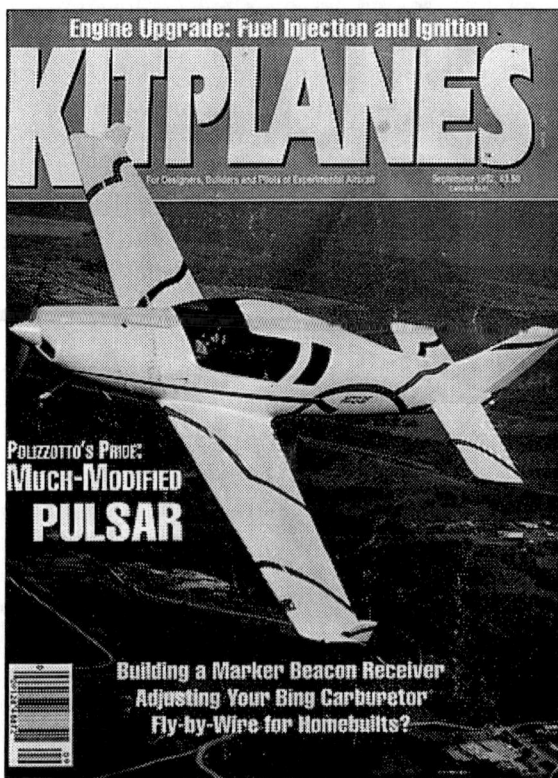

Down The River

~~~~~~~

Around this time I was invited to participate in my second Grand Canyon river trip, all 226 miles of it in my own little boat instead of a 6 man raft. I had done a partial 125 mile trip years prior, but this was going to be the whole enchilada over a period of 16 days and was a privately permitted trip with folks I had a paddled with for many years. (Most Canyon river trips are done with commercial outfitters.)

One of these folks was my near and dear dentist friend Gene who was so excited to be going he almost wet his pants. Little did he know how wet they'd get on the trip. Fortunately for the rest of us, Gene selflessly became our talisman for warding off bad luck by absorbing it himself. For instance, upon arriving at shore one evening and picking a spot to bed down, he threw his sleeping bag on top of a rattlesnake.

That night, I came across the same snake (or a close relative) coiled up on the path to the toilet. Had I not brought a light, I most likely would have stepped on him which I'm pretty sure they resent. The next morning Gene put one leg in his wetsuit and just as he was hopping around attempting to get the other leg in, he discovered a scorpion inside the suit. Ever see a guy dance around with one leg in a rubber wetsuit? One false move and you'll slingshot yourself into tomorrow.

Because of my knee injury, I could no longer get in a kayak or kneel in a canoe (I tried that once and got pinned in the canoe upside down under a waterfall), so I bought a good quality inflatable "open kayak" that I seriously modified for "big water". The changes I made are all fairly common now on high-tech inflatables, but back then, you had to invent and implement them yourself. They included making the boat "self bailing" (self draining after it filled up with water in the rapids), installing a "flip strap" for self rescue and making the boat narrower lengthwise so you didn't get thrown out of it in rough water.

Paddling the Grand was unlike anything in the East I was familiar with and some of the rapids were simply huge with 8-12 foot waves for long stretches. What was interesting to me, however, was I felt safer there then on the Southeastern rivers which were mostly "drop pool" such as Section IV of the

Chattooga in northeast Georgia. Drop pool rapids are fairly short and created by a rock ledge or boulder in the river which then drops you into a calmer pool below. The danger here is getting smashed into, or worse, stuffed under rocks much harder than you. Western rivers, while often much bigger and violent, are also deeper and even though you can take a very long, exciting and bewildering swim, you will *usually* get flushed out the other end of the rapid as opposed to being wedged under a rock.

The Colorado has hundreds of rapids, but there are two that are notoriously infamous: Crystal and Lava Falls. Eastern rivers use a 1-6 difficulty rating scale with a 6 being "Are you crazy?" The Colorado uses a 1-10 scale with 10 being "You *are* crazy!" and both Crystal and Lava can rise to a 10 depending on water release levels from the damn dam upstream. However, more people drown in Crystal and after we pulled out an exhausted Gene from a very long and violent "swim" in it that would rattle anybody, and while sputtering out a gallon of water, all he could gratefully but humorously gush out was

"Oh now that's just *not* right, no that's *all* wrong. That rapid should *not* be on this river!!"

The rapid, mind you, not Gene. But in my book I give anyone a 10 for trying Crystal. Unless they're just crazy.

Gene at his best - hand cranking margaritas.

104

But it's the heart stopping Lava – considered to be the fastest navigable rapid anywhere - that gives one the loose bowel syndrome known as the "Hershey Squirts". And this happens while you're off river high on the right side canyon wall trying to eyeball your route through. (Like it makes a difference. Not.) It has been said that standing next to Lava is like listening to a freight train in a tunnel. I would not argue with that. I do know you can barely hear someone right next to you yelling in your ear. But it didn't matter to me as I couldn't talk anyway.

A few days before getting to Lava, I had lost my voice due to some bizarre throat thingy – probably cactus flu or something. I could not talk, sing (which the others appreciated) or yell for help, so I needed to stay out of trouble like no scorpions in my shorts. So at the top of every big rapid, I hummed to myself the same song "A Kind Of Magic" by Queen. Don't ask why because I don't know, but somehow it seemed to keep me focused. Maybe I think the Canyon is magic (it is) or that I would need magic to survive (I would.) But the lyrics seemed to fit, except maybe the last line which says "The day will dawn of sanity…" Well, maybe someday. But not that day.

Lava Falls is almost 1000 feet long, drops 37 feet and is approached by entering a large, almost eerily still pool that stretches for several hundred yards. This is your first clue there's trouble ahead as the big drop is causing the upstream water to back up and slow down. The next clue is the "747" you hear roaring downstream. The final clue is passing the gigantic tombstone-like rock called Vulcan's Anvil where you toss your loose change for good luck. There are two routes down the river: the "gentler" left side "Bubble Line" or the right side maelstrom.

As by now you know I'm a bit dim-witted, there's no point telling you which route I chose. But I did recall several past truly scary swims where I learned that air is *not* overrated. So, knowing the top 2 feet of Lava's waves are nothing but foam – which I really do have trouble breathing – I donned two life jackets (stuffed with 3 cans of emergency beer in case I got lost.) This made me look like the prototype Michelin Man, but hey, better afloat and breathing than fashion conscious and dead.

Anyway, here we are at the top of Lava shivering with excitement and fear. I paddled hard for the right side entry to miss the humongous center river hole (check out some pics of this rapid on-line.) Now in my mind I have every intention of doing - what?! *"Hey! What the HELL am I doing here?!"*

(Oh, I think I neglected to tell you my boat leaked air and I had to tie in a hand pump between my legs and just before - and I mean *just* before -a rapid, I had to frantically pump up the pressure and then grab my paddle.) Anyway, by that time I was sucked down into the maw of the vortex and in the video, all you can see are my hands sticking out of the water while holding the paddle over my head. And mind you, I'm still sitting upright in the boat but we are both about 3 feet underwater. So, at around this point I'm wondering just how long *can* I hold my breath?

The ride through Lava could only be described as *violent*. But there's also something totally mesmerizing and awe inspiring about the relentless power and infernal roar of thousands of tons of brawling water that almost made being terrorized fun. About half-way through (and on what seemed like next Tuesday), my head popped up gasping for some much needed air as simultaneously more huge waves folded up and over the boat pounding us both deep underwater again.

Long story short and with the grace of God offsetting my incompetence, I made it through upright and when I was finally ejected out, I yelled a victorious victory cry. Or tried to. At first, nothing came out and then, all of a sudden *all* of the noise I couldn't make for the last few days came rushing out at once (along with what was probably a piece of my lung) as one long high pitched cacophony that turned heads on the shore over the rapids roar. (Poetic, isn't it?)

Yep, I could talk again…and now I also had an entirely new voice which remains to this day. A few months later having failed to recover my previous mellifluous tenor, the ENT specialist took a look down my throat and said

"How the hell did you get all that scar tissue down there?"

Cactus and Lava, my boy, cactus and Lava...

About ten minutes after my run through Lava, we came close, way too close, to losing someone in it when a large supply boat flipped over and threw Terri into the churning frenzy. This all happened at the worst possible place in the rapid where there is a huge rock sticking up out of the water, which Terri slammed into. She was then helplessly swept around it like a rag doll to the downstream side of the rock and got caught in the backwash "hydraulic" where it was almost impossible to rescue her.

Several kayaks, long minutes and ropes later, we had her on shore, completely hysterical and in shock, but thankfully, alive. It took almost 2 hours before she could talk again.

As for me, I learned a major lesson in Lava that day: I don't ever, *ever need* to do it again. But did I even "need" to do it this time? Perhaps. Maybe choosing the right side run was not to challenge my abilities, but to confront my fear and was just another version of "If you take out the biggest or the baddest first, the rest just usually go away." I know one thing, after that one very long and insightful minute of my life, I never needed to prove my male-nosity to myself in that manner again.

I'd invent new ways. Like having my heart stopped by something other than Lava Falls.

Post Lava Falls
"May The Ig be with you."

Flatlined

~~~~~~~

R emember how tidy Chapter 1 was about my heart? Here's the rest of that story. Around 1990 I had developed a heart arrhythmia presumably as a result of exposure to a toxic paint I used on the Pulsar.

The first time I went to the hospital, they kept me overnight with a "tele-monitor" around my neck. This was hooked up to the EKG leads on my chest and transmitted a signal by radio to a specialist nurse down the hall "watching" several EKG monitor screens. Anyway, I woke up around 4:00 A.M. and noticed one of the leads had fallen off, so I just reconnected it and began to go back to sleep.

All of a sudden I realized "Hey! Wait a minute! *Why* didn't anyone notice something wrong was going on here?! Why isn't someone yelling 'Code Blue' and running down the hall with the crash cart? Isn't all hell supposed to break loose when someone goes flat line?"

So I got out of bed and quietly walked down the hall to the glassed-in room where the nurse was. I stood outside of it and behind her and one by one began disconnecting my leads. When my EKG looked like a picture made by a chicken with inky feet, I poked my head in the room, pointed to the monitor and asked

"Hey, does that guy need help or something?"

She then finally noticed the screen and jumped out of the chair running down the hall and, yes, yelling something about "Code Blue!" or some other color. It took me awhile to catch up with her to ask whether all these extra unused wires in my hand might be the problem.

She seemed to think they were. Bet she watches those screens now.

Anyway, although the arrhythmia was usually associated with too much caffeine or too little rest, it was an infrequent problem and I had learned some "self-treatment" techniques that usually worked, except this one day at my clinic. Now, when the problem occurs, it comes on, literally, in a heartbeat. Blood pressure immediately drops and you feel light headed and weak. As I could not get the beat to convert back to normal, I went to the emergency room at Emory Hospital, a major teaching institution with a reputation for treating heart problems.

At the ER, the head of cardiology said he would try an IV solution to restore the normal beat. But after two expensive applications, the EKG next to me still looked and sounded like jungle drums on angel dust. He then informed me I just might have to go to the operating room, be anesthetized and get "converted", but he didn't say to what religion. Anyway, that's where they lay you down, take two electrified ping pong paddles, slap them against your chest, yell "Clear!" and zap you like a moth flying into a bug lamp. You then come about two feet off the table flopping around like an epileptic trout.

And that's when you get religion.

But then he brightened up like a happy kid and said

"Hey, I know what we can do!" He then pulled out a needle and said "This will stop your heart. Hopefully it'll restart."

"Hopefully?!" "Yes. Lay down."

If you read the first chapter of this book, you already know my response. For some reason, I had the strong feeling I was about to become the subject of an experiment. But you know me, anything for science. (Remember "Trust me. I'm a doctor"?)

So into the IV goes whatever alchemy is going to solve my problem - presumably. Within seconds, my heart just simply and completely stopped beating. Now, let me tell you, to say that, and to experience it, are worlds apart. I looked over at the EKG which went flat line and blared "Houston, we've got a problem!" But that was nothing compared to the eerie silence inside my head. Up to that moment, I had never realized how much noise the thrum of circulating blood makes inside of you...until it stops. Ever hear the term "deafening silence"? This then combines with the subtle vanishing of all the pulses around your body as the limbs take on a heavy leaden feeling. (If you can't imagine this, don't worry, some day you'll experience it.)

But that wasn't all. As there was now no blood pressure, gravity made my blood settle downward and I could feel it literally pooling behind my arms, legs and along my back. In dead people, this phenomenon is called livormortis. I didn't like feeling dead and, well, I'm sorry folks, but this is just getting *entirely* too weird. After about 10 seconds of this surreal alternate reality, my heart restarted with a lurch. And it was just as bad as it was before and the EKG was still all over the place.

Disappointed at the failure of his Science Fair project, the doctor then said

"I'm sorry, but we've exhausted everything we can do, we'll have to paddle you now." Almost sounds erotic, huh?

"OK, but I *really* have to pee first." I then explained my bladder was in so much pain from all the IV fluids that it couldn't be helping my heart from the stress. He just laughed it off and said it had nothing to do with it. I told him I didn't care, I still needed to pee. Badly and right now. He then handed me one of those little wine carafe type jars and he and the nurse waited outside the room where there was another EKG monitor over the door.

I hurriedly started to relieve myself and within 10 seconds, much of the bladder pain and pressure was gone. And within the next 2-3 seconds the EKG went *entirely* normal. Believe me, "ta-dump-ta-dump-ta-dump" (that's supposed to be normal heart noise) is a very, *very* sweet sound to hear! Before I had a chance to repackage myself, the doctor (and of course, the nurse) burst into the room and said "What the hell...I don't believe it!"

Now many of you probably know the heart beat is divided up on the EKG into separate waves identified by the letters "P, Q, R, S, T". Out of curiosity, I asked the doctor which wave was the aberrant one causing my problem.

He looked around and almost in embarrassment said

"The P wave."

But of course.

I was now back on the road to good health. Which, if you think about it, is the slowest possible way to die...which sounds painful to me. .

But you know, this event made it exceedingly clear in a *very* real manner that we are *all* literally and simply one heartbeat away from eternity. One moment it's beating and the next, well, it's not. And while some things may not apply to you or me, this is the common denominator for every human alive. So, if you knew exactly how many beats you had left to use, would your life be any different? Would your heart beats and Life-*Time* be *spent* any differently or more wisely?

Oh, two more things: Doctors don't "save" lives, but they might get you some more "time to spend"...

And, we all die from the same problem: Our last one.

A Few Good Men

~~~~~~~

It's pretty well accepted the most significant role model for a child is the same sex parent. In the case of a boy, if the father is absent physically or emotionally, the boy will have more difficulty locking in his genuine confidence as a man. It is just not passed down from the father to the son.

When this happens the mother often subtly fills the vacuum as the boy depends more on her for learning his social skills. The outcome can be a man who is comfortable around women but has difficulty with committed relationships. In more extreme cases, the mother can have so much influence that his personality traits become more like *her* later in life.

When a young girl's mother is "absent", the outcome is just the opposite. She will gravitate towards the father and often become a charming woman who is very comfortable around men, but may be unsure of her "worth" as a woman.

If a child is outright *rejected* by the same sex parent, the problem may escalate. When grown, these folks may simply not accept others trying to treat them well because they are often convinced they do not deserve it, so they settle for whatever level of relationship they feel is their due. (See "Life In 3-D")

What is also known is they often incline towards mates who somewhat mirror the rejecting parent, and then try to fix them, and by proxy, the parent. They may also become "high maintenance" in an effort to convince themselves of their worth and they anger easily when denied what they want.

And all of this in an attempt to fill the vacuum left by an irresponsible parent. Put two of these folks together and the road can be rocky indeed.

In my case, and although I am now convinced my Dad did the best he could, as a child I rarely felt like I met his standards. When my little happy kid brain did or invented something (well, maybe not the spider web) and rushed up to show him and hopefully get his *approval* (keep an eye out for that word, it'll be real important later on), instead of telling me how good a job I did, he'd say

"That's nice. But let me show you a *better* way."

And truthfully, he usually did have a better (and often safer) way he wanted me to learn. But I understood *none* of that as a kid. The message I *did* hear and learn was that I wasn't good enough and my immediate source and model for my being a man did not approve of me.

So let me tell you how that played out. As I felt my Mom *did* approve of me, I found it easy to be around the opposite sex. In fact, to this day, plunk me down in a social setting where the guys clump to one end of the room doing the "sports thing" and the ladies to the other, I will eventually gravitate to the women because I find them more interesting.

Besides, they *always* smell better.

And I can easily identify why this shift happens. For one reason, I have almost no interest in typical "guy sports". Truth is, I'm not much for spectator stuff and I get scared when any of the following become an obsession, religion or something that requires lurid body paint:

- Baseball: a guy runs as fast as he can in a square circle so he can get back to exactly where he already was
- Basketball: directionally challenged ex-felons with pituitary tumors
- Football: large angry looking men run after another guy running away holding a fake pig's bladder
- Golf: you take a ball out of your pocket and hit as far as you can...so you can walk after it and pick it up again

So now that I've alienated just about everyone - and even though these sports all involve a lot of balls - it's not exactly what I had in mind. But while the guy sport-talk thing is fine, it really helps me learn nothing about the person except that they possess critical information like who scored a field goal during the World Series 9 years ago. Or what state the "Tar-Toes" are from. And although I can watch some of this stuff now and then, it's just not something I want to commit a lot of brain cells to. (OK, I may as well just say it: I've never seen an entire football game in my life and for a while, I thought the Super Bowl was a $40,000 NASA toilet.) But...I do watch the "Lifetime" channel every now and then and as you'll see later on, Life-*Time* is something of utmost importance to me.

So, does this make me un-manly or something?

I do notice if I bring up basic car or caving stuff like hyper-miling, trailing throttle oversteer or the merits of dangling on static vs. dynamic ropes, they begin to hyperventilate and steer for a rope to dangle me on. In any case, when the talk inevitably turns to sports - or when they become glassy eyed by them on TV, that's usually when I drift over to the other side of the room.

And the reason I find the women a better *time investment*? They are far more likely to talk about things that, to me, actually *matter*. They more freely discuss their feelings, experiences and life itself, which I find of more interest and value. And as those are the exact things that help us better understand and relate to each other, it quickly gets my attention.

Even so, I do want quality male companionship in my life and have been blessed with a few. Unfortunately, as of this writing, some have either moved away or died. I hope I didn't have anything to do with either.

One gentleman was Norbert who was introduced to me by Karla. In spite of my own ignorance, she was wise and sensitive enough to see I still needed a father figure in some areas of my life and some help in understanding what it meant "to be a man". And while she was rarely wrong, this time she was right. Norbert, an architect from Argentina, had an interesting parental mix: a German father and a Spanish mother. The end result was the practical met the emotional in a healthy and constructive way making him the *most* gentlemanly guy I had ever met. He was kind hearted, sensitive and always made an effort to find the good in others while making you feel valued.

So one day I went to visit him. I arrived at his office, he pushed his drawings aside, pulled up a chair and we talked...for two hours. When we were done, I offered to pay him for his time and he just shook his head "no". Then I offered to wash his car...just something to compensate for his time. He simply said

"You don't understand. You have blessed *me* with *your* time." He was right. But I didn't understand then the real value of someone freely giving us some of their Life-*Time*.

But as you'll see later on, I do now.

And we met every Wednesday for several years before he moved to Arizona. And in those years we talked about any and everything with an emphasis on how Scripture might relate to different situations I was encountering in my life and in doing so, I was learning new options for old problems.

Now, to some this might sound like therapy, and it may have had just that effect. (Studies show there are many benefits in speaking openly and honestly to a trusted friend.)

What I did know was I had found the genuine and authentic friendship of a man who simply accepted and *approved* of me based on who I was and not just on what I did. When I did do something stupid, he took the time to understand my *intent* and we discussed what my options really were. And when I did something good, he was sure to say "Well done!" And he did it in an area where my father was just not prepared to go, which was that of my faith. Norbert became, in effect, my "spiritual father" who loved me as a son and by his word and example, Scripture had started making sense. But just as importantly, he believed in me which helped me believe in myself.

Woody, who had moved to Idaho (and sadly passed away almost exactly as I was writing this), was yet another man for me to admire and learn from. He was, well, simply brilliant and had a Ph.D. in physics which he taught along with astronomy and math at Emory University. I recall lunch with him one day where he proved to me math could be made illogical. He explained it so very clearly that I understood it for at least 7 minutes. (Math is *not* my subject. If the sun goes in while I'm using my solar calculator, well, I just have to wait to figure out the tip.) But Woody had such a wonderfully easy and unassuming gentleness that to me made him seem like an earthbound angel in an old checkered flannel shirt.

These were guys who didn't need to prove they were men. They also had some of the very best marriages I had ever seen with *ongoing* chemistry because the man and woman believed in and encouraged each other on a regular basis and always "had each other's backs". And they knew relational success was more important (and satisfying) than personal success. These were the marriages I had always hoped and believed could exist, but had never seen while growing up. They were people you *wanted* to be around, to learn from and to soak up the vitality they had.

No less a sage than Winnie the Pooh said

"If you live to be 100, I hope I live to be 100 minus 1 day, so I never have to live without you." That's the attitude they had.

(Norbert and his wife were in a restaurant after almost 30 years of marriage when the waitress asked them "How long have you two been dating?" That oughta tell you something!)

And there were others such as Dale and Captain Paul. These were men of integrity who had gracefully survived Life-Stations I have yet to visit. More importantly, they lived out their faith in a real and tangible way that benefited others and their actions defined them far more than their words. Simply put, these were all folks who did the ordinary extraordinarily well and I am grateful they all *spent* some time on me. They proved you can learn more in an hour from an expert than in a lifetime from an idiot. Thanks guys. You made a difference and I am better for it.

Twenty years prior, when I had ventured into the "New Age" stuff, I had only succeeded in traveling from whatever ill-formed vestiges of theology I had from my youth to a self-centered "Meology". The outcome after two decades of this was feeling I had been subtly sucked into the ultimate Cosmic Catch-22 as I realized I didn't make a very good God worthy of worshipping. In other words, I was trying to have faith *in me* instead of having faith in something *bigger* (and wiser) than me. And there's a huge difference between the two. As a result of sensing these men knew something about Life that I didn't, it was time to seriously investigate this area once again and perhaps consider where I fit into God's plan…instead of where He fit into mine. So after studying all major world religions for several years, I ultimately found comfort in the words of Christ and the uplifting gift of Grace in the New Covenant Scriptures.

And for you, dear reader, pause and think of the people you have met on the trail of life that have made a difference in you. Perhaps it was a teacher who pushed you a little harder, a parent who believed in you, a doctor who took a chance and had a heart to heart with you or a love who revealed your strengths, and weaknesses. Take a moment and reflect on why they were important to you. These may be some of your Golden Threads.

As for my life, there are those who have treated me far better than I deserved and those who treated me worse. And while I am grateful for one, I learned a lot from the other.

But any poor treatment I may have endured seemed small after I went to the other side of the world to do some studies and met some folks who have lived that way for centuries.

We Have A Failure To Communicate

~~~~~~~~

Back in the pre-9/11 days when most Americans – myself included - had little real awareness of anything to do with "terrorism", other parts of the world were eyeball deep in it - and had been for countless years. One of those countries was Israel, where I was scheduled to visit on El-Al. This Israeli airline has had some of the most elaborate security checks in place for a very long time out of simple survival efforts. If you wonder how far and serious they took this, here's how much: I was told by a Delta captain some of their airliners have heat seeking missile detectors on them. Also, their pilots are military trained and learn evasive maneuvers for missiles. Does that not comfort you, or what?

Their security begins at the check-in where every passenger has to pass a personal interview including questioning of your itinerary, who in the group you are with etc. All the while, the agent would be taking notes and then cross reference your answers with others you were traveling with. Then, you would go through a metal detector as would your luggage which was then hand checked as well. This was just to get on the plane…and it was long before 9/11. As a result, El-Al is considered the best protected airline in the world because of these measures.

The extended trans-Atlantic flight was on a huge 747 which held several (hundred) more people than my Glasair. This made the plane absolutely packed and within a few hours, there was trash all over the innards. About 5 hours out, I got up to use the bathroom, which was also a huge mess and while passing a flight attendant on the way back to my seat, I said jokingly to her

"It looks like a bomb went off back there."

Now in my little mind, this was a harmless comment so absurd no one would take it seriously, right? Wrong. It was also in the pre-taboo days for such words. But not for them. The attendant's eyes got as big as saucers and she flew – not ran – up to the cockpit. At that point I kinda got the clue I did something bad and ran *after* her, which was probably not giving her the impression I was just a harmless lovable fuzzball. So here I am running up the crowded trashy aisle yelling

"No! Yoke! Yoke!" which was as close to "Joke" in Hebrew I could get to at the moment.

Well, she got there first, got the captain - whom I believe was armed - and he and I commenced to having a seminar in the front of the plane all about JAP's. (Jewish Aviation Procedures)

Jeez - I'm sorry.

When our study group arrived in Israel, we were told to pick a travel partner. I picked Terry who was bright, funny and would look great in a bikini. She picked me because I was the only one left. We then all piled in a bus and drove to Tel-Aviv to our hotel. When we arrived, we were ushered into the very crowded hotel lobby to get our keys. While Terry and I were in the exact geographical center of the crowd, she said to me

"Darn, I left something in the bus. I need to go back. Do you need anything?" I said yes and to please get my bathing suit in my day pack. She said OK and turned to go outside. She got about 20 feet away from me and yelled back

"Where is it?" I yelled a bit louder as she continued to walk away in the crowd.

"It's in *the rack*", meaning the coat rack above my seat.

Ever see that old E.F. Hutton brokerage commercial that takes place in the middle of a NYC crowd and says "When E.F. Hutton talks, everyone listens"? In the commercial, an entire building lobby goes immediately and entirely silent while the people strain to listen.

Well, apparently I had just done an Israeli remake of the commercial as the lobby went totally silent and all eyes turned to me. Including the hotel security guards. Now remember that little thing I said to you about what people hear vs. what you said? What this crowd had heard was that my bathing suit "was in *Iraq*." But they heard only the words that provoked a strong response, and it wasn't the part about the bathing suit. So off I go again explaining to the authorities what I *really* meant to say.

But see, now I'm starting to get a feel of some sensitive "issues" with these folks. Two days later we took bus tour along the Israel-Egypt border. There, for as far as you could see, was a double row high barbed wire fence separating the two countries. Every so often, we would pass a large tent on the Israeli side with soldiers in it who would be looking into the Egyptian desert through a huge (and I mean *huge*) set of binoculars set on a tripod. We finally stopped at one tent and the friendly soldiers allowed us to look though the binocs. What you saw was actually a little weird and almost funny in a surreal sort of way. About 200 yards away in Egypt in the middle of nowhere (desert, remember?) was another little structure with some Egyptian soldiers looking back *at me* through their own huge binoculars.

We waved at each other.

After being baptized in the Jordan River, we traveled to the resort city of Eilat by the Red Sea. As we neared downtown I noticed from my window seat on the right side of the bus a small car parked up a hill on a side street. As the front of the bus began to enter the intersection, I watched as the car accelerated down the hill and slammed into us right under my window. This really didn't appear to be accidental. I mean, c'mon, how hard is it to miss a huge bus especially when you were parked?

The bus driver immediately pulled over and me, actually thinking it *might* have been accidental, jumped off the bus and go running over to the guy who was trapped in his car because the front end had collapsed to the point of jamming the doors. At first, I wasn't overly concerned because he seemed to be alright. In fact, he was so alright and excited by the event, he kept punching the inside of the windshield until his hands were a bloody mess while shouting something other than Hebrew. What got *me* excited was the large pool of gasoline I was standing in that was getting bigger…and that his car was still running…and that some people gathering around were lighting up cigarettes.

I attempted to force his door open, but without success. Finally, I just pulled him out through the open door window and off to the side at which time the police had just arrived. For some reason, they immediately handcuffed him and took him away and then quickly searched the trunk of the car. All for an accident? Perhaps not. The police then came over and wanted to take a statement from me in their little investigation panel truck. The inside of the truck had a bench along each side with a long table down the middle and the captain sat across from me. Fortunately, it seems all Israelis speak English and we started to go through the details of the "accident".

At some point in the interview, he asked me my name. Now you need to know something about Hebrew. The words are written phonetically, have no vowels and are read from right to left. So I said "Polizzotto" and his head jerked up and he looked at me and then at the other cops and asked them

"You got any ideas?" After struggling and writing for a few minutes with different variations that didn't get anywhere near "phonating" me correctly, he scribbled something down, looked at it and said to the others "Well, I guess that will have to do."

He then, for some really odd reason, asked me for my *father's* first name. I'm sorry, but I can't resist starting to smile and waiting to see what happens next, so I said loud and proud

"Ignazio! - *I'm Iggy's Kid!*"

He then stared at me completely exasperated, looked at the other two officers, literally threw his pen over his shoulder, closed the book and said

"We're done here. You didn't see anything. Have a nice day. Shalom."

Remember the saying that it's OK to be paranoid if someone *is* really out to get you? I now understand these folks a bit better.

But between the incidents on the plane, in the hotel lobby and with the police, I again very clearly saw two things that appear consistent no matter where you are or who you're with:

1. How easily simple communication between people can go wrong and;
2. People's perception of reality can have more effect on them than actual reality…and it's ever so easy to get comfortable with our "factual" assumptions.

Bigger Isn't Always Better

~~~~~~~~~~

Having gained some confidence that came with building a plane that took me to 17,500 feet and upside down at 250 mph, the next project was to take my life savings and build something to build the next plane *in,* a house, or more correctly, a 2,700 foot hangar with a house over it. The first step was finding a lot, which I did with frontage on a 13 acre private lake about 19 miles outside of Atlanta. At the time, this seemed like a reasonable commute to work.

This was all after I got to watch the "Dance of the Emus". What I had done was take an Atlanta map and draw concentric rings in 5 mile increments around my clinic with the property no more than 20 miles away. In order to expedite the search, I'd get in the airplane and fly a grid of possible areas. After landing, I'd drive to see them at ground level. One such spot was a few acres where the owner had a pen of about 30 emu things. These are big ostrich type looking birds that apparently have a lot of useful parts. It's the new tuna fish.

Anyway, the owner walks me over to the pen and says "Watch this." He then got in the pen where the birds were just standing around pecking the ground and began to whistle "Dixie" (you were expecting maybe something else?) and just like someone had thrown a switch, the birds jerked up their heads, started bobbing them around while flapping their wings and picking up their legs in rhythm. All of them. From where I stood it looked like 30 Drew Careys doing the Chicken Dance. They stomped around to the tune while marching behind him and when he abruptly stopped whistling, they went right back to pecking! Just to prove his point, he repeated the whole scenario.

I passed on what surely was possessed property.

Anyway, the house started as a doodle during a dawdle over coffee. I began with the master suite based on the construction principle that the bedroom is where the foundation of the house is laid. I told my contractor, an elderly friend, I wanted to pay for the construction as I went along with the money I had saved up for 20 years, which he said was enough. (Yes, those of you who have built a house, I can hear you laughing now...)

120

This commenced into the construction phase whereby he told me at the 30% completion point he had underestimated the cost of building by oh, let's say $53,000, which was identical to the 53K I didn't have. The main reason I didn't have it was my stock broker of 18 years, had left me just that: broker after he lost me about $63,000 in very hard earned dollars. Fortunately, he did not suffer in kind and gladly took his full hard-earned commissions based on my following his sage advice.

In any case, it seemed my contractor had contracted a form of dyslexia from a head injury a few years earlier. This resulted in transposing numbers whereby I'd be given a quote of $394 for something that was actually $943. He then dismissed himself from the job. So guess who became the new contractor? Moi. Needless to say, I was once again in virgin territory without a virgin and spent the next 14 months learning a lot of new trades like kitchen installations, tile and brick laying, landscaping, building a dock etc. Oh, and almost driving an enormously huge Caterpillar bulldozer into the lake. (Talk about driving up the costs! – but that was after I got pinned under a tree the regular driver knocked over on me.) So, the project quickly began to wear on me and I can remember days being there by myself, and out of sheer physical exhaustion and mental frustration, sitting in the middle of an unfinished room and just weeping.

Next we discovered the house had been placed too low on the lot for the septic field to work. (As in the government, the main principle in plumbing is that "sh*t flows downhill".) Anyway, as we couldn't raise the house, we had to lower the lot. "That'll be $15,000, sir. Thank you." Need more? While I was out of town, the plumber ruined $3,000 of hardwood floors testing his work. Of course he decided it wasn't his fault.

By the front door, I hung a sign that said "The Money Pit". Those that hadn't seen the movie kept asking me where the "money pit" was. Eventually the house morphed and grew into a fairly nice structure. When it was finished, I had two full size airplanes in the basement along with a 65 foot indoor gun range, so I considered the hangar/gun range part of the house successful. This also meant I'd be out of the way in the kitchen.

The house and I were pretty much finished simultaneously as by that time I had badly herniated (well, actually kind of exploded into pieces) a disc in my lower back from picking up railroad ties to build the dock. (Where's Iggy when I need him?!)

121

This was the source of my next three surgeries. The irony is given the subsequent medical costs, lost time from work etc., I would have been better off paying the $53,000 to the contractor, had he still been there. But at least I now knew that "Experience is what you get by not having it when you needed it." How true.

Completely worthless, but true.

But consistent with my father's advice to "live below my means", when I first put the key to the completed house in my pocket, it was paid for down to the last penny.

Inside the unfinished Money Pit

In hindsight, the whole project became what later seemed to be a monument to my ego with its 18 foot acoustically designed ceiling, raised Italian marble entryway, 25 foot long bathroom (with indoor plumbing), jetted tub and a glass block shower for me and six of my closest friends. There was also a great deal of openness to it and anything smaller than a 12 foot Christmas tree looked like a potted plant. Huey, an adopted, ear mite ridden and starving stray tabby, loved to lay on the 2nd floor railing and swat racquet balls across the room that were thrown up to him. Millie Go Lightly, an abandoned six week old fluff-ball of a kitten from the airport, joined the party a bit later.

The housewarming had about 70 folks with room to spare and eventually we let a displaced pastor hold his Sunday services there as the great room would hold 40 people with ease. To be honest, the house was quite pretty and even impressed me for a while with its design elements almost an expression of art. But its best feature was the steel eyebolt sticking out of the support beam 18 feet up in the middle of the great room. From this bolt, I had a length of climbing rope dangling so I could practice caving rope technique while watching T.V.

For some reason, visitors always wanted to know why there was a rope in the middle of the room. I thought it looked normal. But the 50 people Janie invited for a wonderful surprise "50th" party thought it was anything but and asked me to demonstrate its use. And there, in front of the crowd, I almost hung myself.

Which would have been perfectly fitting one year later.

But the size and total openness of the house eventually began to grate on me and I felt like a BB in a box car. The whole thing also seemed somewhat presumptuous to me. Eventually, the lot next door was built on by a fellow who thought very highly of himself. He was also not what one would call refined or overly educated, but he was relatively wealthy due to a recent business he sold which he felt conferred on him instant class and respect. Unfortunately, while he may have earned the money, he did little to earn the respect and he could not understand why the money didn't buy it or that things didn't equal class. In short, he was a total bore and just one more reason to sell the mega-house.

By this time, the traffic in Atlanta had gotten so bad that my commute was becoming a horror show and more often than not, I was in a foul mood by the time I got home. As a result, I came to resent the house as though it was the cause. Finally, the surplus of black widows sneaking about also inspidered me to move.

But somewhere in the middle of those years and as a cumulative result of several things, I began to notice a change in myself that was, well, new to me. This change was not clearly good or bad at the time, just different and initially interesting to step outside of and just attempt to observe. Eventually it became more predominant and I sensed something dark and ugly was creeping my way. I was heading into unknown territory and within a few months and the loss of almost 15 pounds (which meant I had to run around in the shower to get wet), I realized it was terrain that would challenge not only my survival skills as a person, but almost my entire identity as I was pushed towards the holes in my heart. Like it or not, Gary 4.0 was about to molt.

The Darkness Arrives

~~~~~~~~~

I mentioned before about being in low places such as caves. But there is a distinct difference between choosing to go in a dark cave as opposed to finding one slowly spiraling down to some stygian darkness of the mind and soul, which is where it looked like I might be heading. In hindsight, it was an amalgam of things such as having been in increasingly non-stop daily pain for almost 20 years from the leg and now the back. Next were the closely spaced surgeries on both shoulders, which added yet more painful limitations. These were all combined with the emotional and physical exhaustion of the house building experience and a growing disappointment over the church that was having its services there which also challenged my faith.

So I eventually got to the point where walking, bending and lifting became, well, just so damn hard to do. I mean, if you can't use your leg or your back or either arm, what's left? Tying cherry stems in knots with your tongue? (It also says something about your state of mind when you start looking *forward* to having more surgery because anesthesia is the only time you get any really good sleep. And escape from the pain.) By now I was also a walking barometer. Want a weather prediction? Ask me!

On top of all of this, was a bad legal experience. A few years before when on my way to a birthday lunch, I was rear-ended pretty badly while at a stop sign. This caused a previous back surgery to be aggravated to the point where I couldn't work due to constant pain and the orthopedist now wanted to do a spinal fusion. This did not excite me as the term "FBS" (*Failed Back Surgery*) usually applied to this suggested procedure.

In an attempt to be a "good steward" and save the insurance company some money, I was treated for free as a professional courtesy by other chiropractors and specialists. However, with the MRI and other costs along with the inability to work, I had about $40,000 in documented losses. The offending person's insurance company (which I will not name) offered me 25% of that as a settlement. An attorney friend of mine explained I was being treated unfairly and persuaded me to initiate a lawsuit for an appropriate compensation.

After 4 years we finally went to court in Fulton County, GA. which was overburdened with cases and had called in extra judges. The somnambulist I got was notorious for being eccentric and egocentric with a floppy tired beagle face that, like his mind, was *way* beyond its prime. He also forced the room to listen to the war music "Flight of the Valkyries" during his breaks. Maybe he thought he was an eagle instead of a beagle.

During my testimony, the defense counsel asked me

"Dr. Polizzotto, who was the first person you told about your injuries?"

I replied "When the claim inspector from Progressive Insurance came to my house the next day I...."

Just like on T.V., he then jumped up and gleefully yarbled "Your Honor! I do dee-claire a mistrial!!"

The old and decrepit Honorable Legal Beagle-Eagle peered down from on high and asked me

"Did your counsel tell you not to mention the insurance company?"

"Yes."

"Then why did you do it?"

"Because I was asked a question?"

"Well don't do that again!"

"Excuse me, but how am I supposed to be *truthful in a court of law, not perjure myself and answer his question?*"

The judge said "I don't care, just don't say that. If you do I'll put you *in jail* for contempt!"

My initial response was to tell him "Screw you, you senile old...!" But I politely (and probably wisely) refrained. He then rushed my own and others testimony to suit his scheduled breaks – probably due to a weak bladder. However, in the middle of the trial, he stopped the entire proceeding because (and this is the absolute truth) *one* of the fluorescent bulbs in the ceiling was bad! This took over an hour to replace. In the meantime I sat there and counted how many bulbs *were* working. It was 47. I guess at his age he needed all the light he could get.

After three long days of trial during which the lady who hit me admitted it was all her fault, her counsel closed by telling the jury I was a hero for getting her out of her smoking car and should get *something* for my legitimate injury. The judge then dismissed the jury at 4:20 on a Friday afternoon to deliberate. They were back in 15 minutes. Gotta be out by 5:00, no?

When they returned, and in a generous display that truly "No good deed goes unpunished", they awarded me…nothing.

And what was the judge so upset about? Well, I wasn't supposed to mention the insurance company because the jury was "not aware" they were involved. This was after they were sworn in with secret questions like:

"Do you work for Progressive Insurance? Do you hold any stock in the Progressive Insurance Company? Do you have any conflict of interest with Progressive?" So as you can clearly see, they would be deeply shocked by my mere mention that Progressive was involved in all of this.

I will refrain from the demographic specifics, but did I mention the woman who hit me had worked for the Atlanta mayor? Or that her citation had "somehow" never been recorded and therefore couldn't be mentioned in testimony? And that the first judge assigned to the case was her neighbor and he didn't recuse himself so we had to request a new judge? Just a few small details. Needless to say, this left me sadly disappointed with the state of our legal system. And it just reminded me once again of "It's not what you know, but who."

So the physical problems were one aspect. This rolled over into making it very difficult to treat patients in the office and I had to cut back my hours and depend more on the income from the two other jobs I had for years. One, a major insurance company I was doing medical Peer Reviews for, lost a key client contract and dropped my income by about another 80%. Yes, life was going well. This then compounded with yet other problems and added to the stress under whose combined weight I was beginning to sink. Another funny thing was that after more than 15 years, I had let my "FUNDOC" license tag expire…which was not so funny and spoke volumes about my internal state of affairs. Simply put, I was not thriving – meaning to prosper and flourish - but only striving to survive by exerting a lot of energy and effort with little benefit.

While I was certain there was something to be learned here, I still had no idea what it might be and I hoped someone would rescue me from the deepening isolation I was beginning to feel. At this point, aviation was one of my last remaining joys. Little did I know the next "flying lesson" I was about to receive.

Cloud Rocks

~~~~~~~~

My next aviation project was when I discovered a 20 year old Zenith CH250 aerobatic aircraft up in the wilds of Canada that had become a "hangar queen", meaning it just sat there in its faded glory and never saw the light of day. It also happened to be the next plane I was considering building. As such, it made much more sense to fly the plane to Georgia and rebuild it rather than start a new plane from scratch.

The deal was made and I was on my way to Canada by plane, bus, taxi and 4-wheeler to a far-off in the sticks airport whose Kawasaki tribe Indian name I couldn't even pronounce, much less remember. When I arrived, the seller gave me some "check-out" time in the aircraft, signed the papers and away I went to the U.S. of A. The first stop on the way back was at Niagara Falls Airport to clear customs and pick-up my good friend Billy, who had never experienced a long cross-country flight in a two-seat aircraft. Since he was building his own plane, we thought this would be a great experience for him. Little did we know just what kind of experience it would become.

After Customs, we loaded the plane with gas and gear and off we went. Our first goal was to do "the" scenic tour of Niagara Falls which was as breathtaking as you'd imagine.

Niagara Falls from 4,000 feet. Can you hear them?

We then headed to the heartland of America with a planned overnight stop in northern Tennessee before the final push into Georgia. As we flew south and reached the Kentucky Mountains, we were above broken, but increasingly dense, clouds. Although clouds can appear from "somewhere else" and just float along to where you are, they can also form spontaneously around, under or over you under the right atmospheric conditions, which is what was happening to us.

Because I had plenty of fuel, we first tried to fly around the weather system. But it was forming faster than we were flying. In short order, the mountains below us became almost completely shrouded in the thickening cloud layer with only an occasional hint of green peaks. These conditions began to make for tense moments for a simple yet rock solid reason: lotsa pilots have been known to fly into "cloud rocks" (i.e. mountains that are hidden in the clouds) much to their permanent demise. And although the clouds are soft, once again, it's those pesky rocks that make for the sudden stops.

The pucker factor increased when we discovered the database in the plane's GPS (a navigation instrument which directs you to an airport) was obsolete, meaning it couldn't identify the airport we needed. Unfortunately, we'd earlier realized we didn't have the navigational instruments to fall back on. Some of them were too old to be accurate and, worse, others had rolled over and simply died as the trip progressed.

Anyway, at this point I was looking real hard for a place to set the plane down. And almost *any* place would be fine. As we flew on, I could spot ridges and valleys far below us through an occasional hole in the clouds, holes which were quickly becoming few and far between. Through one of these, I briefly saw a short gravel road on the top of a ridge I thought might be long enough to put the plane down on, at least in a condition we could possibly walk away from.

But we had no way of knowing how close to the ground the cloud bottoms were in this area – which is somewhat vital information that would affect our approach to a landing. At this point, I recalled having seen a Wal-Mart somewhere in the valley, but I had no idea where it was. As my mind raced, I thought I could even put the plane down in the parking lot – if I could only find it. At least help would get to us quickly if necessary. Better yet, there might be a McDonald's nearby.

The weather rapidly deteriorated and I lost all concern about saving the plane. All that mattered now was getting us on the ground unharmed – regardless of what I had to do to accomplish that. By this time, Billy was beginning to look somewhat concerned, a look that only intensified when I told him of my landing intentions. He was probably considering this trip may not have been such a good idea, but to his credit, he remained calm and helpful as I focused on finding a solution to our predicament.

As we flew on, the clouds massed together over and around us. Then the world simply disappeared into a murky cotton ball.

All of a sudden, that 1/8 inch thick Plexiglas canopy didn't seem like much between us and the thick gray gloom outside. And without functioning instruments, a pilot has no reference point of what is straight and level and trying to fly by the "seat of the pants" without seeing the horizon is the classic pilot killer. We were no longer in a position to safely fly and the only option left was to climb and hope for clearer air above. I then rechecked the aviation map and confirmed there was a river somewhere nearby with an airport alongside it.

But just *where* was that river?

I began to sweat more than I like…and while trying to ignore the faulty instruments, I began to pray and try and control the slowly rising knot of panic forming in my gut. I asked God to help keep me calm and to show me the way out of this worsening dilemma while keeping the plane in controllable flight. I had also slowed the plane down from 130 mph to 90, but that's still a lot faster than I'd like to slam into something unmovable, like a mountain. Silently, I could also sense Billy praying alongside me as we truly became "a wing and a prayer". While doing this, I was making a shallow circular climbing turn, hoping to possibly locate the gravel ridge road or at least get up into clear air. As I was almost completing the turn, I looked straight out of the windscreen and saw a small tear in the clouds.

But this was no ordinary hole. To my utter amazement, what I saw for the briefest of moments was like a scene from the original "10 Commandments" movie as many miles away, I could plainly see the sun reflecting off the lost river like a silver homing beacon, and then it winked out.

I could not believe our "luck." Like sailors being led by the Catatumbo lightning, I knew we were safe from colliding into a mountain if I just flew a straight line. I then headed toward the lost hole at full throttle and soon shot out of the bottom of the clouds over the river where it had begun to rain. From here, it was a process of flying the shoreline until we found the airport.

However, we now had another problem: I did not know whether the airport would be east or west along the river as the rain came harder and we were losing visibility again. I need not have worried as our "directions from above" were not over. As I looked to the west, there sticking up 200 feet above the ground was a smokestack with a 20 foot blue-gold flame jetting out the top like a torch! In yet another Biblical analogy of "follow the fire", that was the town that had the airport…and that was where we headed in the fading light.

But the best surprise was yet to come…

As we approached the airport, I set the engine, carburetor heat and flight controls and flew the standard pattern to the runway with no hint of any additional problems. Upon turning onto our final approach, I lowered the flaps and did a final gauge check, all of which were fine. However, no sooner did the two main tires touch the ground during the landing "flare" with the nose wheel still in the air when… silence. Right before our eyes, the propeller came to an abrupt and complete stop as the engine quit cold in the span of a heartbeat.

Stunned, Billy and I just looked at each other wordlessly, not knowing whether to laugh or cry. Laugh because we were safely on the ground…or cry, because it could have happened just moments earlier with a very different outcome. Needless to say, it was with grateful and humble hearts we silently rolled down the runway for our unplanned overnight stop.

We spent that night in a lovely little town where at least 5 people had a full set of teeth and at a hotel that offered free earplugs at the check-in desk. When we signed the registration paper, there was an illustrated train running along the bottom of it that said "No Refunds!" Little did we know how close the real train was to our room. In fact, it thundered by between the bed and the bathroom every hour on the hour. But most importantly, we were on the ground to hear it.

And to me, that made it very sweet music indeed.

After I got the plane back to Georgia, I replaced the engine, installed actual functioning instruments and because it could do some sick aerobatics, people referred to flying it as a "metal illness" and me as a Wing-nut. I then flew it for another year when suddenly without any warning after a short flight one day, I simply lost all interest in flying.

Just like that.

On the drive home I remember saying to myself "What the hell was that all about?" and then decided to sell the plane.

The rolling shadows had stolen one more joy.

When I got home I told Janie what I wanted to do. She looked at me like I just told her I had decided to stop breathing. Her advice was that I give it some time to think it through before doing anything, which I thought was wise.

As we were having this conversation, I opened up my email and saw a name I did not recognize. This turned out to be a fellow in Alabama who one year prior, had wandered out to Berry Hill airport that I flew out of. When he was there, we talked about "home built" aircraft such as mine. Well, in his mail, he told me he wanted to buy an airplane and did I know of any Zenith's like mine for sale?! To me, this seemed like a reasonably well timed "sign" from above I was to sell the plane. So that's exactly what I did.

In the process of training him to fly the plane, and during a botched landing, he ran us way off the side of the runway at about 80 mph and straight towards a 6 foot high ridge of dirt. Compounding the problem was he had frozen on the controls and would not let go and I had no brakes on the co-pilot's side. Three hundred feet later, we finally stopped about 10 feet short of the berm after I had killed the engine and manhandled the controls away from him. He was so shaken up that he wanted to get out and have a cigarette to which I said

"No, we're going back up. Right now."

We immediately took off again, corrected the one thing he was doing wrong on the supplied checklist and his landings were almost perfect from that point on.

So, after that auspicious day and 37 years of flying, I walked completely away from aviation. I think.

Well, maybe.

But I had some other walking to do.

Back Into The Abyss

~~~~~~~~

Shortly after selling the plane, Gene called saying that after a 9 *year* wait, he had gotten his permit for a private river trip in Grand Canyon and would I be interested in going? Without thinking, I said "Yes" and immediately began to try and talk myself into it. But then I remembered how much work a trip really is - unloading a thousand pounds of gear in 110° at days end, setting up camp, the kitchen, latrine, your effects, cook, go to sleep and then reverse it all at dawn with sand in your sleeping bag, food and shorts. (After 16 days of this and 47° water, the orgasmic experience of a hot shower is almost debilitating.) So, I decided to do another middle of the night hike and meet them partway downstream. I could handle a 10 Day Shower Orgasm.

Now, when one chooses to enter the Canyon, they have also chosen to leave behind whatever remnants of our decaying impersonal society remain. We walk away from civilization, as it were, and all familiar forms of reference fall by the trailside.

There is no place to spend money, no gas to buy, PDAs and watches become meaningless reminders of our slave masters and cell phones cease to function. We cut ourselves off from almost all daily transactions and diverting stimuli except the ones we often use the least - that with ourselves and others.

Left behind are such amenities as our rolling steel isolation chambers we drive to work so we can further border ourselves in pale grey partitioned cubicles where we interact not with people, but with a glowing screen. Ah yes, syphilization, which I believe just like the physical disease, will ultimately result in (with deepest apologies to Coleridge's Ancient Mariner guy):

"Borders, borders, everywhere we're not to stop and think.

Borders, borders, everywhere and all our brains did shrink."

And a nighttime solo hike takes this to the extreme. Once you drop below the rim you are in an alien landscape where there is no light (other than star or moon), no sound and *no one*. It is also the time in the canyon when the snakes, scorpions and tarantulas become active. And while they attempt to avoid you, sometimes you come upon them before they can get out of your way. So it's the old fight or flight thing on a primal level. Theirs…not yours.

Moreover at night there isn't even the magnificent view to distract one from their thoughts, fears and deepest concerns. And I think of how we try to defy those by mortgaging our lives to create the perception of safety and stability. But in doing so, it seems we simply become like spiders firmly held hostage in the center of our own steel webs tethered to past obligations, present duties and future responsibilities of appointments, work and payments. And the Canyon offers none of this predictability. I don't even know where I will *be* in 5 hours, where I will lay my head down tonight or where I will be tomorrow. Each billowing footfall of dust is taking me back to basics in an immediate and rudely gentle way and moves me one step further away from all that is familiar and "safe".

A journey without schedules. A journey in self-trust.

But for this moment, this little spider is hanging by only one slim thread anchored squarely and solely in the present – and wondering, wondering which direction the soft Canyon breeze will take him on this quiet and vast moonless night.

So perhaps it is better to let darkness introduce the Canyon. To let the unhurried creep of dawn graciously reveal this portal into eternity as we slowly release our rational railing on a scene that staggers.

However, even while poised on the darkened rim, instantly overpowering is the dense cloak of silence of the 10 mile wide 6,000 foot deep void that returns no sound and reveals no movement whatsoever. It's an immense stillness so palpable it seems to wash over you in waves. Yelling into it sends your voice into an infinite amount of black velvet as the sound stops three feet from you. And it's overwhelmingly unnerving to submit yourself to this black nothingness…until you accept it as part of the canyon's ever changing personality.

So, at 1:15 A.M., I shouldered my pack of essentials and with a sense of the Canyon waiting, over the edge into the silent black velvet void I went. And the truth is, I was afraid. Not because of the things I mentioned before, but because of things I had filed away in my heart and my head. And these files were *really* big and really heavy. I turned on my light to push the darkness away…and immediately felt like an intruder.

I turned it off. The darkness swept back in around me.

And then I knew. God, I so not wanted to be here.

133

God In A Bottle & The Whisper

~~~~~~~~

As I began my 11 mile journey down into the canyon, Snoopy would have called it a "dark and stormy night." I would agree, only it wasn't just a night, but by now, several months of darkness of the soul. Try as I might to look forward to it, I had been struggling with a disheartened state and would have done anything to back out of this trip. I could not recall a time when I felt so deeply broken and *lonely* in so many ways. Through the night, I wended my way down to the river - about six thousand vertical feet in silent darkness, both inside and out. During this odyssey, I stopped several times, turned around and began to climb back up. But each time I would realize my friends would not know if I was hurt on the trail, or worse, and would spend a lot of time worrying and looking for me. No, I had to be when and where I was supposed to be. But I also knew a canyon sunrise always brings heart as it slowly cascades its golden halo down the cliffs above you.

Unfortunately, things began to go downhill again when I backed up into a cactus plant and had a needle break off in my butt which was pulled out two days later. Even getting on the river began on a bad note as the first major rapid I had to do was Crystal - and you already know about it. Here's how that went:

Crystal Rapid, Yoda and me. I take all the help I can get.

134

For some reason, I decided to put my helmet on even though I was in a big supply raft. Within seconds of entering the huge rapid, a very good run quickly turned very bad as Don's oar got jammed in between some rocks. In his effort to dislodge it, the retaining rope broke and the tip of the 12 foot wooden oar slammed into the back of my head throwing me to the raft floor. By then we were getting trashed in the Big Hole and like Gene a decade before, I have vivid memories of the next 90 seconds of my life - mostly because I thought they'd be my last.

Over the next few days I had almost no sleep, way too much caffeine to stay awake, helped row a 2,000 pound supply boat 15 miles a day in temperatures over 120 degrees and was flat out exhausted. This was the perfect storm for what I had feared would occur and one day at lunch, it spawned a serious episode of heart arrhythmia. Not wanting to alarm anyone, I motioned for Don to come over. (In yet another of life's ironies, Don, whom I hadn't seen in 25 years, was my first year physiology teacher at Life College and had started me in whitewater paddling in 1977.)

Some years before while using an inversion machine for my low back pain, I had accidentally discovered I could often stop the arrhythmia if I got upside down. So I asked Don to help me up the sand dune to the base of the cliffs about 200 feet away knowing that in the heat and my lightheadedness, I couldn't make it alone. When we got there, I was very weak and not paying attention as I did a handstand against the rock. What I realized a moment too late was that I had put both hands right into a bed of prickly pear cactus. Could this day get any better?

By this time I was hoping I might actually be able to use my helicopter evacuation insurance. "Unfortunately", the inversion maneuver worked and the heart problem corrected itself but I was also certain I had made a huge mistake being on this trip.

But as the days went on, I also observed parts of myself I hadn't planned on seeing. In the past, there would be many rapids I would run or "sketchy" side canyon hikes I would go on just for the rush. This time, however, the draw was not there and I decided the risk and the adrenaline hit simply weren't worth it and deferred when I thought there was too much chance of injury. Hell, I even walked around Lava Falls. Wow! These were actually like grown-up decisions! I didn't need to prove to myself – or anyone else – that I was a "man"! And all of the hair on my chest stayed right where it belonged. Even so, like the persistent susurration of the river, the deep sadness remained.

One night, the other fifteen people had a beach "party" (read drunk around the campfire), during which I slipped downstream to try and sort out my thoughts. As I sat on the hot sand listening to the river slide by in the dark, I looked up at the narrow slot of clear desert sky framed by the black canyon walls. And there among the explosion of stars, was yet another river, the Milky Way, cutting a celestial swath of gleaming diamonds from rim to rim, its massive silent shimmering grandeur punctuating my insignificance. At that moment I felt like God no longer knew me or what was happening in my life. Surely in the vastness of the heavens I saw so clearly, I was not to be found. Worse yet, my heart felt like I no longer knew Him. This was in stark contrast to the joy and presence I was accustomed to having.

In my crushing loneliness on that beach, I did something I thought I would never do. I asked God

"Give me a sign you are even out there, that you know I exist. You don't need to fix me, just help me find you again."

I then went for the kill by recalling many of the hurtful and selfish things I had done in relationships over the years - the guilt and sorrow of which pulled at my last fingertip hold on the edge. Finally, I could hold no longer. At that moment, I succumbed and went sailing soundlessly off into the cold starry sky.

The next morning a cool and crystal clear dawn eased over the canyon wall as we loaded up the thousands of pounds of gear on the supply boats before the rush of heat arrived. After jump starting my stiff and sore body with coffee and aspirin, I made some tea in a plastic bottle that had joined me on every adventure for over twenty years. I then placed the bottle under a rock in the river to cool. When we were ready to go, I went to get the bottle and, to my sadness, realized it had washed away into the Colorado's countless rapids. Oh well.

Our plan that day was to row 15 miles downstream and camp on the left side of the river. By midday, we had gone 9 and stopped for lunch after which we sent three kayaks ahead of us to secure the campsite for the night. As they are first come, first served and located far apart, it's imperative to claim one early.

After repacking the boats, we continued rowing through the thundering afternoon sun with the river averaging several hundred feet wide in most parts. By the time we were at the 15 mile point, we had traveled through several major sets of large rapids and uncountable smaller ones. But there were no kayaks or fellow travelers on the left side of the river.

We scratched our heads, consulted with one another and agreed there was nothing else to do but continue downstream. Two miles later, we found our companions on the *right* side of the river on an irregular area of shoreline. As I pulled the supply boat to the shore, a kayaker came up to me and said

"Dr. Gary, I have your water bottle!"

I replied, "Thank you! Did you pick it up this morning before we left?"

Her response made the hair stand up on my neck.

Pointing behind her she said, "No, it was right over there behind that big rock in a little calm spot of water."

No way.

Because I found this impossible to believe, she took me exactly to where she found it. To further my disbelief, she said they first stopped at another campsite, decided they didn't like it and paddled right past where we were now standing. They then turned around and paddled back upstream about 300 yards - unknowingly to exactly where the bottle was quietly floating around and around in a little eddy *hidden* by a huge boulder.

Now, this may not seem like such a big deal, especially if you are not familiar with the Colorado River. But here's a fair analogy: Let's say you live on a very long hill and one morning, you place a ball in the street. Your goal is to let it roll downhill fifteen miles through hundreds of curves, heavy traffic, turns, streets, etc., to see if it will wind up in your *assigned* parking spot at work.

Pretty slim so far, huh? Well, let's increase the odds even further. On your way to work, you change your destination to somewhere else another 2 miles away...only to find the ball went *there* instead and was waiting for you! And waiting in the correct parking spot.

I'd wager the statistical odds of this happening are about the same as a completely disassembled 747 jumbo jet being put back together by a tornado. Rivets, wires, bolts and all.

So ruminate on this: My little bottle spent 8 hours traveling to where I *wasn't* supposed to be, got there *before* me, stayed put after arriving there (after traveling 17 impossible miles!) and managed to be in a place where the kayakers would find it. What could I say or do about the "chances" of that happening? Not much. In all honesty, it made far more sense to realize and believe God does indeed go before us in life and will manage to be in a place to be found, sometimes, even if we're not looking. To me, that was more believable then considering the whole event a "coincidence".

But maybe coincidence is nothing other than God choosing to remain anonymous. As for me, I had heard that small still voice that Scripture talked about…and it had called me by name.

You see, lest you think they had found just any old bottle bobbing in the river, that morning, after 20 years of using it, I finally took an indelible marker and wrote "Dr. Gary" on it. Those words were still legible after banging along 17 miles of rocky rapids. Had I not identified the bottle *that day*, it could have been any of the countless similar items in the river and the kayaker may never have even picked it up in the first place.

So, did God get "a message in a bottle" to me? You decide.
I have.

I do know that night I once again found myself alone on the shore, but this time with a grateful heart and feeling I had been answered. My hurting soul had been shown Grace and Truth and if it's right that we become the way we perceive God to be, I was also a changed person. I had not only heard the Whisper

…but watched as ghosts of my past silently drifted off into the deepening canyon twilight…never looking back.

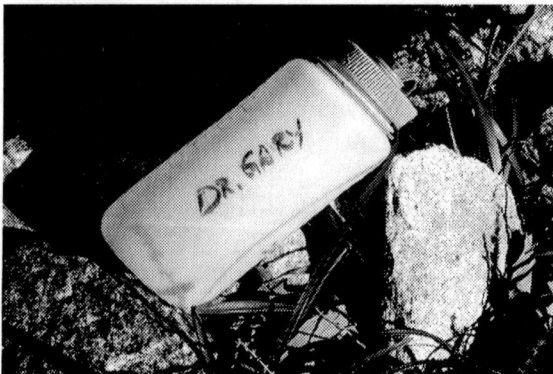

A nd that's when I had my "Big Oh!"…when I finally grasped what had been controlling and discouraging me in such a dreadful way for so many months.

Anger fueled by anxiety anchored in uncertainty.

To me, anger is the result of not getting what you want and anxiety the product of not knowing how something will turn out. My problem was I was fighting an internal battle and I was "losing" - and that made me mad. But I had suppressed the anger and allowed myself to be trapped between believing the *words* of trusted people versus the truth of their *actions*. Sadly, the words became unreliable illusions that left me feeling betrayed and hurt. And while words have consequences we are responsible for, I had forgotten that people are truly what they do.

The anxiety was because I wouldn't let go of something and kept trying to affect its outcome which was beyond my control. This made my *life* feel out of control which caused me to keep working backwards in my belief system to where I questioned just where was God in all of this - and why wasn't my constant prayer for guidance "being answered"? This breach made me feel abandoned and confused because while a man can accept bad news, he is certain to be drained by uncertainty.

But when I had just about let God go, I was letting Hope go with it. And what I didn't know at the time was that hope is often stronger than love…and I was becoming hopeless in a prison where *I* was the warden. Only after I understood *and accepted* the cause of the anger and anxiety, did I begin the long walk back to being whole, and part of that journey was to question my understanding of my core beliefs including who I thought I was. This was to affect every aspect of my life and I was finally on the road to learning what I didn't know. (One of the most dangerous – and immature – places to be in life, is to not know what you don't know.) Likewise, *if we're not first honest with ourselves, it's impossible to be with others.*

It was then I also understood why in the past I had been attracted to so many high risk activities - the wild stuff in the airplanes, the car and motorcycle racing, hanging on the side of a cliff, dangling on a rope in a cave or in the relentless power of whitewater. It wasn't because I had a "death wish" as some had said. It wasn't because I was "stupid" – I had the training and equipment to face the risks. No, it was my misdirected attempt to find "Life". And while I enjoyed many of my adventures, the adrenaline rush was often my unconscious substitute for a lack of satisfying emotional food in my life. This had caused me to become "self-sufficient" and in order to feel "something", I'd risk everything with the irony being the closer I cheated death, the more I thought I was "living life to its fullest."

Truly, this was Stupid Math at its worst.

And the reason I'd not allow the emotional connection with others in the first place? Well, that might mean I was not in "control", no? More importantly, it could also mean I'd have to trust God as well as the intent of others which was way beyond my control. And things I couldn't control had caused me pain which taught me something basic the hard way:

Every betrayal is born out of trust.

But up to this time I had just considered my activities the normal expression of a happy go lucky adventurer. Little did I know of the void inside I was trying to fill. Perhaps going back again and again to the huge void of Grand Canyon was my symbolic attempt to tell myself just that. What I now knew was an extreme experience wasn't necessarily meaningful.

And meaningful experiences didn't have to be extreme. In fact, while the experience could be enjoyed on its own, it often became secondary to whom it was enjoyed with.

What I never did understand was if my activities - and the presumption I'd survive them - was done out of confidence... or innocence. Perhaps it was a bit of both? Either way, I now had a new and healthier sense of humility that, in a way, felt like the bruised but still hopeful heart of an abandoned dog in a shelter. The one with the lowered head but upraised pleading soft brown eyes that when he looks at you, still trusts beyond hope you'll take him home and love him.

And the same one that just wants a chance to love you back.

It was then it became implicit to me *that when we hurt in our heart, we hide in our head.* And I had *distracted* (see p. 162) myself from that pain for so long it seemed normal to feel that way. But now I knew for certain that while the mind can be forced to bow to an ultimatum, *the heart cannot.* Give it a chance for Hope and it will always move towards a source of Life.

My personal Trilogy was now complete. I had danced with my demons physically, emotionally and spiritually. And while close to being completely broken, I exited humbled, but stronger

– and most of all, my heart, gentler. I was also mindful of Thomas Paine's words "That which we obtain too easily...we esteem too lightly." This had not come easily for me.

During the next few days I recalled a dream in which I was a desperately poor man. I was on my hands and knees in the darkness below the floor of an Old West saloon scrabbling for gold flecks on the dirt that had fallen through the cracks of the floor from the gamblers above. As the sun came up after a long and cold night of useless searching, its bright fingers spiked down through the spaces between the floor boards above me.

And there like the countless specks of dust one usually sees in a sunbeam, were instead, countless flecks of gold shimmering in the air that in the darkness, had covered me as well.

I was rich all along and had not a clue.

By this time I had experienced or suffered all the typical physical problems I was to treat in the clinic – and some far worse. So I clearly knew what pain was and how it could steer one's life and I could pass that compassion on to my patients.

I also had an elementary change of heart. In the past, when encountering those struggling with depression or similar problems, my internal (and I suspect, judgmental) attitude was to want them to "Just get over yourself." I now had a clearer sense of the dark hopelessness that haunts these folks. They say you can't understand what you haven't experienced or give away what you don't have. Well, what I had experienced was near enough - and the Grace and sense of forgiveness I received, I could now gladly give to others.

But when all was said and done, and after more than 30 years of "being someone else", I was returning to the tender hearted fellow who wrote the early journals of Trust and Hope, things we often trade too easily for a shallow cynicism. This was the person who wanted so much to be honest with himself, and just as importantly, with others.

This was *Me*.

The Gary 4.0 that had gone down into the Canyon...was not the 5.0 that came out of it.

And the lesson was clear as the streaming Canyon sunlight:

In life there is room for sadness combined with reflection. There is, however, no room for sadness combined with surrender.

141

Parts Is Parts

By this time, I had 11 surgeries on various body parts with a fairly large amount of very expensive hardware put into or taken out of me over the years. (See thigh x-ray below.) As a gift, my surgeon always left the stuff he removed in a little baggie in my hospital nightstand. So now I have a place setting for two along with a pretty good collection of $100.00 screws, bolts, plates, nuts, washers and nails which someday I think I'll make into a mobile.

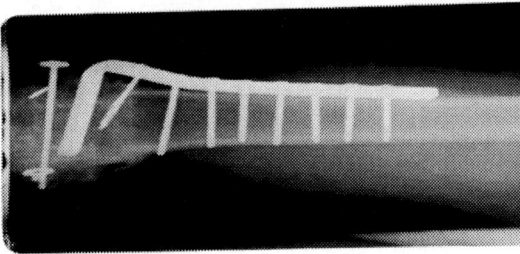

But the best part of my parts is yet to come. When I had my entire knee joint replaced in 2004, I had to make an addendum to my will which previously was for me to be cremated with my ashes spread from the top of Stone Mountain in Georgia. This change notes that most likely the titanium knee will not melt in the cremation, so I requested someone take the pieces home and make a wind chime out of them. Then, when someone asks "Where's Gary?" they can always say
"Oh, he's hanging out by the deck."

But stranger yet was when I went for my regular eye exam. The doctor looked at my eyes through the machine and then back at my history card and back to my eyes. He was at a complete loss to explain how somewhere in the midst of all this, my eyes went from brown to dark hazel.

Oddly enough, this happened at a point in my life right after I started to "see" things quite a bit differently.

Well, I had always wanted to be 6 feet tall, 180 pounds and have green eyes. The last item took about 54 years to do, but hey, 3 for 3 ain't bad.

What Goes Down Must Come Up

~~~~~~~~~

After my 2004 knee replacement, I was utterly miserable and exhausted from nearly 5 months of extremely high levels of 24/7 eye-crossing pain. And while this was my 11th surgery and I was used to pain, this was off the charts and short of narcotic medications which I refused to take, nothing touched it. But experiment we did and every week I had a different prescription to the point where I think the pharmacist suspected me of having my own little neighborhood drug cartel.

Because there was nothing to distract my mind from the pain when I tried to sleep, nighttime became my foe and there were months of nights where I would sit and simply weep while rubbing my leg incessantly just to feel something other than pain. My internal "equilibrium" became so stressed that for 6 weeks I could not maintain a normal body temperature and bounced all day and night from sweating to uncontrollable shivering. (I can now relate to a woman going through menopause.) This is not the typical outcome of this procedure, but much to my delight, I was the "exception".

Whereas this procedure usually takes about 1 hour with an 8 inch incision, mine took 4 hours with a 23 inch cut as orthopedist Dr. Bill had to pull out a lot of old hardware (see page 142). He also had to separate all my thigh muscles which had become fused to each other and to the thigh bone itself before he could glue in the new parts. (Yes, glue.) Part of the post-operative problem was ongoing internal bleeding from the holes left in the bone from removing 9 screws. This blood had to be periodically drained with a syringe needle about the size of a #2 pencil.

He said after the surgery it was the most "challenging" procedure he had performed in 25 years. Great. As always, glad to donate the raw material for an educational experience.

It's a fact your brain can process only so much information at one time. Mine probably does even less than yours. Such was the case when I woke up from this surgery. (A pre-op detail to remember here is that a nurse used a razor to shave my entire right leg bald as a cue ball from crotch to toes.) When I became semi-conscious post-operatively, I realized there was a naked woman in bed with me. But confusing my investigation was when I looked down at the sheets, there were only 2 legs and both appeared to be mine. Where were her legs? So I looked *under* the sheets…again, only my 2 legs. My brain, however, was screaming "Find the woman! I know she's here!" In my haze, I kept looking around for the person who had this incredibly smooth leg rubbing up against my Yeti left leg as my brain was short circuiting trying to comprehend all of this.

This turned into a somewhat frantic search for the woman. The others, who were now in the room, stood there wondering just what was going on with me picking up the sheets, looking under them, looking around the room, asking where she was etc. Of even greater concern was the fact that all this rubbing and stuff was starting to actually feel pretty good. Finally, even though I was looking right at both legs touching each other, my brain still couldn't process the sensory overload and just gave up and let the morphine carry me away back to a silent stupor.

Overall, quite a unique experience. So what did I learn from this? Nothing whatsoever. I just thought it was interesting. Try it some time. It's positively Machiavellian.

So now I have a mechanical knee that clanks and clunks with every step – no more sneaking up on anyone with my old stealth ninja moves. It's kinda like having a cow bell hanging from my crotch. I then spent the next 6 weeks at home in an electric hospital bed and had to give myself 2 injections in the stomach every day to prevent blood clots. That was fun, sorta like 20 bee stings on your belly. The worst part however (besides the pain) was the loss of confidence I had in myself to do, well, just about anything. I was simply too weak and could barely support my weight. As I am a guy, this of course, challenged my guynitude. What to do? Hey, I know! Go for a walk. And so I did – in a place where art comes to life on a majestic scale.

As I was very familiar with the "inner canyon" down at the river level, I wanted to explore more of the mid and upper canyon levels. So I got busy planning a goal to hike 4 miles down into Grand Canyon on one trail (I only said I would never do the *river* again, right?), 4 miles through the canyon on the Tonto Platform and then 4 miles up and out yet another trail. My goal? Twelve miles in one day with more than 6,000' of elevation change while remembering "a mile" in the canyon is quite unlike a mile most anywhere else on the planet.

When I told the surgeon of my plans, he became unglued because he thought my new knee parts would become unglued. He told me in no uncertain terms the *only* thing he wanted me going up and down was stairs, with 2 handrails. I promised him I would think about it. I just didn't say for how long.

Or exactly when I'd do the thinking.

After much preparation, including over 6 months of hard knee rehabilitation, the day of the descent arrived and we began our journey down the very abrupt South Kaibab trail. This is one of the steepest and most direct ways into the canyon. It is so steep, in fact, that it is not recommended as a return trail to the rim as it offers no shade or water supply. So, if you've gone down the initial 4 miles, you are pretty much committed to do the remaining 8 miles of the "loop" using the 2 other trails. Janie had planned to do 3 miles and then return on the same trail as she didn't feel up for the entire 12 miles. This she did while Anne and I continued on. Janie would also "rescue" us at trails end.

Anne is a little girl with a big heart who was married to my caving buddy Ray, who was in Iraq serving his country. At times, Ray and I can talk Anne into going caving and once there, we can sometimes also stuff her headfirst into holes we cannot fit in. This is to see if the cave "goes". If it does, we may need to use a blasting system we devised using different sized bullets like we did to open up "Whacked on Crack" cave. Anne is also an avid photographer and in one cave I had discovered, she tried to lower her Nikon camera box into a pit on a rope. But as the knot was "not so tight", it failed and the camera plummeted to the bottom. The "sproinging" noise heralded a bad outcome. Because of this, she suggested we call the cave "Nikon Plunge" but it's a courtesy among cavers that whoever discovers the cave, gets to name it. So with consideration to caves being formed in different types of rock and her failed knot, I chose: "Knotsotite" – Now I ask you, is that clever or what?

Anyway, while figuring out the logistics of the canyon hike, a good deal of time was spent on weather projections, expected temperatures, the sun's position relative to canyon walls for possible shade, potential water sources etc. As such, we had expected around 85 degrees as a day high for the month of May while the Canyon had decided on 100. And boy, do those 15 degrees make a difference. But hey…it's a *drrrrry* heat, right?

Uh-huh. It's dry all right. That's because it sucks the water right out of your liver, and if you're not careful, your frontal lobes.

Hiking the canyon can only be described as beautiful and harshly severe. They sort of balance each other out and the only way to get to see the beauty is to deal with the severity and harshness. And it was turning out to not only be more beautiful than expected, but more difficult as well. About 7 non-stop hours into the trip, we were close to the half-way point which is where we rested and had a bit to eat. By now I had blisters *between* my toes and fingers from using the wrong boots and walking poles. It was also at this point Anne informed me her knee was hurting pretty badly, so we shared my meds. The next section of the "trail" - a dusty 18 inch wide path - was unknown as I had been able to research very little about it. (Although one can now use "Google Earth" and "walk" the entire trail from their living room. Talk about "armchair adventure"!) One report simply mentioned it as being "sketchy" and that was all.

Sketchy indeed.

That definition was a bit specious at best. When we got to this section, the trail itself skirted the edge of a 400 foot vertical drop into a side canyon. This would be OK if the trail was 50 feet away from the drop on flat ground, but it twern't. It was 50 feet away on a 60 degree slope and paralleled the drop. From the trail to the lip of the drop was nothing other than loose gravel and small scrub. In other words, nothing to grab onto if you slipped and slid. Anne, who is a climber, did not really cotton to these types of heights and drew to a halt when we got to the start of this section. And we talked about it. Anyhow, she cornered up all her courage and on we went finally stopping to rest about 4 P.M along the esplanade before turning south…and the long, steep walk up to the canyon rim which took yet another 6 hours.

Perhaps the 2 biggest problems for new canyon hikers is the "Reverse Mountain Syndrome". When one goes hiking up a mountain, the return trip is downhill – which is good, because you are tired by then so gravity helps. In the canyon, if you go down….you gotta come *up* and usually when you are completely exhausted. So you get to do the most difficult part of your trip when you are the most worn out. And gravity hinders your efforts most effectively in your slow upward grubble.

The other problem that gets far too many people is simple dehydration. Now this seems like an easy thing to cure – drink more water, right? Well, yes and no. If you drink too much of it, you will dilute your electrolytes (primarily salt) which can cause hyponatremia. This starts out as headaches, muscle spasms and dizziness often followed by brain swelling, coma and death.

Sounds attractive, doesn't it?

The Sketchy Spot. Trail is thin horizontal line above cliff.

Well hey, I know all about this stuff and I've done over 500 miles of serious walking and paddling in the canyon, right? Yes, but apparently only theoretically. Even though I had taken great care to carry the appropriate foods, liquids and electrolytes, at about 9 P.M. I began to experience hyponatremia about 2 very long and steep miles from the top. That's when I noticed the headaches coming on. Next I felt a bit woozy and unbalanced (and not the way you are by now thinking I am) on the narrow trail. Then my back spasmed so badly when we stopped to rest, it took me almost 5 minutes to be able to get up and walk again.

This all got worse as we got nearer the top but Anne and I continued to encourage each other. At one point I thought she was hallucinating when she said she was getting attacked by a bird in the now total darkness. It wasn't until I saw the spooky glare of two red eyes go swooping by in my headlamp that I actually believed her! (When I later saw a picture I took of her in the darkness with a flash, there was the evil flying creature with the beady red eyes sitting on a rock right next to her.)

Well, by the time we stumbled out of the canyon after a 15 hour ordeal, most of which with the sun roaring down through the clear desert air, I was entirely spent, totally exhausted and barely able to move. Literally. When I was driven and dragged back to the hotel bed, my body jerked and quivered for another 2 hours as I tried to get my electrolytes rebalanced.

It was great!

The next morning, I felt like I had been flogged on a torture wheel and the only 2 things on my body that did *not* hurt were my eyelids and...oh the irony of it all...the new knee. But I guess titanium isn't supposed to feel pain. When all was said and done, the trip did *exactly* what I wanted it to do which was to be so difficult for me to complete there was no assurance at the outset that I *could* complete it. In other words, if it had been any easier, I would not have accomplished my goal of finding my new post-operative limits. On the other hand, if the trail had been 100 feet longer, I'd still be there buried under some rock.

Did I tell you it was great?

~~~~~~~

But the logic of knowing my different limits is simple and pragmatic. If I could build an entire airplane, then I knew I could fix one. If I could build an entire house, then I knew I could fix a broken toilet. It was all a matter of creating perspective and that perspective gave me the confidence to do things I may not have attempted. So now, if I could do 12 miles in 100 degree heat in Grand Canyon, I do not hesitate to go on an enjoyable 5 mile hike in the woods because it's well within my limits.

Now if you are thinking back to when I used hazardous activities for an emotional fix, and that this is much of the same, I'd beg to differ. There's a difference between being in a rapid that will not stop for you while you get yourself together. Or a climb where there is no way out. Or lost in a cave. No, here, I could simply sit down on the trail if I needed to and sort out life. So, in that sense, there was no immediate risk. Nonetheless, that did not make completing the trail any less strenuous or exciting for me, which was exactly what I wanted.

Besides, there was always that helicopter evacuation ID tag hanging on my backpack. (It didn't occur to me until hours after the hike there was no place for one to actually land...)

And really, it *was* great. Actually, it was the best. Ever.

So here's my conclusion after all of my Canyon trips: Its majesty will hush all but the most insensitive and if you want to take your soul on a long...slow...quiet walk to sort things out and hear *Life's Whispers,* there's no Grander place to do it.

~~~~~~~~~~

Well, that's a small sampling of my good resume stuff to date which neatly helped me avoid a mid-life crisis. But walking away from aviation, the house and high risk activities signaled a major change in my life path. I now understood that life was not about things or activities, but had everything to do with people. And if it involved people, then by default, it included time and relationships...both of which I sometimes managed poorly as you'll see in just a little bit.

And, oh, about the airplane stuff being history? Well, there's a possible addendum there as I'm 90% done building an original design ultralight affectionately named the "Aluma-Tub".

So there is that.

But overall, I find myself now thinking what most people naturally do at 58: "Jeez...How am I still alive?"

The Aluma-Tub. Test pilot anyone?

Part II

It's About Time

Money: Something we try to get value for when we spend it. And we can always get more of it.

~~~~~~~

Time: Something we rarely consider the value of when we "spend" it. And we can never get more of it.

~~~~~~~

Heaven: Someplace everyone wants to go to. But usually not right now.

The Midward

~~~~~~~~

OK, let's get off the roller coaster and go for a walk and talk some of this stuff over. So far you've been able to sit back, be a voyeur in my life, watch my foibles and think "Jeez, what an idiot this guy is. I would have never done that." And you're probably right. So here's where I attempt to untangle the messiness of things by considering how our personal truths affect ourselves - and others. Part II is also the result of over 20 years of deliberate conversations with folks, 25 to 95, about their relational successes and failures. The spectrum spanned from one being married 60 years to another married 5 times in less than 10. My goal? To better understand the most complex but essential of human activities: Relationships. And while I discovered none are perfect, it seems many can easily be made better. I also think much of what I found is universally applicable. (Unless you live in California, then all bets are off.)

You'll also notice an emphasis about comprehending and apprehending the unstoppable role Time plays in our lives and how we use it as "currency" in our relationships. So, here's what I find myself now considering: When I willingly trade some of my non-renewable Life-*Time* at work or in a relationship, do I get satisfaction and fulfillment in return? Or boredom and strife?

In other words, when I "spent" that time, exactly what did I "buy" with it? And was it time "well spent"?

It's often said the best place to hide something is in plain view. Like an elephant in the room. After reading Part II, you may find some elephants in your life disguised as furniture as I did. You may also discover that any relationship is only as healthy as the least healthy person in it. As such, you may find yourself considering whether your own are honestly fulfilling, just OK, or maybe even somewhat toxic.

But here's the good part: It's a fact everyone has some unexplored potential that can better their lives. So if you put two people together, and they willingly *choose* to combine that potential - any situation can be improved! And as we are the ones that have the most control over the ending of our story, we really don't have to "give-in and give-up" if things are not quite what we'd like them to be.

From this point on, I'm sure you'll also notice the tone as being a lot more passionate. And it is - because *Life-Time* and people are worth being passionate about! It's also a bit more detailed. But I can't help that. I build airplanes, remember? And missed details often make planes – and relationships – crash. But even if you don't agree with some of my ontological opinions, we're still all in the same boat on the same river when it comes to Time. And we all consume it at the same rate. You'll also detect a definite distinction made between "life" and "Life" and about how I think both effect us. But take heed, this is not a self-help book. There are thousands of those out there so you can pick your poison. (Just stay away from the ones about "Issues".)

Now, is what you're about to read fact or opinion? Let's just say it's a fact that it's my opinion and that none of it is fatal (even though some events leading to this point almost were.) And my ideas may or may not work for you - and either is OK. But, if something makes you uncomfortable, perhaps it's worth asking yourself *why*. Above all, please understand I'm not trying to play amateur psychologist nor do I intend in the least to be preachy. Just know after I honestly combined my thoughts and experiences, this is the "mechanics of life" I saw before me.

The Good, the Bad and yes, there's some Ugly.

Anyway, at the very least, you'll read some good quotes. In fact, here comes Einstein now with one:

"If at first an idea doesn't sound absurd, then there is no hope for it." Based on that alone, there's great hope ahead!

And, oh, almost all of the dumb things I'm about to suggest you not do? *Guess how I know they're dumb.*

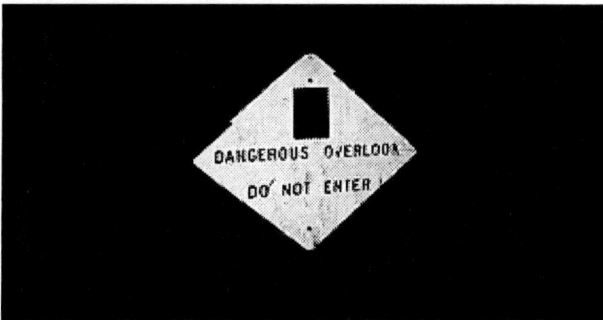

So, take a deep breath and c'mon along while we take a closer look at…….

It's About Time

~~~~~~~~

Good for one ride only.

I've been through Grand Canyon on the Colorado River numerous times now and often see the trip as an *almost* perfect analogy of life.

Hop in the boat with me and perhaps you'll see it as well.

Like birth and death into the stream of time, one puts onto, and takes off of, a river trip. There's a definite start and end, and once you enter its flow, you become part of it. And this flow *will* take you somewhere regardless of any actions you do, or don't take. Just like time, there is no "pause" button.

And this river can take you to some of the most breathtaking places you could ever imagine with sights, sounds and scents that delight beyond description. Or, it can thrash you through its rapids, throw you over a waterfall or slam you up against a rock and kill you mercilessly. But because you have not traveled this river before, you know not what course the water will take, whether it will be peaceful and smooth, or turbulent and rocky. Therefore, you'll not be forewarned of exactly what training or equipment will best suit your needs to insure the safest and most enjoyable journey. Nor will you know what – or who - you'll meet around the next hidden bend.

So because of the unknowns, perhaps you were wise and learned how to *read* a river, understand its flow and plan your course accordingly for the safest passage. In doing so, you learned the probable skills required and had some equipment to help influence as much as possible your journey in the unstoppable current.

But at some point in this odyssey, as the days and river rolled lazily off to the horizon, you realized you would only come this way this *one* time. You would never again hear that same rustling breeze in the willows on the sun dappled dampened sands of the shore, the lilting cascade of a canyon wren or glimpse up that beautiful and inviting side canyon in the soft evening twilight. Those moments in time, just like the quiet murmurs of the river were gone forever, never to be repeated.

155

Nor would you ever again travel this course with these same companions and you may sense a pull of sadness thinking of the promises that could have been with one of them. And just like the many possible outcomes of choosing your run through a complex rapid, you realized how quickly and easily the entire course of your life might have changed had you or another said something...Or not said something.

Or took a chance when you had the chance.

Because of that awareness, the passing moments and views suddenly came into such clear focus that your choices of companions and skills took on a new significance.

You learned some fellow travelers were more prepared and willing to make the trip better and safer for all concerned, while others were focused entirely on themselves. Some exposed your known weaknesses, others, your unknown strengths. Some were like a piece of driftwood and were in for a frightening ride as they tried endlessly to control things around them. Others were paddling along in wonder and amazement of their trip and handling the difficult places with purpose and grace.

And then there were the exquisitely hushed moments between rapids while drifting along only to look to your side and see leaves on the river's silken surface keeping perfect pace with you. Entranced, you moved in graceful and whispered harmony, a motionless pas de deux framed by the river's silent reflection of the canyon's golden majesty. For that precious instant, time seemed to stand still and only when you raised your eyes to see the shore, did you witness how swiftly you were both moving upon this river of time. And even as you watched, sometimes those very leaves were whisked away by some unknown and invisible current. While others were left behind as they spiraled off to an unseen destination taking with them some of your time, and sometimes, a part of your soul. And it came to mind how profound the dealings of a human heart can be...sometimes it'll never let go...and other times, it'll never come back.

Just like some people in our lives

But the sun and seasons came and went as we learned the better our skills became, the better was our time spent on the trip. Such as it is with our lives when subtle and unnoticeable forces take us to some shores we never intended to visit, or be.

And on we go.

So where does this all begin? Well, from where I sit, I'd say the entry point is how we *spend* our Life-*Time*.

"But at my back I always hear
Times winged chariot hurrying near…"
To His Coy Mistress
Andrew Marvell, 17th century

Spending Time

~~~~~~~

Spend wisely...spent inexorably.

When we "spend" time (use it doing something), we *spent* something we have a limited amount of. In doing so, *we no longer have it*. We actually "bought" something with that time and a "one time" transaction occurred. So was it worth the cost and did what we get in return have any real value?

But before we go there, what exactly is "time"? Well, as you'll see, Ben Franklin had his thoughts, but here's the dictionary definition: "A non-spatial continuum in which events occur in apparently *irreversible* succession from the past to the present to the future." But it's also the ultimate stalker that courses throughout our body, mind and soul and moves it from birth, growth and finally delivers it in due "time", to the exit sign. It's a concept coined by man to describe change and often referred to as something we "spend". And it's a coin that can be spent any way you want, but you only get to spend it *once*.

And "spent" means GONE as in "POOF!" You *never* get the chance to "earn" it back and you can never create more of it. No recycling allowed. So, considering in reality we can neither save nor lose time, I define its qualities as follows:

1.   It's a "tradable commodity" whose usage we can direct as it is automatically being "spent". Think of time as money in the following: "I spent time, I saved time, I can't afford the time" etc. which all put Ben Franklin's phrase "Time *is* money" in a different light! And while we can make more money, we can only do so if we "spend" more time to make it...if we have the time!

2.   Like different currencies, it has differing values. I may value time with you more than you do with me.

3.   Once a moment of time is gone, then that moment is "spent" just like an exhausted athlete who is physically spent and can do no more. You can't get that moment back and you can never really do anything "again". (Heraclitus said "You can never step in the same river twice.") Actually, you do not even have to use the time *deliberately* in order for it to be exhausted (spent). Much like your tax dollars, it's spent regardless if you direct its usage or not!

Perhaps if time was actually given to us in "coin" form, we could see just how much we've spent vs. what still remains.

But it's not. So why do we so often assume we have an endless supply and then *spend* what we do have, so poorly?

Now we all know our time is limited and we'll die, we just *don't really believe* we will *before* "our time". I mean, you *totally* expect to wake up tomorrow morning, right? But at some point, *everything* we do will have been done for the last time. Like last night. Problem is, we'll never know when that will be. And what we thought we could put off until tomorrow...really?

So, suppose you were told today
"You have cancer and about 2 weeks to live." Whoa.

What would you do with those few *precious* days left? Eat fattening foods? Be with someone in particular? Probably not sleep late! What would immediately jump to the front of the line for you and what would you say or do that you have not yet done? Remember: *We* can delay, but we can't delay time. Whistling past the graveyard only works for so long.

So, let's do a "Real-Time" check on this <u>right now</u> – and I'm betting the results may surprise you. Write down what you think are the 5 most important people or things to you in order from most to least important. (Example: spouse, money, sex, work.) I'll wait... OK, now turn it over and write in number of hours how you *actually* spent your time last week. Now compare how much time you spent on what *you said* was most important against what you actually did. Learn anything new about your "priorities"?

Franklin's understanding of this was simple and profound:
"Do not squander time for that is the stuff *life* is made of."
If you're weird and actually like math it looks like this:
Wasted time = wasted life = wasted Life-*Time*.

Ever watch the display on a microwave as it counts down? That's *your life* ticking away in seconds. But what really makes the time we do have so precious? One reason: *It will end.*

Immortality would actually make time worthless. Selah.

So do some people make better use of it than others? I think so, and there is evidence they have an *involvement and quality* in their lives that appears appreciably better than those who use time "poorly". And I think they've also discovered that time is like love...you can *invest* it - in people.

And invested time can be *the foodstuff* of relationships.

So how does one get to that point? I think for some its wisdom gained with age or a sudden realization of the "timeline" of their lives, meaning there's not much left! But perhaps the largest category had a life altering experience such as a near death event (recall the climber's stories after their failed attempts on Everest in 1996 or K2 in 2008), a serious or life threatening illness (ask any women who has been diagnosed with breast cancer), or even meeting the love of one's life and experiencing the joy of truly connecting with them. I've been "fortunate" enough to experience some of these and it *does* make a difference. But regardless of the reason, most would say they had *"The Wake-Up Call"*. As a result their life was enriched by almost a sense of responsibility to *live* their Life-*Time* with more intent and passion, especially in relationships.

Ben Franklin also gave this some thought and concluded

"Time makes more converts than reason" followed by the laconic irony of it's "...a great teacher, but unfortunately it kills all its pupils." Simply put, time, or the perceived lack of it, can add a perspective to life like nothing else.

Even so, in order for time to have any *practical* value, it needs to find a source of *expression.* Some may create something with their hands or minds. And others, a treasured investment of the heart. And while the former have worth, the latter has *"Life".* And I'd argue whatever has Life has the *highest* value.

To acknowledge this means making the best use of the only time frame we have: *The Present* with the understanding that *any and everything* we do consumes some of our limited supply of time. In terms of creating quality time with people and relationships, I think it means literally hearing what's in our own hearts and then being willing to let others experience who we truly are. Simply stated, it means "putting ourselves out there" and risk letting others approve – or disapprove - of the real us.

But I also think this process can get subtlety sabotaged by the 2-D's in life of Deny and Distract. These tricky two are the antithesis of valued time. They are the *thieves of time* that come and go unnoticed and make days, months and years invisibly slide by until it is too late.

So let's go drag them out into the light while we still have "the time".

Life in 2-D

~~~~~~~~~

We hide in our heads when we hurt in our hearts.

It can all begin with Denial, the main breeding ground for invisible elephants. See, if I can pretend not to "See the elephant in the room", well…then I don't have to deal with it! I'm sure you've heard "Denial is more than a river." That's a great analogy because the Nile is one of the few rivers in the world that flows north which is the opposite direction of most every river in that hemisphere…much the same way denial usually flows away from the truth. It's also the longest river in the world. Maybe some folks hold onto denial longer than anything else as well, even if it drains a relationship of its "Life".

For me, sometimes I'll try to deny what I'm actually thinking or feeling when I've learned there's "no point" in talking to another about what's bothering me. After, all, why do what history says doesn't work? So I learn to make the elephant "invisible". (In medical terms, elephants would be called a "space occupying lesion" - and they are never good news!) But does ignoring it make it go away? Almost never.

As folks get caught up in this process, I've watched denial get expressed in 3 ways: suffering in silence, anger or just abandoning (physically or emotionally) another, sometimes without any explanation. Friend or lover - and whether we intend it or not - each one of these sends out a hurtful message.

But when one's heart is troubled, it will *always* interfere with the quality of time "spent" with another. Why? *Because we hide in our heads when we hurt in our hearts.* The heart is then "off limits" as it tries to heal the hole in order to become whole. Or, it gives up and walls itself off with a moat and barbed wire. And we isolate ourselves like this not because we're crazy, but because we are hurting somewhere inside. But even in our attempts to "partition" off the corners of our lives, the elephant still peers down at us over the partition itself. Do this long enough and I believe we can become walking sponges of emotional and eventually, physical pain, as we'll see more clearly in "How a Broken Heart Breaks a Heart". So if home starts to feel like it needs a neon sign over the door that reads "Abandon hope all ye who enter here", well…that's a problem.

But denial doesn't always have to involve another person. For example, remember my Dad's brain tumor? A few years after he passed away, I began to get unrelenting headaches and definitely wanted to deny the possibility that I too, had a brain tumor. Finally, after screwing up all my courage because I was terrified of the possible outcome, I had a brain MRI. But I needed to know the truth more than I was afraid of the truth. (Yes, the scan was completely normal. And yes I also know you're thinking "Mabel, that's just too hard for me to believe.")

You may also recall that the last time I tried to find comfort denying the truth and believing an illusion, I paid an awfully big price. (*The Whisper,* page 139)

So what's the next stage when denial no longer works...like with a *really* big elephant? Well, how about:

Distraction. This is where we find any number of ways to divert our attention from the situation or heart hurt at hand. Again, if we can't connect with *someone*, then we'll try *something*. For me, this was often done on a long term and "grand" scale, such as building another airplane, and, I suspect, the house. Projects like these could distract me for *years* with a believable excuse. For a quick fix to help me "forget about life for awhile", I'll find relief in the computer, reading or perhaps ponder if sterility is hereditary.

But hands down, I think the best relational anesthetics to drain time from our life...and Life from our time are the "Plug Drugs" TV and PC. Perhaps you know some folks physically separated all day long who, after they get home, remain "virtually separated" all evening long by a 54" flat screen or the alternate world of a PC addiction. Sometimes even in different rooms around the house. But these are "safe" because there's no interaction required when minds and eyes are glued to a screen. And as there are only so many hours to use, this can help put off for days – or years – things we might really need to talk about.

Like that there elephant.

About TV in the bedroom: Really, aren't there better things to do in there? You know, stuff like snuggling, sex and sleep? (OK, and maybe a little reading...) But shouldn't "Prime Time" in a relationship *really* mean something other than TV?! ☺

Other "immersion diversions" can be work, sleep, exercise, sports, pets, food, alcohol, medications and even sex. And none of these are bad in themselves (and some *are* more fun than others) unless they are used to avoid, or become substitutes for, communication and connection to the point we forget who matters most - and what really makes us happy.

For some shopping can become a metaphor for life and the perceived prestige of having the "best of everything" helps distract them from what's not the best in their personal life. Ironically, these relationships can appear simply fabulous on the outside and be a struggle for survival on the inside. Like a fresh coat of paint over a badly corroded bridge, things may be on the verge of an imminent collapse and the relationship itself may be less fun than having their eyeballs tattooed.

If any of this sounds familiar, maybe the canary in the mine is gasping its time to query if there's a preferred anesthetic.

And if so, what's it being used to numb us from?

Remember, we can't change what we don't identify.

For me, diversion would sometimes be another high risk adventure. And because this often had the penalty of injury or maybe even death, it consumed my attention and, better yet, hey - if I survived, it gave me another adrenaline hit! It took me a long, long time to understand I was using this as a replacement for the lack of emotional truth in my life.

But in doing these diversions, really, *what* had I gained?

Absolutely nothing.

I "spent" (lost) time and only managed to push the same pain producing problem into the future so I could repeat this process over and over, year after year. In doing so, I became the modern day equivalent of the mythological Sisyphus who spent eternity trying to push a boulder up a hill, only to have it forever get away and roll back down. So, how smart a choice is that?

Not very. And when you combine Denial with Distraction, what you get is a "2-D" life. Wide, flat and not very deep.

Just like the 54" flat screen.

But not only can we divert ourselves, others can do it to us. Like when I'm genuinely trying to understand someone and they simply offer a "little bit of truth" or no information at all. (Old Ben Franklin said "Half a truth is often a great lie.")

So then I get to guess the rest. And of course, I'm usually wrong and then "spend" far too much time trying to figure it out...or worse, apologizing for guessing wrong - which all feels rather controlling to me. Then there are those who if asked a question, change subjects and presumably, you aren't supposed to notice it happened. (Useful tip: Don't even attempt doing this to them. They know the trick.) Of course, there is also the "Selective Memory of Convenience" as they recall – or forget – whatever works best for them at the moment.

Maybe their "payoff" is they never have to commit to a statement because they're not used to people actually listening to them? Or maybe they simply have nothing to say. I don't know.

But I do know it's virtually impossible to understand someone if they don't - or won't - talk to you. It can also be a lot of work to be around them. (Maybe that's why they call it "guess-*work*"?) In the end, when these folks shut up, they shut things down by shutting you out. I also often notice one other trait. When they "give you an inch", they'd have you believe it was 10 feet...as they themselves think it was.

And while the above seems to be a lack of communication, it's just the opposite. In actuality they are communicating they really *don't want* to communicate! But when we avoid the problem, we avoid the relationship by default and what we don't address, we'll inevitably act out in some form or another. To me, this seems like trains on parallel tracks heading for opposite destinations as the distance between them increases with time. And though I said it's good to invest time in people, sometimes like picking a bad stock, it can be a losing investment.

So if for whatever reason it gets to this point, then maybe it's time to ask if it's still a relationship - or is it simply a full time job? Without pay. Makes me tired just thinking about it.

And just to round this all out is the "Classic Crazy-Maker" who says what they think you want to hear, and then deny they ever said the very things they told you. (Remember the Mad Hatter saying: "Words mean whatever I want them to mean when I use them"?) Smooth-talkers? Yup. Straight-talkers? Not. So when they say "See you Friday", it may really mean something like "Oh, I meant I had to clean the litter box."

Either way, the end result is usually a load of poo. ☹
Huh.

The Elephant Crap Trap

~~~~~~~

Belief determines behavior.

OK, so what's all this stuff about elephants? These are problems we'd rather pretend don't exist but then sweep under the carpet of our heart - where they eat at us from the inside. They are "unsafe" topics to talk about and there never seems to be a "good time" to discuss them. Even minor elephants like "This relationship isn't really working, is it?" can be off limits. And as talk often leads more to assigning blame instead of accepting responsibility or finding solutions, why bother?

As a result, we can become hostages of our own thoughts in our own homes while a quiet storm of resentment forms dark and threatening clouds on the horizon.

And in the shadows of those clouds, hides the elephant... invisibly taking up room, quietly stinking up our lives and its very existence making us do extra work to "get around it." But this elephant is a "living" creature that eats up Time and Hope - and craps Despair. And we fantasize if we wait long enough, it'll just wander off someday and the relationship will magically transform itself. (Some call this futile fantasy the "Hope Hook".)

But we know it won't. Even so, sometimes we'll try and make the *relationship* "work"...even if it's not working for the *people* in it...and then rationalize we're getting something back.

What is clear, however, is that it's hazardous to bring some things up. (Heck, we can't even *mention* the elephant much less get rid of it.) We even know the response: the roll of the eyes, the big sigh or "The Look"! (The real irony here? Like vomiting, you feel better when you finally get the elephant out.)

As for me, well, with much resistance, I finally admitted I can easily pull Scarlet O'Hara's "I'll think about that tomorrow" - knowing I can find an excuse not to then, too - as all the while Fridays, Decembers and years came faster and sooner in my life.

But the real cowards are those whose only exercise is jumping to conclusions and want to "punish" us when we bring up something *they* just can't handle. So instead of engaging in finding solutions, their impatience often finds it easier to dismiss or discount us by saying things like *"You're* just wrong! *You're* the one that has 'issues'! *You* need therapy, not me!"

Uh, OK. At this point you're most likely dealing with a sulking child who refuses to even consider *any* culpability. This also means you often have a moody person whose "default mode" is anger -as opposed to kindness, hard to know and nearly impossible to talk to. Oddly, they often believe they are lovable simply because they exist. (If you're one of these Pod People, Jesus *does* love you. Others probably think you're just a clod.)

A gentleman I spoke to about this had been married for over 50 years and said for decades he has felt almost like a prisoner in his own home. Why? Because if he went where he was "warned" not to and tried to discuss a "forbidden" topic (an elephant?), he would be punished by silence or attack from his spouse.

As a result, over time he learned not to talk about what was important to him which caused them to never be as close as they could be. And he was only one of many to tell me that. To me, it would be infinitely sad to give someone your entire life - and not be able to share your true heart with them.

> OK, so let's chat about this logically for just a minute:
> We choose someone to spend our *whole* life with (you know: rocking chairs holding hands sunsets on the porch stuff) because we want to know each other better than anyone else and then we don't or can't talk to them about what matters to us? In other words, the *person* matters, but what they think and feel *doesn't*...even though what they think and feel *is* who they are! (If anyone out there is successful with that routine, call me.)

Communication - usually considered to be talking - doesn't necessarily have to be nor is it the universal cure-all. In fact, problem resolution can be whatever works for everyone involved and is compatible with each having their needs met. However, what won't work is our old duplicitous friend Denial.

But while we all mess up at times in relationships, our long term survival and fulfillment depends on how successful we are at repairing our problems. And that hinges on the relationship having more inherent goodness and similar sense of humor than negatives. Even so, in some manner we need to communicate to others who we actually are, so don't be afraid to give your heart a voice. Just be careful not to let another intimidate you. You are not responsible for their response nor do you have to validate what you feel. It's also wise not to say "always or never".

Those words are almost always never true!

Of course, being openly honest with another (even with the best of intentions) may still cause us to be misunderstood and seen as nothing but fools. However, this risk does not make being authentic wrong! Both are simply vital ingredients that must be stirred together to be of use – and to make elephants go away. Even so, some will say if you want to win the war, pick your battles carefully. But who wants to be in a war?!

Also, be wary of one final trap in discussion with others: Almost all the time our *perception of reality* is what we believe is true regardless of the facts and we often have well formed – but fact-less - opinions. Or as author Ferrol Sams, M.D. puts it: "Things are not what they *are*; they are as they *seem* to me" and we often collect evidence to support *only* what we choose to see. Because of this, don't be surprised someone insecure will find it quite convenient to hold onto their old ideas of you than to acknowledge any changes that may have been hard won.

I also know the fallout of wrong perceptions firsthand. An example of this was a gal, who right after she said she was in love with me because I treated her so well, moved back in with her old boyfriend. Her history with him? He sold drugs and beat her. Now isn't that special?

But perhaps her childhood where her mother told her she was unwanted made her believe he was the best she could do. And because he "needed" her to fix him, he became the project that gave her "worth". So I ask, did her perception become her reality? (See "Life in 3-D".) However, the oldest pattern of human nature is to repeat our past behavior, especially if it's to avoid feelings we think might be painful. Unfortunately, it's sad that sometimes those who least deserve to be treated poorly are the ones that tolerate it the most. Go figure.

Because of this, it may be worth remembering that *belief determines behavior.* (Maybe that's where "My mind's made up don't confuse me with the facts!" actually came from?) Even so, Mark Twain offers yet one more option:

"Get your facts first, then you can distort them as much as you please." And the final line in this drama? As mentioned before, we are often more influenced by the *conclusions* we reach - than the actual *experiences* they were based on.

Know Ifs, Ands or Buts

~~~~~~~

The nekkid truth.

I t's common sense that if we want to get better at a skill or ability, we get the training or learn how to do so. It's a normal thing to do when we don't know all we need to and smart people *want* to learn new things. That's how they got smart.

But how many of us ever had even the most basic instruction in the core skills of things like relationships and communication? In my case? None at all. It was just assumed (incorrectly so) I would "know" how to be successful in the two most necessary but potentially perplexing of human behaviors!

As noted in the last few pages, communication (*especially listening!*) is a skill worth some time developing because it's so easy to create confusion. For instance, does the word "current" refer to electricity, water or being up to date? Or, if I said "Don't judge a book by its cover, especially one as weird as this", am I referring to the book or the cover as weird? Without context (which we often incorrectly *assume* we understand), it's impossible to know. So just for fun, here are a few words we all know and use a lot, but whose unspoken meanings we often overlook when they're slipped into conversation.

IF: Right off the bat, this tiny word implies there's a condition attached somewhere to something. "*If* you do this, I'll do that."

AND: This means there is something extra being added to the subject at hand which may be good…or bad. Pay attention!

BUT: This essentially means "Forget everything you/I just said because I'm about to refute or contradict whatever it was!"

WELL: If someone habitually begins a sentence with this word, it usually means that in their mind, they have pretty much discounted whatever it was you just said and they are now about to set you, and the record straight.

NEKKID: On this, Jeff Foxworthy reminds us that in the South, "Naked means you have no clothes on. Nekkid means you have no clothes on…and you're up to something." ☺

Inside the Egg

~~~~~~~~

The small world of self-sufficiency.

I think it's fairly obvious we interact with one another by word or touch for the *sole purpose of a response*. And a "response" can be ignoring us, an indifferent grunt or some form of healthy and positive attention. I also believe in our heart of hearts, we truly want someone who absolutely delights in us *and* finds ways to show it. After all, love is "Show & Tell", no? (Wouldn't it be great if someone actually thought you were *half* as wonderful as your dog does? Think of the possibilities!) Maybe Robert Frost said it best when he coined the line
"Love is an irresistible desire to be irresistibly desired."
So if someone *doesn't* "delight" in us, why are they *with* us? And why are we with them? What's up with that?

But the response we get from others depends a lot on the level of "togetherness" we have, which often gets confused with "proximity". And there's a big difference. Two people can share a room or bed for years and not be "together". Many married people who think of themselves as "roommates" do just that: Live parallel but emotionally divorced (ED) lives in proximity to each other while addressing the practical details of everyday life.
Simply put, they are alone together. But this type of ED rarely gets *anything* up, especially your happiness level.
To me, when this occurs, the obligatory "celebration" of such things as holidays, anniversaries etc. can become Life-less events because while *desire creates Life, duty often drains it.* I mean, which holds more value for you: Getting a gift just because it's "that day" again, or, because someone really wanted to celebrate your Life-*Time* together? How about just giving a gift for no reason at all on, oh let's say, September 1st? Consider this: If you were to ask three masons working on a wall what they were doing, one may say "laying bricks", another "making a wall" and the third "building a home".
Which one defined duty, desire or passion?
Which would you want in a relationship?
But being "together" means giving deliberate attention to another and - *doing* good far outweighs feeling good about them.

And it can be the simplest of gestures.

For example, doesn't it really feel much nicer if someone takes the effort to make eye contact with you when you talk to them (even a dog does that)...instead of staring at the TV or newspaper at the same time? It does for me because of all the things we wear, I think our expression is pretty significant.

How about in the car? This is a great place to talk – we're both a captive audience! That is until we send the message we'd rather not by popping in a CD and staring out the window.

But whenever two people are "together" *something* is always being created. That creation can be companionship, comfort, security, love or some other positive benefit.

On the other hand, proximity is more likely to create anger, distance, sickness or depression and do it all against a persistent background hum of unhappiness. The bottom line is *something* will always result from time spent together during which we can be "turning" toward, or away from one another. The difference is the more we turn "towards" them, the more we stay connected and keep the pilot light of connection and romance lit.

So what's it mean if we find ourselves living in proximity with someone, or that regular negative responses have become "acceptable"? Well, I'd reckon if we are relying on ourselves to compensate for a lack of togetherness, we are then living in "self sufficiency". This is where we put little or no dependence on others to meet our emotional needs so we won't be disappointed by not getting what we want. The fallout is we learn not to ask for "what we know we won't get" and, as a result, we become self-dependent because we can't desert ourselves. I mean, really, where are we going to go? And while we can cause this our self, sometimes others force us into this mode. Ironically, (and as a result of their high awareness level) they are often shocked when they realize we don't need them anymore!

My experience has been these relationships often become a mile wide, an inch deep and surround us like the fragile veneer of an egg shell that must be handled "just right". (Squeeze an egg end to end and it's virtually impossible to break. Turn it slightly sideways and it crushes easily.) Ever hear the saying "like walking on eggs"? That's how a fragile relationship often feels. And sometimes our hearts become just like that egg ...hard and fragile at the same time.

I've also discovered that the habit of being self-sufficient can manifest in some well disguised ways.

Paul had a hard life. He was deaf, struggled with his weight and had several other health problems. These all made staying employed a difficulty. He had been a patient for over 20 years and as I knew "charity care" felt demeaning to some, he paid me $5-10 a visit. One day after his treatment, he said

"Dr. Gary, do you remember what I told you a few years back?" I confessed I didn't recall what he was referring to. He then related to me he had "nothing" of value in life other than some equity in a small house where he lived and rented rooms to a few other men to help pay the mortgage.

He then looked me in the eyes and said

"In my life only three people have always treated me kindly. You are one of them and my Will says each of you get a third of the house money when I die."

I sat down for a moment, digested this and said

"Paul, you don't need to do that. I don't need the money. Why not give it to a charity instead?" He said that was what he wanted and that was that. I began to object again…and then it hit me like a brick to the head: Here I was insulting this man's show of appreciation by rejecting the only gift he could give me. Could I be a bigger jerk? I stopped talking mid-sentence and with a newly formed lump in my throat said

"You honor me and I thank you." Right then I learned the art of giving by receiving. I had allowed another to feed me.

Now, having personally *spent* far too long being "self sufficient", I believe the danger is that after enough time, this thinking becomes completely normal and unquestioned.

So what's "normal"? The thesaurus defines it as: ordinary, common, mediocre, mundane and average - all of which you'll see later on might be really bad for our brain. But here's a question: If we wouldn't want a mediocre income, health or doctor, why is an "average" relationship any more acceptable?

But how do we move away from this? Communication in countless forms certainly helps - including letting others know of our needs and then *allowing* them to fulfill them. Also, a genuine appreciation of the people in our life can be golden to others. And both can easily be displayed by a word, letter, simple touch or even a subtle eyebrow flicker and a smile from across a crowded room.

Susan, an energetic and thoughtful patient for 25 years, came to see me recently. She sat and as we were catching up, she saddened and I could see the water brimming in her eyes. When I asked her was there something she wanted to say, she told me

"I have breast cancer…and it's not a 'good' one." It was one of those times when life just didn't seem fair – she is a good person who treats others kindly and had always taken excellent care of herself. We then talked a bit more and on her way out after being treated, she gave me a quick hug and said

"You know Chris and I love you and we want to know your thoughts when things like this come up."

As we walked out to the reception room, I quipped that "Well, I'll never get rich doing this stuff, but I've sure met a lot of wonderful people." She was halfway to the door when she stopped, turned around and with a small smile said to me

"Doc, you're richer than you know." And then she left.

Out of Susan's gentle display of Grace under duress, I was taught another lesson in the fight against self-sufficiency.

Other ways of confronting self sufficiency can be when we take the risk of being real with others and discover they are reliable keepers of the heart. It can be "going the extra mile" without any praise because we believe another is worth it. It can be sitting over a glass of wine and asking "How's your life? What can I do to make it a bit better for you?" And it's *allowing* others to provide for *our* needs. But regardless of the "how", it always causes an *enlivened* sense of being and satisfaction because *we are better*. And why are we better? Because it is Life-giving and *living* people need Life!

I can recall a few years back when, literally in a moment, my life changed - *I was better* - and unchained from a problem that had shackled me for years. But I could have never done that by being dishonest with myself living in self sufficiency and denying some elephants – or by holding on to old patterns that had stopped working. This meant I had to allow something dear, but unhealthy to die so something better could live.

But sometimes we don't want to give up what is familiar.

However, like a child's hesitation to surrender an old worn out stuffed dog, one only needs to replace it with a live puppy and a whole new relationship blossoms on a far more satisfying level because it now has "Life"!

Yet for this to happen we need to be open to the winds of change and we can't let others convince us it is not obtainable. To them, perhaps the fear of loss outweighs the hope of gain. This is when I try to remember that people will usually judge our ability to respond based on their own limitations in similar circumstances. But in life and relationships, the possible upside of *some* risk versus the downside of *no* risk – can be huge.

So if you're feeling uncomfortable "in your own skin", perhaps like a caterpillar it's because you've simply outgrown it. And the message? Maybe its time to become a butterfly! However, *you* make the decision for yourself if you want to change things. If so, I'll suggest three ways change happens:

1. When dissatisfaction intersects with opportunity to have a need fulfilled.
2. When the discomfort of *not* changing exceeds the discomfort *of* changing.
3. When someone or something brings you "Life" in a way that *inspires* you to be "other centered" (as opposed to self centered.)

Oh, and in terms of "genuinely appreciating" others?

I think God gave us senses not only to function in the world, but so we could add Life to life by more fully *responding* to one another and enjoying what only they can provide – and in doing so, move us away from self sufficiency! Also, what we take in through our senses is the food for what we literally think and feel - which results in w*ho* we are. So, at the risk of sounding mushy, I could use my sight to be captured by the flash of a woman's eyes or the sultry sway of hair swept shoulders, my hearing to be soothed by her voice, my touch to feel her soft warmth and my sense of scent to surrender to her fragrance. (The last of which I discovered can often turn my brain *to* mush.)

And these are all easy things to simply enjoy about another. But in doing so, I also choose to be grateful for the unique sweetness she can so easily bring into my life.

Double Huh.

You Can't Always Get What You Want.
You Just Do It.

~~~~~~~~~

We choose our choices.

Ok, this is going to give you a headache just thinking about it and I'm only going to write enough to aggravate you, so take an aspirin now. I believe the following to be 99% true: You always *choose* to do what you *want* to do.

"How could you even say such a thing?! I have a crappy job-spouse- life (fill in the blank) that I absolutely *don't* want."

If that's what you just thought, let me explain a bit more. The first mistake you made was thinking I was referring to you *having* what you want. That was not my premise. I said "you always *do* what you want" which references our decision making abilities. Clearly, if we have an illness or someone smashes into our car, those are *not* things we usually "want". But neither were they in our control to make a decision about. So let's discuss the things we *do* have control over: Our mind and our decisions.

I believe any decision we make, we *choose* it because at that moment, it's simply the "best" choice we can come up with under the circumstances, even if we know it's wrong, illegal, harmful to another etc. It's still the best concluding idea we could conceive given the information available under those conditions. And we choose it because we think or feel we have a good enough reason to do so. If we could concoct something "better" (i.e., more certain to get our desired end result), then we'd make that choice, no? I mean c'mon, be dumb not to, right?

So, in other words, whatever decisions we make, they are made in the hope they will get us closest to what we desire. Therefore, that's the decision we'd "want" to make.

But there's a difference between wanting *to do* a particular thing vs. wanting a particular outcome. In most cases you make the decision you think brings you closest to the outcome you want but the truth is - your "intent" doesn't guarantee the desired results.

So let's say you want to pursue that gal you find so alluring and do everything you know how to, but - she resists your irresistible charm. Well, you still *did* what you "wanted" to do, which was pursue her. You just didn't "*get*" what you wanted."

174

One should also not confuse "wanting to do something" with "liking" to do it. For example, a woman rarely likes to bring her car in for service, but she has the greater "want" of knowing it is safe to drive. Likewise, most men I know don't like getting a digital prostate exam, but they do want the assurance of knowing they don't have a dangling participle or worse, trailing arbutus growing somewhere up inside them.

Then there's the notion of "having" to do things versus wanting to do them. Ever "have" to do something just to keep "peace" in a relationship? In that case, I would still opine the greater "want" of keeping peace outweighed the supposed "have to" item.

As an example, your spouse asks you to do some yard work, which you *don't* want to do. But you do it anyway because escape by self-immolation makes you feel burned out. As such, I will propose you did exactly what you wanted to do. Here's why: To not do it would mean a possible argument, guilt, no dinner, sex – whatever. Those would be the expected "penalties" for not doing the work. Therefore, your "want" to avoid those things was stronger than your "want" to *not* do the work. So, weighing all the possible outcomes, you chose what gave you the "most" of what you wanted to have - or - the least of what you wanted to avoid.. In doing so, you still *chose* to do whatever it was.

Now folks generally don't like this whole idea because it makes them entirely responsible for whatever their life decisions and subsequent situations are (again, barring health problems and other items beyond their control.) But remember even "no decision" *is* a decision. And as the saying goes, there's always a pay-off at some level for our behavior and choices. Even so, not all "smart" decisions are wise choices!

But here's the good part. If we are indeed in control of this process, then we can also make different choices which will have...drum roll...different outcomes! So, not only are we responsible, but we are in *control* of much of our life as well!

Because you are a free agent of your own thoughts and have the freedom to choose your actions, this then allows you to have your own "Hands on Life". And the life your hands are on and managing? Your own! What a concept...unless it becomes an "Issue"...which is another issue altogether.

Need another aspirin?

The Issue with Issues

~~~~~~~~~~

And I only thought I had problems.

S ome consider the fact that life ends to be an "issue" (which the dictionary defines as "A point or matter of discussion.".) Others might call it a problem. But it's neither. It's actually one of life's good points. Now am I saying dying is a good thing? Not really, although I have known folks who eagerly anticipate it. Like my Mom. For the longest time, she was so ready to "head out of here" she refused to buy green bananas. But here's why death is a healthy part of the life process. As mentioned before, if we had an endless amount of time, it would lose its value. The very fact Life-*Time is* limited is what makes it so precious – and is exactly why we should *spend it* with the utmost care.

So why waste it on something dumb like "issues"? Let me get this on the table right up front: I am *so* over hearing this word that it makes my ears bleed. Really and truly. Aren't you? I mean when I first heard the term used 20 years ago by someone I respected, I thought "What a unique an appropriate term for the subject matter!" Before that, I thought it only referred to next months "issue" of Road and Track magazine.

But years later (by which time I was hearing it 217 times a day) when I heard a 12 year old patient of mine telling me she had "issues" in school, well, it started to lose some relevance for me. Then I heard the T.V. dude talking about a "weather issue". (Now, let's be real folks. I don't know about you, but when there's a tornado watch about a 300 mph wind coming my way that can park a locomotive on my roof, I don't consider that a "matter of discussion". I mean, I'm not a meteorologist or anything, but to me, that appears like a BIG *problem*!) But I finally lost it when a fellow on a call-in radio show about cars said he was having "issues" with his carburetor.

The "issue" had finally gone from the sublime to the ridiculous. Why? Simple. These folks were no longer talking about "issues" as it was intended to be used. Now the word had become the abstracticated universal replacement for "problems".

Too weird.

As a result of all this constant and irrelevant usage, I'm convinced it really has lost all, well, relevance. I wrote Dr. Phil about this out of control verbal menace to society, but he apparently had an issue with it and never responded back.

From my perspective, it seems we now use the term as a conversational convenience: a reference to a perpetual subject that has no solution or, if it does have one, it's a solution we never intend to apply. (Or a problem we don't intend to resolve?) Sometimes we use it in a derogatory manner like "Oh my, *she* has issues…" (And you don't?) In short, it gives us something to talk about without ever having to do something about *what* we're talking about.

Or said another way, it's easier to complain than change. However, a consequence with going too far down this road is when change is inevitably demanded, it may be the equivalent of taking a pee on the way to the electric chair.

It'll make no difference in the outcome.

But what I've seen over the years has been the more honest and secure one is with themselves, the more capable and willing they are of resolving "real" issues. Likewise, I've known those who no matter how much a situation required their own truth, admitting it became a perpetual obstacle. In a sense, they became pathological liars to themselves. (Others just give up and become pathological sighers.) Either way, it makes it wearisomely difficult for folks around them.

Problems, on the other hand, actually have implied solutions which when applied, make the problem go away! What a concept, no? Which is why I told the child in my office

"Gee, when I was your age, issues hadn't been invented yet. All *we* had were *problems*…which we found solutions for." When I said that, her mom perked up her head like she had just heard a revelation. Maybe she had.

But then I recently heard a woman say she had "Problem Issues"! As I have absolutely no idea what that means, I'm not sure there's any hope for her.

In any case, while you're waiting around to die, my advice is try not to make it an issue.

Anything But Lonely

~~~~~~~~

Just a state of mind?

Do you remember a place called the "Hanoi Hilton"? And that instead of clean sheets, room service and drinks by the pool, that insect infested gruel, sleeping on concrete floors, "locked down" in lonely isolation and daily physical torture were the height of the social activities? The "Hilton", was of course, the POW camp captured American pilots were kept at during the Vietnam War. After being released, prisoners were asked to recall the most difficult thing they had to endure. Their one word answer?

"Loneliness."

I couldn't have said it any better. But let's make a clear distinction between "being alone" and loneliness. Solitude and even living alone can be healthy or healing when freely chosen. But while human beings were designed for many things, loneliness (defined as the absence of meaningful contact with others) is not one of them. This is the root reason why solitary confinement is considered the harshest of prison punishment.

Now, it's obvious to the casual observer the best way to avoid loneliness is to "not be alone" which means you need other people around which also generally implies they need to approve of you in some manner to want you around. Whew.

Bruce Springsteen simply said: "Ain't *nobody* like to be alone." Bad grammar but point made. Genesis 2:18 puts it this way: "It's *not good* for man to be alone." Either one, the *soul* reason the glorious web of life works is: *We need each other.* And not only to *connect*, but to help solve each others problems!

Keeping in mind approval's ultimate goal is to get us what we want and to prevent loneliness, think about some relationships you are familiar with, including your own. Now, while understanding *no* relationship is in reality perfect, how many of them are unhappy, unhealthy or even "poisonous"? And if it is one of the above, why would we choose to remain in them unless it still seemed *better* than being alone? (When discussing this with married people, I was stunned by the number who defined their relationship as nothing more than "roommates".)

Out of this, my little brain concluded that at any point we probably remain in a situation for one of three primary reasons: desire, guilt or the fear of being alone.

And those relationships include friendships, a place where we have to trust in the intent of others and where our choice of people is a reflection of our character. I also think real friends are reliable in word and deed and can be believed in. If not, well…I reckon it's pretty easy to figure out how much of a friend they really are, no?

In terms of our "one and only", our choice should be based on a heartfelt desire to be with *that particular person*. We should not be with them simply to distract us from a void in our life or to use them (or things) as a life raft. In other words, we should be moving *towards them* as opposed to moving *away* from something else. Even so, there is one thing more dispiriting than being alone: Being with someone and *still* feeling that way!

But even though none of us would do well for long without human contact, loneliness isn't really solved just by having someone physically present. I mean, we can be in a crowd and still "be alone", no? It is solved when those in our lives *know* and care about us *at a level that matters*. And in doing so, remain emotionally, mentally and physically available and accessible. This, of course, is quite different than knowing how much milk goes in our coffee. And real different than a life long roommate. Remember that "proximity vs. togetherness" thing?

When we are known *and* accepted at that level - meaning when another knows the "why" of us as opposed to just the "what" - *then* we are in reality approved of, which is the opposite of rejection. Rejection, of course, can ultimately result in loneliness and is probably the most painful of all emotions because, as Occam's Razor would suggest, it essentially means

"Go away, you're not good enough to be in my life. You're not *worth* my time."

And I'll say from personal experience that being rejected after you've given someone the best you have to offer can hurt a bunch. But listen, no matter what they do or do not give back, never ever regret giving someone your best. If you truly care for them, you will always regret having given anything less.

Even so, it's the oddest of ironies that sometimes it's better just to want someone…than to actually have them.

Because Of You I Am Me

~~~~~~~~

Who are you?

I magine for a moment you were born on a ship that sank near an island. Everyone was lost except you and somehow, you survived and washed up on shore a giggling little nipper. In some miraculous way, you stayed alive, perhaps out of sheer luck, being raised by monkeys, wolves or just an act of God.

But you never saw another human being.

Who are you?

When the day came another human set foot on the island and asked you who you were (and somehow you understood the words), what would you say? You really don't have any identity, do you? You have no name, no known relationships, no one to be identified with and no job to define you, so there is no way to embody the sense of who you are to others.

So, who are you?

I create this highly unlikely scenario for one reason only: I submit we primarily define ourselves by the others in our lives and who we are "relative to" them. (Consider the root meaning of "relatives".) You are your father's and mother's son or daughter. Because of them, you are you. Literally and figuratively. You are your children's parent. You are your spouse's spouse, your friend's friend, your neighbor's neighbor. You are your employer's employee and your God's child. And on it goes. We use all of these to build an intricate web of relevance around us to construct our identity. And I believe it's because of this essential need for "self", to know "who" we are, coupled with our drive to avoid loneliness that becomes the principal reason we *have* to have others in our life. Maybe this also explains why we hurt so much when someone we care for goes away or dies. Perhaps they really do take a piece of "us" with them – and in doing so, we have less to "belong" to.

And without them…who are you?

But I'm lucky…I've always known who I am.
I'm "Iggy's Kid".

If I'm Not There, Neither Am I

~~~~~~~~~

"The Law of Unintended Consequences"

Life is *not* easy. Truth is, it's only slightly less work (and money) than owning a German car. OK, it's a *lot* less than the car on both counts. I also believe that about every problem we have in life - including many health related - will involve people or relationships. And as relationships require our participation and presence on more levels than merely being physically present, here's how I think we ambush ourselves.

Our "software" makes us inescapably relational to the point where I'd say without at least one really good relationship, life is barely a shell of what it should be. And once again, for a relationship to even exist, someone else needs to approve of us.

So, with your permission, let's return to the subject of approval and its corollary, loneliness. Norbert once mentioned that "Relationships are born in approval and die in disapproval" which was a tidy way of stating what we all intuitively know. Springsteen simply says "Two hearts are better than one." If this is so, and we want to avoid being lonely, we usually will develop a "strategy" to protect against possible rejection by others. But the rub is that every strategy also has its own built in weakness.

Now here's the sticky part. When fear drives us to avoid something we think might be painful (like being lonely or rejected), then whatever action or decisions we do, will seem completely reasonable at the time. Even if it's the wrong course to take, we are blind to the method we use because the "end justifies the means".

And the "gotcha"? Often when we want the approval of others, *we do it by concealing parts of ourselves* we worry they may dislike. In doing so, we only let them see or know what we feel keeps us safe, while hiding the rest. (see "Persona" p. 197) In order for us to be accepted, we need to be acceptable, no? And when we do reveal something, we watch how the other reacts and then, we either take a step towards, or away from them. If we step away, this can *cause* the very thing we are in relationships to avoid: emotional disconnection.

This is a great way to make yourself nuts.

181

For example, sometimes I'll hide (isolate my feelings) that I'm frightened and try to come off as brave or unaffected. Or when I'm angry, I may just appear indifferent or even courteous. And when I'm lonely and sad and need to be held, I tell no one. But the real paradox? All of the above self-protective junk seems entirely reasonable while I'm in the process of doing it!

But functionally, these strategies are about as effective as a Kamikaze pilot wearing a helmet and a seatbelt.

Which *is* nuts.

But there's more! I may not want to be *completely* truthful for several reasons such as: I'm afraid I might be burning a bridge behind me. Or, it's too much work and I just don't care that much about things. But no matter, in hiding the truth it only serves to move me further away from those I supposedly want to be close to. Which is a bit counter-productive, no?!

And you know what I mean: it's just seems *easier* to "shade" the truth - even though I'm still bothered by whatever elephant is dancing about the room while I try to avoid stepping in E-poop. Besides, I'm "Too *tired* to deal with it now. I'll do it tomorrow." But – oops - I'm tired then, too.

(Maybe I'm just retired?)

So, do we finally have a high enough Nutz Factor?

And that's usually how I know I'm going down this road - the feeling of being tired and "worn out" and all too often sleep becomes the escape from the problem. (Ironically, no matter how much sleep I get, I still feel weary.) But because only the brain – and not the body - needs sleep, I think the fatigue is more due to the energy I expend trying to ignore and compensate for whatever is going on inside of me.

So, I have three thoughts on that:

1. "One of these days" usually really means "None of these days" and not dealing with a problem until something finally has to give may make the "applied cure" the equivalent of taking an aspirin for terminal cancer.
2. In the meantime, by continuing to isolate the truth of myself from another, I live the lie.
3. This then leads to my being angry at *myself* because I have *chosen* not to express these thoughts or feelings, so I repress them by *depressing* them. Hmmm…that can't be good.

And why do I do all of this? I think it's because over time, (and possibly a subtle resignation?), I allow the "unacceptable to become the acceptable" by rejecting my own truth. I became the frog sitting quietly in the pot of cool water on the stove, which as it slowly heats up, does not recognize the change of temperature and boils to death. In the end, what I did was let my own choice of "strategies" trap me while I learned to exist on what I had, instead of thrive on what I want and need.

And out of all this I became the unwitting casualty of
~ The Law of Unintended Consequences ~

Do y'all remember the rooftop scene in "Annie Hall" where Woody Allen and Diane Keaton are talking to each other? Although we hear them speaking, the screen sub-titles reveal what they are actually thinking but are just too afraid to say. And why didn't they say it? Simple: they each wanted the approval of the other. Or, said another way, they didn't want to be rejected.

This principle is so simple it confused me at first, so in case I confused you, let me say it again:

In our need for approval so we aren't alone and emotionally isolated, we often do the very thing we were there to avoid: Isolate key parts of ourselves to *prevent* us from being isolated! And once again, there we are...alone together.

Swiss psychologist Paul Tournier says it much more elegantly:

"Nothing makes us so *lonely* as our secrets."

And it's this hiding of who we truly are that will dissolve the closeness in the relationship from the inside out, leaving only a shell of what it could be.

Think that'll help a relationship? Even if it all looks good on the outside, what's it like on the inside?

So here's the irony of it all: We look for the comfort and happiness only relationships can provide and then we "protect" ourselves from having it! *In short, we create loneliness in an effort to cure it.* And then we see what we can change around us to provide relief for not having what we really want.

The bottom line? It is easier to take control than to take risk. It is easier to doubt than to trust. And both will wear you out.

So, are you feeling worn out for "no reason"?

How A Broken Heart Breaks A Heart

~~~~~~~~~~

Your body believes you. Why don't you?

Do "heart" problems cause heart problems? In my opinion, absolutely! I couldn't be more certain about it. Before we go there though, what is "heart" in the non-physical sense? I would define it as "the center" of one's being, the summation of our mind, emotions and will and who we are at the core. It is, literally, the "heart of the matter".

I have been in practice since 1980 and have known some of the same people as they go through the many phases of life. I have seen folks meet, marry, have children, divorce and their children have children. And I've seen them die. Almost 3 decades. That's a long time to spend with what I consider my extended family and people whose lives I care a great deal for. Even so, I am a "professional observer". I watch the way someone walks, how they sit, their unconscious moves and postures. I pay close attention when they say it hurts on the left side but point to the right. Once while performing a history on a patient, I asked if she ever had any surgery. She said she had "a tubal litigation." I then asked if her attorney was moonlighting, which confused her. So I explained it was probably a tubal "ligation" but she insisted she was right. Oh well.

But I listen even more closely for what they are *not* saying about their troubles and try to tie in lifestyle actions to health problems. For instance, if someone says they have a constant "pain in the neck" and upon questioning tell me that things are not good at home or work, well, I may want to know *who* is the pain in the neck and why. Because if that part is left unresolved, it's unlikely the physical problem will go away. Sadly, many never connect the dots - or are unwilling to - and their "solution" is to deny whatever "elephant" is making the problem and hope it goes away. And away it goes – right to the body which physically expresses what the person won't verbally express.

However, the stress of "isolating" our truth (especially from ourselves) can have long term physical effects and, as mentioned before, that's too high a "heart currency" for anyone to pay. While I'm at this, I'll suggest even some auto-immune diseases (where the body attacks itself), and definitely digestive and headache problems can be seeded in emotional stress. So while I absolutely believe some folks are worth dying for...I also believe that none are worth getting sick over!

On the positive side, new research indicates that regular *emotionally* satisfying sexual relations (not just the physical act) lowers stress and abates chronic pain which may lead to a longer life span. This of course gives you more time to have more sex. (My personal theory is that if you have enough sex you can live pain free forever.) There's also a very low divorce rate among couples who describe their sex life as "great". ☺☺

Recently, the University of Washington completed a 14 year study which was able to reliably predict with a 94% accuracy rate not only if a couple would stay together, but when a split would occur if the relationship was doomed to fail.

Another outcome of the study was that couples will *not* be compatible *69 percent* of the time. That's no typo either. And the stress of pretending otherwise does eventually find us. (A 2008 British study showed psychological "distress" increased strokes.)

Consider that statement. And consider again if our parents – or anyone – ever really taught us *how* to choose a mate, solve problems etc. in a relationship? If they were like mine, probably not, most likely because no one ever taught them.

But I do know this: Two of the most important decisions in life you will ever make are your faith and who to marry. One will usually set the blueprint for your life to follow and the other who you'll share that life with. (There's also good evidence that an actively shared faith adds measurable quality to marriages.)

So, do you think incompatibility might be just a little bit stressful? And I'm about to tell you the heart is not excluded from that stress. In fact, it appears to be the target. (Ever wonder why a "heartache" always seems to hurt in your chest?)

Cardiologists have identified the "Broken Heart Syndrome" or, Stress Cardiomyopathy, which affects women more than men and is often misdiagnosed as a heart attack. This is a condition where elevated stress hormones actually make the heart's shape deform to the point where it becomes a defective pump. It is then, literally, "broken" and cannot do what it is supposed to.

What generates these hormones? *The mind.* Although this can occur at different levels, perhaps the most extreme example is when a spouse dies and the other passes on soon thereafter from a "broken heart". It is also known that those who isolate themselves emotionally or are depressed *double* their chances of a serious heart problem.

If you think about it, we easily accept people can have *physical* problems such as diabetes, ulcers, arthritis etc. But then for some reason, perhaps because we can't see or touch it, we almost disconnect from the body an emotional problem as "not real". But because there is a physiological chemical connection between every thought and the body, then it's easy to understand why *your body believes every thought you have.* (A hypnotized person can raise a skin welt just by being *told* they were burned!)

Here are some more direct clinical observations to adduce this further. During almost 30 years of treating people, most men consistently come in with lower back pain, and women, almost *exclusively* with upper spine and arm problems. The common explanation is men do more heavy work and lifting while the women do more secretarial type duties such as using a computer or holding a baby etc. which places more stress on the upper spine. (The upper back and neck nerves affect the heart, arms, digestive organs etc.) All of those *physical* reasons are true.

However, here's the politically incorrect possible connection. Traditionally the man has been the "supporter" of the home, and the woman, the "nurturer". (Hint: Who is more likely to hug someone, the guy or the gal? Or would you rather have the guy hand you a wrench when you are sad?) Is it possible in some way the body takes these symbolic roles and expresses them physically? Can a woman's "heart" (not the physical one) that is unable to nurture or express itself or that is dominated eventually affect the physical heart or even the arms? Can that also cause spinal pain at the levels that are associated? And is it also a coincidence that many women with low back pain are single and must be both the "nurturer and supporter"?

Many years ago, I treated a patient who had severe upper back pain that responded only temporarily to care. After a few visits, and out of nowhere, a thought occurred to me and I said

"I don't mean to pry, but how are things at home? Do you feel like you are being stabbed in the back?"

She slowly shook her head up and down and became very sad. At that moment, my heart knew hers was hurting - and I believed her body was expressing the pain of a woman's heart that received little real appreciation in the home. But I could never get the problem to go away permanently and over the years, I watched it slowly morph into what I felt were related and more serious physical problems including her arms and stomach. ("Coincidentally", the stomach is supported by the same level of spinal nerves where she has the back pain.) Ten years later she still had back and stomach problems and I wondered if the situation at home was simply becoming "too hard to swallow"?

Recently a 70 y/o woman told me with great sadness that her stressful 49 year marriage now seemed like "a joke" she had played on herself. "He's a great guy - but I don't really like him" she said. "Unexplainably", she has also had a serious auto-immune disease for over 45 years. Any connection there?

(For those "wanting out" but afraid to make the change, it's not an entirely uncommon "wish" that the spouse be in a fatal accident. I've actually heard this several times.)

But the truth is, we can only fool our body for so long, and ultimately, the ability to lie to ourselves is only a "lie-ability". On this subject, Einstein observed, "Problems cannot be solved at the same level of awareness that created them." Ya' think?

If you are still not convinced, consider the fact a woman will have *4 times the chance of dying from a heart attack if she is unable to express or resolve emotional problems with her spouse.* Yes…four. Is that high enough to get our attention? She also risks high blood pressure and cholesterol levels - and more wrinkles! - for the same reason.

Now, let's connect the dots here. Of the 2 sexes, who would you say functions "more from the heart"? You know the answer. Now, is it too great a leap of logic to connect the fact heart failure is the greatest killer of women? (Heart disease strikes 40% of them.) Could it possibly be that because her "heart" is not being fed, the physical heart simply weakens and dies?

Are we killing the hearts of our women?

Maybe we need to listen to them more so their headstone doesn't say "See, I told you I was sick!" So please, make no mistake, your mind and emotions *are not and cannot* be separated from your body. *Our bodies are talking to us.* But will we listen? And will we hear what is being said in time?

187

A friend said his dad was never sick a day in his life and "When he died, it wasn't from anything serious." My brother's wife went to bed at 57...and never saw the next sunrise.

However, even if our body is screaming at us, please don't make the mistake of always looking for a single large event to get your attention. Although that can be the case, it is often a series of apparently unconnected and possibly insidious problems such as headaches, chronic muscle pain, fatigue, sinus or a variety of digestive problems as well as high blood pressure.

These may all be indicators our system is breaking down from stress we refuse to recognize or admit. Therefore changing doctors, diets and medications will have little effect if the habits of a haunted heart go from *cobwebs to cables*. And while a doctor may be of temporary help, the final cure will not be found in their office if the cause is in the patient's house or "heart". I know this from experience. It has taken me years to discover and confront some of my own ghosts.

Sadly, there are also those who apparently would rather *not* get well and just want to give the appearance of correcting the problem. Whether this gives them some leverage or control over others or is the only way they can get attention, I don't know.

But then again, I've always told my patients it's not how you feel, but how you look that counts.....

So here are some final thoughts to mull over: There are two major principles that affect how the body runs itself:

1. *Stress vs. Resistance.* Whichever is higher is the one that wins and when stress wins, something breaks down in you.
2. *Structure Determines Function.* Stress can damage cell DNA. This means from the cellular level on up, if the structure is altered, then so is its ability to function correctly.

With those two points in mind, is it not reasonable stress can cause a problem by interfering with the body's normal function and we get sick? For me, I had this sobering thought: Is my own arrhythmia the result of a "heart" problem?

This was closely followed by yet another lightening bolt:

Perhaps when a part of the soul dies, a part of the body goes with it. Ever hear the saying "The truth will set you free?"

Pretty smart guy said that. Maybe being truthful with ourselves really *is* essential to staying healthy!

The Grays

~~~~~~~~~~

"You can observe a lot by just watching." Yogi Berra

When I say I am an observer of people, that's all I do. In no way do I judge the intent of their hearts. That's God territory. Further, it'd be presumptuous for me to even think I could fully comprehend any problems they may have. (I have enough difficulty understanding my own!) But, in spite of my shortcomings, that does not mean real problems do not exist.

I also know that what I find desirable or fulfilling in a relationship is not what everyone else would. But I do think there is a universal and normal hunger for happiness and comfort that occurs when we "connect and belong".

So here's a 30 year observation: I have seen a goodly number of relationships where the people in them simply didn't seem to "bond" in any significant way. (Maybe they're the incompatible 69%?) And one did not need a Ph.D. in psychology to see the boredom or indifference in their eyes and manners towards each other. There was nothing there that would make another say "Yes! That's what I want my life to be like!" Or "I'd really like to spend an evening with them just to learn the secrets of their relationship!" And I thought to myself "Surely they see this and want to make things better, no?" But some were being killed so softly, they never saw it coming.

As I watched many of these same folks for another 5, 10 and sometimes 20 years, to my complete surprise, many never changed and some passed away no different. (Ben Franklin, also an avowed observer, said "Many people die at 25 and aren't buried until they are 75." I now have reason to believe him.)

During that time, I began to see the loss of "color" in their lives. There seemed to be no sparkle in their eyes or vitality in their words and even their clothes often time reflected drabness. It became like watching a battery running itself down. But even if they were visually unchanged, they began to get more "aches and pains" and other problems then would typically be expected. Research has now shown unhappy relationships result in higher cortisol levels – a stress hormone – which results in 35% more chronic infections from weakened immune systems.

Interestingly, holding others in contempt appears to have the same effect as well. Conversely, people in happy and fulfilling relationships are usually sick far less.

So even though I don't know what caused them to become like this, there was no denying there seemed to be little or no joy or passion in their lives. (Possibly relevant to this is the link between depression and high TV use – not to mention how all its gratuitous violence can numb us to another's real pain.) But simply put, they seemed sad. In an effort to compensate for this, some of them tried to equate financial success and the ability to buy whatever they wanted, with "life" success. But the stimulus of something new or expensive never seemed to dissolve the sadness you could sense just behind the smiles.

Over time, these folks became "The Grays" to me – a static display that seemed to forget what they wanted their Life to be about and who didn't *grow* old, but *became* old by not growing, something you'll see the proof of in the next chapter.

But I also believe this is all reversible, it just needs folks willing to do it. However, there's a catch: Nothing can be done about anything until we identify it. *And we can't identify something we are unwilling to believe exists.*

And as noted before, relationships cannot be any healthier than the least healthy person in it - and one form of unhealthiness is becoming the "victim" by not knowing that *we train* others how to treat us. An example of bad training was a patient having agonizing stomach pain at 3 A.M. on a rainy night. After pleading to her husband to take her to the emergency room, he finally did - and then drove away making her take a cab home by herself hours later! So if you don't like how another is treating you, then *you* have pretty much *allowed* them to believe their behavior towards you is acceptable. Ouch.

However, just identifying something does *not* correct it. That's yet another step. And that's where many of us go south in spite of the many possible benefits.

Now am I saying these folks have "wasted" their lives? Nope. Some may have been perfectly content in whatever situation they created for themselves.

However, in some cases, I *do* think they lost precious time. And those that *did* change their lives for the better confirmed that suspicion.

Which means the good news is, yes! I *have* seen some "Grays" have the color return to their lives. Some had counseling (which takes some personal strength to have an objective outsider say what may be uncomfortable observations about us, especially for men.) Others had a life altering event or learned better skills at communication and problem resolution while yet others needed medication to help balance out their chemistry. In any event, *they* felt the quality of their life had improved dramatically. For the first time in a long time, some felt as though they could breathe again. "Life" had returned!

And that was *after* they had lived what they considered a "normal" life for years. They had finally learned that pleasure can be more than just the absence of pain.

~~~~~~~~

When I was in my teens, I already believed there could be something very wonderful that could develop between two people - but didn't really know what it was. I only knew it existed and seemed to be broadly divided into two categories: Those who had "it", and those who didn't.

In an effort to observe this, I would drive to Newark Airport and just watch the people come and go. And as you have probably seen at airports for yourself, these folks span from the intensely ecstatic to the prematurely interred and everything in between. For example, sometimes I'd see the boundless joy of two lovers reuniting or the deep sadness when they were parting. Other times I'd see a bored husband meet his bored wife and give her a mechanical "welcome" home peck on the cheek and off they plodded to the baggage pick-up, each in their own different worlds...life as usual. If I had to boil down the behaviors I witnessed to the bare essentials, I guess much of it would be defined as: Desire vs. Duty.

I came to view these differing levels of relationships (and what each has to offer) to be like swimmers: Some will only swim on the surface where they see and experience what anyone else can. For many, this "lack of depth" gets so life-less or boring they have to find other interests to occupy themselves with. Others put on a mask, snorkel and fins and catch a glimpse of an entirely new world below the surface.

Still others will choose to scuba dive and immerse themselves into a beautiful and deeply three dimensional place perhaps few know exists - and even fewer will pursue.

However, it's only the divers that get to experience the entire spectrum *by choice* and are not stuck in any of the levels. And this is important because people really are like icebergs - 90% of who we are *is* "below the surface". But over the years I have come to believe *we gravitate towards the level of relationship we are capable of participating in* at any given time. Because of this, to dive deeper in water takes a bit more skill and even a bit more risk. Just like in a relationship.

The good part is that in relationships the skills can be learned which in turn, minimizes the risk. Just like in diving.

But some may not want to "dive deeper" and are perfectly satisfied with where they are, and of course, that is fine. Others may be likewise satisfied because that's all they've ever experienced or their current situation is simply at the limit of their skill sets. And yet others out of laziness or personal belief may be existential about their lives and accept that whatever is, "is" and do not want to extend any effort to see what they can improve. This limitation then infects the others around them.

However, in the acknowledgement that it takes all kinds, I still vividly remember a personal ad I saw in an Atlanta tabloid over 25 years ago. It read:

"Retired one legged ex-sea captain with pet seal looking for very obese woman for normal relationship." So there ya' go.

But the reality of *any relationship* is no matter how good things are, improvement is *always* possible

And that's because while change is inevitable in life, *growth and fulfillment are optional*. And the folks I mentioned before ("A Few Good Men") that I had so admired and had so much "Life" knew that. So for the most part, life becomes what you choose it to be. Grow? Don't grow? Paddle around on the surface, snorkel or dive? But just know there's a lot of really good stuff – and less crowds - at the deeper end of the pool.

And that's a good thing to know in spite of others sometimes telling us "things are what they are". I think Yogi's response to them would be

"Don't always follow the crowd because nobody goes there anymore. It's too crowded."

The Real Know Brainer

~~~~~~~~~

Change is inevitable. Growth is optional.

Neuroplasticity. That's high zoot for The Plastic Brain. (And no, it's not something really cheap from China.) It is, however, an exciting new area of research that is changing our understanding of how we age, learn and the quality of life itself due to the brain's ability to be "moldable" and rewire itself.

We all know that when we exercise, our hearts and muscles become stronger and function better. Well, challenging the brain with *new* learning and physical activities likewise turns on switches that keep it healthier and working better too!

And the best part? They can also make it grow.

But as adults, we need to be pushed beyond the familiar areas of thought and activity in order to "turn-on" the necessary switches which actually results in forming *more new brain cells*. This was not thought possible a short while ago. There's also good evidence that diseases like M.S., Alzheimer's or brain injuries, for example, may be helped. This means it is extremely beneficial to go learn something new that motivates you, especially if it strongly engages the emotions. This may also explain why some folks experience a distinct euphoria and sense of well being with the learning of new things and being around others who involve them in healthy emotions.

When I began Life College, initially the study load was so beyond my abilities, I was forced to "grow" into them. For example, one professor helped us develop our touch sensitivity (in order to palpate a spine under layers of clothes, skin and muscle) in the following manner: He'd have us pull a hair out of our heads, close our eyes and lay it on a page of our textbook. We would then keep folding pages over it and see if we could find the hair under our fingertips. Eventually, I was able to get up to 61 pages, which I would have thought was impossible. But as my brain didn't, it just went ahead and made the new connections needed to form the new skill! As a result patients often joke about having "eyeballs in my fingertips" when I find something even they didn't know was there.

So while the old "use it or lose it" maxim applies, the use must be beyond what we are familiar with doing on a regular or daily basis and be coupled with a *motivation* to grow. This is the only way to cause new growth and ward off deterioration. (A fine everyday example might be learning ways to improve our relationships!)

It's a know brainer, no?

But it's also a 2-way street. We can *cause* it to grow, or *allow* it to weaken - and there appears to be little middle ground in between. It's now known if all we do is the same old thing (job, activities etc.) for years at a time without being "upgraded" to newer more challenging levels, the brain begins to stagnate and becomes less functional. It simply knows its job too well and over time, literally "turns off" switches and causes internal disconnections. At that point, we become less engaged in our lives. (Could this possibly explain "The Grays"?) Also, this "negative plasticity" can occur from such things as hair dye, fingernail polish fumes, chronic pain, an ongoing stressful environment at home or work and of course, being in a trance watching a lot of literally "mindless" TV. (Stress also makes the brain perceive we have less time.)

One of the best examples of prevention I've seen was my 93 year old friend Orion. He fascinated me with his ability to discuss politics, engineering, faith, literature and maintain 4 acres of land. His hearing was bad, but his mind surely wasn't!

One day I asked him how he kept his "edge". He walked me to his upstairs study where there was an entire wall full of classic literature. You name, it was there. He told me he would start at the top left and read through all of them, and when he was done, he'd do it over again. He had a positive Plastic Brain.

My point? In life, just "getting old" should not be our goal. But getting older while keeping our "self" - and life meaningful, should be.

So as I look back, I can now see how pushing my curiosity and desire to learn and doing things like building the house, airplanes, learning aerobatics and even attempting to write this book were quite beneficial to me. But thinking about fractals, well…that may just do me in.

But I also have a great gratitude for those in my life who help turn-on those switches, such as Norbert and Chris who always push me a bit harder. Yet others have forced me to think through many things (this book is the result of that) and some brought me emotional experiences that were at first, completely out of my league, but are now deeply valued and appreciated.

Here's a thought: Have you ever had someone (or yourself) "just not get it" and then at some point there's the "Ah-hah!" moment? Well, most likely that's when the actual nerve connection was made. But here's the catch: this works better if they really *want* to "get it" in the first place! Like *really* listening to another when they are talking. Something about desire and focused attention literally adds brain cells.

As a result of all this, I now realize why I enjoy so much being around those who make me think and feel more. It's yet another sign of "Life" and if you want to "get more out of life", you simply cannot avoid traveling this road. So deliberately learn more and exercise your body and your brain will continue to grow and connect. Do neither and it will wither, disconnect and who "you" are will fade with time. Remember, if you lose your brain, you lose your mind with it.

And you *are* your mind.

But if you take the initiative to literally change your brain – your life will change as well! Conversely, if we insist on limiting ourselves, the brain – and our lives - will politely oblige. And some *will* choose not to grow. That's just how it is. But given the evidence that seems like a slow form of suicide to me. By the way, it's a myth we only use 10 % of our brain.

We use all of it.

That's why it's there.

So if someone says you're wasting time being passionate about learning or doing something new, it's like I said before: Others tend to critique our abilities based on *their* own limitations. Simply put, we're judged by their frame of reference.

And remember, their frame may be BIG...or very, very small.

Brain Test: Quick, name the Seven Dwarfs.
(See bottom of p. 225 for the one I bet you missed.)

195

Heart Mountain

~~~~~~~~~

Living with strangers we know well.

A few years back a large truck found my lane more desirable than did my little Miata, Black Mambo, and totaled the car. This would have been OK had I not been in it at the time, but the moment his fender came *over* my hood and the windshield shattered, I said "This is it" as the airbag exploded into my face. (Health Tip: Glass sunglasses *will* shatter and cut you when the airbag grinds the shards into your face.) Later, after recovering from a gallon of adrenaline and tending to my hurts, I found myself going through what is probably a natural post-accident reflection about my life and those in it. Things like, what if that truck simply took me out, would I even be missed for more than a few days? And *who* would miss me? But more importantly, do I make a difference in anyone's life?

These thoughts reminded me how foolish I am sometimes when I assume tomorrow is guaranteed. Listen, in spite of what your agent told and sold you, *there is no "Life" Insurance.* I also discovered how we *view time, determines how we live life.*

Because of this, I got to wondering how often I'm really willing to "go up the mountain of my heart" and risk connecting with others when I have the chance. Or do I just talk about it while only stumbling around the bottom over and over? Well, I first considered the reasons (excuses) not to go up. Reasons like the higher I go, the further I may fall if I stumble. And this is possible as the path seems less used the higher one goes up - and I still ache deeply from some old falls. But loving another is always a 2-edged sword for one reason: It only works when my *heart is so open I risk giving another the ability to hurt me...and trust they won't.* But they had. Several times.

So why bother? Why set myself up once again?

Well, for one thing, the view is certainly better. I also think we should bother because connection with others is a destination our heart calls home. But for many, what they call "home" is not what they expected or want. And for others, any home seems "better" than no home because "something:" is better than nothing, right? At least we don't think we're being rejected.

But the irony is I think sometimes we reject *ourselves* as touched upon in "If I'm Not There, Neither Am I". So let's take a closer look at our own unique form of Identity Theft.

As noted before, I think rejection means "Go away, you don't meet the standards to be in my life." So to avoid that and play it safe, we put on our "persona" (the actions and words we think will be acceptable to others) as opposed to our real "person", which is who we are when we're alone. And we can have different personas for work, friends, home etc. However, when my persona caters to others, I feel empty because they're not relating to the *real* me. And if I consistently depend on this to be accepted, over time I may actually become more like the persona *than* me! (I know folks who from habit "bend" the truth when there is absolutely nothing to be gained by doing so.)

And really, that can't be good, can it?

This can make yet another problem. Because I *need to be needed*, whoever gives me my significance now "controls" me and I become a "victim" of what they think of me - which can make me angry and resentful. The bottom line? If we have to be so disloyal to ourselves by becoming "someone else" just to make a relationship "work", surely we have paid too high a price, no? I mean, at that point, *what's* the point?

So like snow softly settling around a silent mountain at night, we can cover who we really are and write the history of our future long before it ever happens. But the truth is, only by being more of the "person" can I ever have any real intimacy.

Now that I think about it, maybe even animals can do the persona thing. I remember Susie, our ersatz guard dog who liked to watch the Ed Sullivan Show from the couch. If she sensed danger, she'd roll one baleful eye towards it and let out a half-hearted bark while still in full lounge mode. For years we thought she was a Beagle until we discovered she was actually a very rare Barkalounger.

But concealing (isolating) these parts from others to keep things "smooth" can find us years later *"living with strangers we know well"* and have almost no real connection with. We learn their habits but not their hearts and discover too late that familiarity doesn't equal fulfillment…or that the short term gains pale in significance to the long term losses. And instead of saying "I *get* to spend the rest of my life with this person!" we wonder "Do I *have* to spend the rest of my life with this person?" Once again, we have paid too much and gotten too little.

But every decision has it consequences, no?

The reason the above doesn't work is that connection with another requires the assurance *we can be the real us* (not the persona) without any concern of rejection. It means we feel safe to say what are our delights, concerns, fears and flaws knowing they will *not be used against us*. And it means that our heart has a protected haven in theirs. And if not? Then maybe the time has come to ask how much of our Life-*Time* we're willing to give away to another. Or how much we'll let them steal.

So, is it worth thinking some of this stuff over? Well, that'll have to be your call, but Socrates said "The unexamined life is not worth living." And while that might sound a bit harsh, if "knowledge equals power", then it might be time well spent to see if your own beliefs are really working for you.

More importantly, we really do have a choice to be who we actually are, instead of whom *others* think we should be. And if we climb our own personal mountain first, when it comes time to have another join us, it won't seem nearly so scary. Robert Louis Stevenson said of a successful man

"He got where he is by starting where he was."

And that's exactly how you start being "You" by paying attention to what your heart is speaking. It's talking - we just have to listen and the more we hear, the more we become the "real" person and less a persona. Why do that? Because we have to first connect with *ourselves* before we can with others. (The folks I know who have chosen to do this are, to me, simply a pleasure to be around. You never have to guess who they are!)

After doing this, you are ready to become the person *you* want to be. Change our personal truth by learning more and we change with it. It's that Plastic Brain stuff, remember? Personally, I also believe God honors this level of self honesty.

And when the right time comes, a walk up the mountain can offer extraordinary moments of clear views, fresh air and warm sunshine that will never be found around the shadowy bottom. And really, there *are* those willing to take the walk up with us, help when we stumble and share the rewards the destination offers. But as always, it's our choice to discover if it's worth the climb. You already know I think it is.

And finally, when two connect on Heart Mountain we have the prize of our efforts: *the creation of Life between one another.*

"Life" – that intangible spark that jumps across space between two people and literally *fuses* their souls and hearts together in a connectedness as nothing else can. And when one has reached this point, our former unspoken deep and heartfelt sense of longing is replaced...by an even deeper sense of *Belonging.*

And the ultimate irony?

When two experience this together, there are moments of bliss when something magical happens:

Time truly seems to stand still.

And *that* puts me right in the middle of my Happy Place.

How about you?

Some personas just don't work out. At all.

Where Do You Live?

Are you there because that's where you are?

I often wonder how phrases came to be. For example: "Good grief!" How is grief supposed to be good? Or "Home is where the heart is." Now, does this *have* to mean your heart is at your house? Or, can it mean wherever your heart is, *that* is home? (I believe the latter.) In the South, some folks will ask "Where do you stay?" instead of "Where do you live?" Now to me, "where you live" is obvious: you live in your body! If it is supposed to mean at home, then does one "live more" and have more "Life" there then somewhere else? Well, maybe that's exactly what it *should* mean. As such, the question of "living or staying" may very well apply to the "condition" of our life with others inside the home.

This concept of "Life" is difficult to put into words but I think you do know when it's present! Part of it is a comforting vitality between you and another along with encouragement to explore your talents and reach your goals. It's also satisfying to just be around them, even if they're in the next room reading a book. But mostly, there is shared purpose and meaning based on a strong foundation of friendship.

I think we're all drawn to what we believe is Life giving, because without it, what is not growing is dying. No aspect of life is static and simply put, *Life is motion.* And not just the physical - but emotional, mental and spiritual. And while some will attempt to find Life in their possessions or work, I believe the main source should be found in our primary relationships. And it's there some people can fashion and experience more "Life" together than with others.

These folks form a genuine "togetherness" in their own little world by validating each other and combining their energies to create fulfillment. In short, they admire and bring out the best in each other! And while I know of no one who would not want this, I know of only a few who actually pursue it.

On the other hand, we can create a Life-*Time* stalemate by using that energy to oppose and cancel each other out. (Two people can be "good", but not necessarily good together!) So, are we helpful Life-*Time* partners...or obstructive opponents?

200

If it becomes the latter then it's important not to confuse the resulting "drama" (silence, arguments, sickness) with "Life". This emotional stimulus is a counterfeit of the Life I am writing about and is probably an unhealthy attempt to recover some type of lost passion. These relationships too frequently feel like work.

The result? The whole is less than the sum of the parts.

I used to date a gal whose life was in a constant uproar with one distraction after another that pulled her attention every which way. This kept her - and us - continuously off balance. Finally one day I told her I could not be in a relationship with her anymore. She asked why and I hesitatingly told her

"Because your life is a non-stop soap opera. A really bad one." Her thespian response floored me:

"Yeah, isn't it great?!"

No, it wasn't. It was exhausting and stressful. Not to mention very unfulfilling because where Life creates inspiration, drama delivers frustration. Remember that old break-up line

"It's not you, it's me"? Trust me, it was definitely her.

Scratch one elephant. Life was too short for that safari.

To me, these folks never seem to be more than just "happily miserable". If you know anyone like this, ask them "Hey, how's that working for you? Would you like some cheese with your whine?" Truth is, sometimes it's just smarter to observe what behavior achieves rather than try to figure out how it got that way. (At which time, it may be best to just get away!)

But truly, the *pleasure* of our being together depends on the extent the needs of *both* individuals are being met on a regular basis. *This is Life-giving in itself.* However, having our needs met depends on us knowing who *we* are in order to know *what* our needs are! If *we* don't know them, how can another? And this means a look-see beyond the "inner doors" of our own heart to find what truth is in there for sharing. When Mark Twain looked behind those doors, he saw his wife and said

"Wherever she was, there was Eden."

That's more than sweet. It's an attitude that brings Life to both.

So, wherever you are, are you "living" or "staying" there? Is your home a fun and safe place for you to be? Or do we stay with the familiar solely because...it's familiar? If so, at what point does a "home" simply become a house where we've boxed up and stored our dreams?

...*Musical Interlude*...
Footfilling Stories.

Time out for two short stories that have nothing to do with anything. Back in '85 on my earliest trip into the Canyon, I did my first solo midnight hike from the rim down to the river. It was in October and I expected, and was prepared for, somewhat balmy overnight temps. The Canyon had other ideas.

Like below freezing.

About 5 miles down and 4 hours later the cold had deadened my hands and feet making for unstable footing on narrow canyon trails at nighttime a bad idea. So I sidetracked off the trail and did a park no-no: I built a fire and then pulled off my boots and socks and thrust my unfeeling feet towards it.

While basking in the warmth of the fluttering flames in a small rocky alcove, something else decided to bask as well. In fact, quite a few somethings made this executive decision. In moments, the heat had attracted bountiful amounts of spiders, scorpions and lizards scuttling from all directions to join the party. I quickly decided I had an urgent appointment elsewhere and clumsily tried to get my boots quickly on my sandy feet.

Speaking of quick, sand and feet, a few days later I made another memorable side trip. While we were pulled off the river for lunch, I decided to go rock climbing up a side canyon river bed. At one point I had to do a difficult overhang climb – which dumped me into a deep sheltered pool above and well out of sight and sound of my compatriots. After this spot, it was much easier hiking upstream which alternated between wet and dry.

Thirty minutes later I got to where I had to cross a 20 foot long area covered in about 2 inches of water. At the midpoint, I stopped to gaze upward in awe at the soaring saffron, auburn and cinnamon canyon walls that appeared to converge overhead. The view was a bit dizzying and for some strange reason, the walls seemed to verrrrry slowly get higher and higher...

It was then I felt the cool water around my mid-calf. And it was steadily rising. Actually, I was steadily sinking. All alone.

And quick...sand.

Oh crap.

We now return you to your regularly scheduled program.

202

Moments to Live For

~~~~~~~~

Conspire to inspire.

So I got to wondering. Is there really any good way to "capture" the value and rewards of time? I think so. I started by discerning what were the "moments I lived for". You know, those times – and people – that are just plain satisfying to be around and add "Life" to life? The ones I just naturally smile more around and leave me feeling full inside? Once I knew that, then I could work towards creating more of them. If those moments involved another, then I needed to *spend* more time with them because that's great soil to grow heart food in!

In a relationship, we either contribute Life or suck it out like a tick on a dog. One of the best indicators that we are contributors is when others feel better about *themselves* after spending time with us. This happens because we recognize and bring out their "best stuff" and are as concerned with their well being and comfort as with our own. Over time, this creates a mutual admiration society that causes us to believe in, and support each other toward our personal and shared goals.

As a result, we *conspire to inspire*.

So why is this important? Because it helps release the passion they have about their lives and themselves. It also allows them to feel safe knowing they have our support and the freedom to pursue what's important to them. And that benefits us as we get to know and enjoy more of them growing more fully into who they truly are. (I've known several people who absolutely blossomed because someone believed in them.)

When both feel enhanced as a result of the other, then time together is pure heart food. Time itself becomes a precious *gift* to one another as it creates worthiness and gives us what we find so nourishing: *emotional food* and Hope. Listen, I don't know about you, but I like that idea. So does Twain who said

"I could live for two months on a good compliment." (Personally, I'd need at least three.)

Love and Hope...gift wrapped in Time. The three most precious of gifts. That's all we really have to offer each other, isn't it? And all good things flow out of them, especially those moments to live for.

And Some to Die For

~~~~~~~~

Conspire to expire.

If one is so insensitive or arrogant as to have no awareness of both sides of the "time and love coin", then they may simply presume they have a *right* to your time (which in my opinion, calls for a "time out"!) These folks typically have an easy ability to display anger and are content with relationships that have the depth of algae. They also have a scary level of certitude that makes problem discussion and resolution almost impossible. From the start, "they're right and you're not" and they are more concerned with being "right" than *doing* right as they go about their business of judging you. (The *less* someone values you, the *more* likely they are to criticize you.) In short, they have more quiet contempt then consideration for another and often treat friends better than those they "love".

At that point, it's worth remembering the only rights others have with us (other than expecting honesty) are the rights we extend them. And those rights can be rescinded at any time!

But it's a certainty that *people* of certainty have little patience with the human heart, especially those of others and sometimes, they're simply mean folks. And someone can have a nice *persona*-lity but not be a nice *person* - particularly if they practice the "3-C's" of Criticism, Condescension and Complaint. Folks like this don't *get* angry – they are anger driven which has a lot of energy behind it. This is exactly what gives them their perceived certainty (and snobitude) and makes their patience and promises to others measurable in minutes. Also the less substance their position has, the louder they sometimes get to "prove" their point! I mean, *that* should really convince you, no?

But then, and perhaps just as bad, are the so called "passive-aggressive" type who veil their anger with a silent attitude of "I can handle the truth and you can't...but I'm afraid to tell you" and in the meantime they grow a tumor. To me, they seem simultaneously quite arrogant - and insecure - at the core

However, the difference is *where love blesses and bonds, anger drains and divides.* And the real irony? The person least interested in the relationship is often the one in control of it. But like rights, whatever degree of control anyone has over us, it's the exact amount we have given them and that should *never* include giving away our dignity or self-respect.

Unfortunately, the target of this divisive behavior is often driven to other affairs of the heart as they go looking for caring, friendship and respect from somewhere else – which were the very things the relationship was supposed to provide.

One thing is for certain, however, affairs are rarely about sex and they are not the root cause of divorce. But emotionally starved marriages are the root cause of affairs because by that point, regret and sadness have usually replaced the friendship and admiration that has been missing. (In divorce, people are gone emotionally long before they go physically.) Too often we forget we need to respect, admire *and* like those we say we love.

As I write these words, I can't help thinking of the sad lyrics written by a young - and recently deceased patient of mine:

"All the time you were here…I never felt you near."

So, if it's true that past behavior is a reliable predictor of future conduct and we allow ourselves to continue being treated poorly, then our future simply becomes an extension of our past and life is nothing more than a series of re-runs. And how many times do you want to watch the same movie? (In the South they say you can't plow a straight line by looking behind you!)

I also have to think that if someone makes no effort to hold us accountable for our words and actions (which they should even if we don't like it when they do!) then our presence may actually have little real significance in their life. People who *care about us* want to know what's going on when we do things they don't understand. This means it's abnormal to behave normally in an abnormal situation. (Like around an elephant?)

Finally, as noted before, it's useful to be aware if we are unknowingly getting more comfort from the "home" itself and our daily routines there, instead of from *who's in it*. So unless you're single, if it's the home that matters most then it may simply be just a "staging area" for our "real" life which takes place outside of it with other people, work etc.

Remember, if it's not working for both, *it's not working*. Without connection to another, a "home" is just a house where people are *spending* what's left of their time alone together.

And those can be moments to die for.

Vampires and Tuning Forks

~~~~~~~~

Truth is always true.

As we just discussed, in life there are those that just feel good to be around...and those that don't. Some are delightful and others are bête noires. Some leave you walking on air, others feeling buried alive...and you know who they are. "Vampires" are mobile black holes whose self absorption simply sucks the Life out of you. Sometimes rude (which really means "You don't deserve my attention.") and often late or thankless (meaning "My time is more important than yours."), don't expect *them* to be inconvenienced. Quick to complain and slow to forgive, spending time with them is more akin to chewing tin foil while combing your hair with a cheese grater. Sometimes alarmingly charming, they can turn the death ray on or off.

"Tuning Forks" on the other hand have an inviting vitality and, well, you just like being around them! They seem to "light up" the room (or our day) when they enter it. What's interesting about real metal tuning forks is if you have two of them rated at the same frequency, you can start one vibrating and then, if you bring it in the *presence* of the other fork, it too will begin to vibrate in harmony without them ever touching. In essence, it exhibits the universal law of like affects like and in doing so, it has caused the other to do what it was created to do. In a sense, the two share the same source of "Life".

I believe one of the wonders and a blessing of life is to meet another that has our "frequency". And you know when you are in their presence because you simply "resonate" with them and things just "feel right". Why? Because again, like attracts like and "Life is motion" (dead things don't move.) This analogy may be appropriate because these people can be separated for years, and upon reconnecting, the "Life" returns as well. Truth is, I've even noticed I have less physical pain around these folks.

This can also be likened to chemistry whereby mixing the same chemicals will always give the reaction. (In a somewhat related manner, studies also show that the most fulfilling relationships are a combination of chemistry *and* commitment.) In mathematics, the same equations always give the same results.

Perhaps it is so with people, no?

Truth is always true.

It's been said that the two hardest things we ever have to do in life is to *accept* love and to *offer* forgiveness. In accepting love, we get two of its greatest gifts - the infusion of Life that comes with the *real* thing - and the inspiring strength to believe we can be better then who we are alone.

And we can help this along SO easily by offering a kind word, smile, touch or even a simple email - a little bit of "Life" each day to help get through the day, no? These all have the ability to create Life IF they have the most essential ingredient: *Sincerity*. Without this, all is as a vacant smile or an empty promise...worthless. (For some to say "I love you" holds the same assurance as "I love tofu".) Even Shakespeare referenced insincerity when he mused "We are damned by faint praise."

(And, I'll add, by desperate politicians.)

So be wise, for while some people use words to express the truth, others use them very effectively to obscure it.

In the end, each of us is nothing more than a tiny island of sand in that river of time. And every moment, another grain of us washes away until finally, we and our time are spent...only to linger on in the vault of another's memory. I did not really appreciate this until recently when I was asked to participate in a memorial service for Susan's mom, both of whom I knew for 27 years and have shown me much of the South's graciousness.

As I stood in front of the church speaking to the gathering, I suddenly realized all that was left of Carolyn was the memories we had to share with each other about her. *We* had become the living breathing walking repository of her entire life. Who she was and all she ever did lived on in us sheltered in the vaults of our memories. We had become the caretakers of a Life-Time and were attempting to pass it on to others to remember. And although she was gone, what we said about our shared past became her future.

But even as we tried to hold on to a part of her, she stole away a piece of us. It was then I knew that when someone leaves my life by decision or death, they take with them a bit of me only they were able to draw out. Because of this, I will never relate to another in the same unique way I did with them. They are, in a literal sense, irreplaceable.

And so it is when anyone leaves our life for any reason.

I then thought back to my Dad in the hospital and my determination not to wait until someone dies to say something nice about them or to add Life to their life. And I hoped everyone in the church had told Carolyn something wonderful to her before she passed. The truth is the people who will be there in the end and what will be said about you, and me, is the harvest of the seeds we spent our entire lives planting. Perhaps in part this becomes our "After-Life"? But only the memories that were created can be drawn upon. If nothing happened, there'd be nothing to remember. *There would be no Bookmarks.*

So perhaps in doing these small daily events that touch the hearts of others, we can find what we sometimes feel we've lost:

The faith and passion to keep looking for what matters most to us while creating memories worth remembering.

And that's useful because we are one thing above all:

The sum of our experiences as a result of our decisions.

Or, said another way: Life's rarely the way its "supposed" to be – but it's always the way it is – and the way it is depends mostly on the way I am!

How about that?

Sometimes just when you think you've got life all figured out, the unexpected happens: You get attacked by tumbleweeds. Again.

The Hope of Romance

~~~~~~~~

*"Hope deferred makes the heart grow sick, but a desire
filled is a tree of life." Prov. 13:12*

Romance. Do you have it? Is it too idealistic to want it?
Not at all! But to have romance, (and unless you are
really in love with yourself) it helps to be in a relationship, no?
So, what's a relationship? I'll offer the following:

A relationship is when two people make a deliberate and
conscious effort to "relate" and know each other by surrounding
themselves with a vehicle (the "ship") that takes them on a
mutually fulfilling journey and goal. In doing so, it provides
them with comfort, purpose, meaning and emotional food.

But I humbly offer its even better when it includes romance.

Even so, I've come across an awful lot of people who say
"Long term romance is overrated" which just makes blood want
to spew out of my eyes. Listen up: romance is not overrated - it's
"underused" and I've never come across someone who didn't
enjoy it when they had it. But I *have* come across "a million"
who were unwilling to create or sustain it and believed that it
can't last. But ships built with care *can* last the trip. (Remember:
one guy built the Ark and a bunch of "experts" built the Titanic.)

Am I a "hopeless romantic"? – a term used by many in a
sweetly derogatory way as in "There's no hope for him!" Nope.
In fact, there is no such thing as the very requirement of romance
is to be hopeful. So realize if you think things are hopeless, then
there is no hope and all is lost. I am, however, a *hopeful* romantic
and it is what drives me and is part of my passion for life. And I
believe passion is what gives life so much of its color.

But there is a difference between hope, wishes and fantasy.
Hope has an "object", such as a person or God we can believe in.
*It is the desire for something with the expectation of attaining it
that activates the will to pursue it.* Wishing, on the other hand, is
"hoping" for the attainment of something to place our hope in.
It's almost like the step before hope, and if it's a person, it's the
one we are most likely to dream about. And fantasy, well, we all
know what that is - a complete fabrication with little or no
chance of becoming reality at all.

But to make hope realistic will depend on what it is based on. If we have an unrealistic expectation placed on someone, then we are only setting ourselves up for disappointment. So, we need to consider if there is really a chance they can and will "deliver" the desired end results. If not, it becomes a fantasy.

When we love another, we place our hope *in* that love for our future success as the love becomes the vehicle for our hope to ride on. However, even if we "fall" out of love, one or both people can still "hope" for the return of lost passion. Hope can persist even where love doesn't because "There's always hope".

Likewise, if you have a vision or dream for something in your life, you don't "love" that it will come true, you "hope" that it does. So, under some circumstances, hope can be the stronger of the two forces as it forms part of our faith in God and others.

And that's why when life turns crappy and there's little left to believe in, hope lost can hurt like nothing else. It is for this reason I will never belittle the hopeful.

Some think the "color of romance" lives quietly only in the heart of the woman who "learned" to settle for whatever shade of gray replaced it, or that the man only considers it sex. But it's much more than sex and while *making* love (meaning to literally create more love) includes romance, sex doesn't have to. I do know I've seen the brightness dim in the eyes of folks who have let hope and romance walk out the door. Little did I know I was also witnessing the death of a part of their soul.

And this is how it can look: Two people having an entire meal together in polite but disinterested conversation while spending most of the time looking around in silence. Their only connection is their disconnection. (You can almost always tell in a restaurant who is dating or is married, no?)

And this is how it can feel: We get to the point where we have nothing more to give, or care so little, that even the pretense of the "acceptable" persona is dropped and their approval is no longer important. Words that were once right from the heart now too often carry an edge that cuts straight through it. Sexual pleasure may become as frequent and mechanical as tire rotations and even if sleep is used as an escape, no matter how much we get, we still feel tired. Finally, it feels "hopeless" and where we are today is only because we were there yesterday.

And this is how it can happen: We no longer hold hands on a walk (or stop walking altogether), no longer snuggle, no longer provide the little courtesies we once did. In our efforts to make the unacceptable become acceptable, Hope just quietly slips away, a distant voice that fades from despair to resentment.

Finally, in failing to find comfort in our discomfort, we may eventually admit there's just too many "no longer's" and place the final and fatal nail in the coffin of disappointment: Apathy. We simply don't care anymore as life may convert to being more about our house, our job and our daily rituals instead of the two people who once really enjoyed each other. Where has the affection and comfort gone? When did it all become so *dry*?

And *when* did The Roommate move in?

And "they" will say "Oh, it's natural to feel this way...it happens to everyone." Which may be true...for the Sheeple.

So guess what? They're wrong on both counts and I have the evidence to prove it. Besides, as the Chinese proverb says,

"The person who says it cannot be done should not interrupt the person doing it." (Unlike those just *saying* they'll do it!)

But let's be honest, most folks would have never gotten together if they first didn't experience the colors of romance. So why do we let the colors go to gray so easily? Is it yet another frog in the pot? I mean if it's true all marriages are *made* in Heaven, why do so few of them seem to remain there?

Now on the other hand, have you ever been so *delighted* with someone that even the anticipation of their presence often made the little boy - or girl – inside of you jump up and down? That sometimes just thinking about them gave you a warm fuzzy? That "time spent" with them simply left you feeling good? And was usually, well....FUN?! And some of that joy was from an unexpected source: Doing things that please *them*?

And none of these really seemed to fade much with time?

Can that even be "real", or is that something that goes south with the infatuation phase? Well, I believe it is real because I've known couples married for decades who still exhibit this inviting energy. Simply put, there are some folks that you share more energy with and whose very presence inspires you to become a better version of yourself. That's "Life" and a desire fulfilled!

And it's also a damn fine reason to hope in the passion of romance for a very long time. Gee, I feel better already. ☺

Passssion

~~~~~~~~

Livalot by staying alive.

So, exactly what is "passion"? Well, the dictionary has numerous definitions, but aside from the sexual, I use the word as a reference for a strong emotion, appetite or enthusiasm towards another as well as to life itself. One can be passionate about a person, romance, art, writing, vocation, their skill with a car or an airplane etc. It is an "energy" that draws one forward and helps them thrive in life and especially in a relationship. Honestly, I really don't think life would be very interesting without some form of it. Nor can I live without it.

And while we don't need to be "great" to have passion, I think all great people have it. (Look at DaVinci, van Gogh, Shakespeare, Beethoven, Ben Franklin or Jesus.) I also know that everyone of us can be great in our own unique way.

For me, to even be writing this book is a passion and because I am in pain all the time from injuries, surgeries and the like, it's a healthy means for my mind to loiter on something more comforting and inviting. And while hope provides food for the future, passion helps keep me fed in the present.

(While on the subject of food, I remember someone's subtle display of passion for another during a mundane meal. She simply said the food didn't matter, but that the company did. I wonder what it means if the "food does matter" at home?)

But once again, we come back to hope! So, to expand: Passion can also be fueled by hope which I believe is the strongest *drive* we have, even more than love, although the two are intimately intertwined. Why is that? Because even love has its foundation in hope as it is usually in another we have our expectations, dreams and desires.

To this end, there is nothing more devastating than to be "hopeless" because it represents the end of the road with nothing left to believe in or on. One simply can run out of hope in their vision, dreams or a relationship. And when hope runs out, so does passion. I also believe the more depressed a person becomes, the less hope they have because as was noted before, "Hope deferred makes the heart grow sick."

Frankly, I don't think the human heart can survive without hope and relationships truly become Lifeless without it. To this end, if you are a passionate person and there is no passion in your life, you'll feel like the walking dead for one reason:

Passionate people need passionate involvement. The following is paraphrased from something I once read that I think states this nicely: "We always feel more alive when we get near what we don't possess, *but need.* It brings parts of us to life that have little chance of surfacing on their own." That sense of Life can often be found in the object of our hope. But hope is both durable and delicate and sometimes a single word from another like "Yes" or "Goodbye" – can create it...or crush it.

A long time ago Fred invited me to participate in speaking to a group of homeless men at the downtown Atlanta Mission. As I foolishly believed I had many of the "answers to life", I agreed to go, but found myself afraid to just be driving in the area. When I finally stood in front of 100 black men, the thought suddenly occurred to me "How on earth will we ever relate? What should I say?"

Over time and in order to have something to talk about, I would prepare a "sermon" with notes and talk *at* them about how "wonderful life" could be. I did this for quite awhile, but it really was a waste of time. There was no connection happening, they would talk while I was talking, the information was useless and they couldn't wait to get out of the room.

This went on until one night when I was really feeling the effects of my own state of despair with little hope. In the midst of my and their talking, I just stopped. In a few seconds they too stopped talking and looked at me as I stared down at the floor for about 30 seconds. I finally looked up at them and said

"I can't do this anymore."

I then wadded up my notes, took a deep breath and spoke *to* them from the heart for the next 20 minutes. I told them truthfully what I was in the middle of, how much I hurt and how it affected my life. I explained how everything I had built my life on seemed to be crumbling before me except for a few strands left of my faith and that I felt like a public success but a private failure. And, I confessed I would never again stand before them unless I had something to say. I would never again talk just for the sake of talking.

The silence was deafening. They had heard someone being painfully honest.

And when I was done? The entire room of previously disinterested and disengaged men gave me a standing ovation!

In that moment I learned by example two very old lessons: Others want us to know how they feel before we offer them advice – and, we always need to *earn the right* to speak into their life while remembering it takes time for the emotions to catch up to the intellect. But that night I saw first hand the immediate Life giving power of hope and passion of a different form and many years later, being authentic works as well now as it did then.

And not only there.

But listen – everything we do, have and are, will end in "time". We've only got so much of it to accomplish and enjoy what we want and need. If so, perhaps it all gets down to this: Are we *willing* to passionately make the best use of our Life-*Time* with ourselves and others?

Well known author Max Lucado once said

"Changing directions in life is not tragic; losing passion in life is." In the Song of Solomon (8:6) we are told that passion is "…as fierce as the grave." That's pretty fierce, no?!

I mentioned before about how "One of these days" is separated by only one little letter and all too easily becomes "None of these days" until eventually we "Run out of days". The real truth is that *one tiny little letter* can separate me from a "lot of nothing", and a life of wonderful people and experiences.

And it's ever so easy for me to let it do so.

To thwart this, I simply remember an even simpler truth:

"The time is now."

And right "now" is the *only* moment all 6.6 billion of us on the planet will *ever* exist in. We are all captured in the exact same slice of time. No one is before or after us. The question is what are you and I doing with the moment *we* occupy?

So, will we savor what time we have left and choose our time investments wisely? In short, will *our involvement* in our life be more true to the passions that define who we are?

If that is indeed our choice, I've got only this to say:

It *will* be time well *spent!*

Having A Seinfeld

~~~~~~~

So there I am standing alone perusing the wine selection in the local Publix grocery store when over the PA system, comes the classic oldie "Pretty Woman" by Roy Orbison. While reading the back of a bottle, I am absent mindedly tapping my foot and sorta moving with the music (as best I'm able to with a wobbly knee making distinct mechanical clacking noises) when out of the corner of my eye, I see a fellow shopper coming down the aisle toward me doing much the same.

So I turn and look at him a bit more directly.

And he's really getting into the music. I mean, he's high stepping along and slapping his feet and swinging his head side to side in wide arcs so vigorously it looks like he's holding on to the buggy just to keep from falling over and I'm thinking

"This dude is really *free*. I mean he just doesn't care who thinks what! Look at how much he's enjoying the tunes."

As he sways closer to me, I find myself getting drawn into the rhythm and motion he is so enraptured by. So I start stomping a bit louder and moving around a bit more and give him a little smile of simpatico as he closes in to go around me.

He looks back at me like I have three eyes.

As he passes by, the song ends…and I watch his floppy body gyrations and convolutions continue as he goes down the aisle and out of sight around the bend. Then it hit me: Sixth quarter Life Chiropractic College Neuro-diagnosis class.

"Stomping Gait" due to brain dysfunction.

Oh my. He's not dancing, he's not jiving - he's just trying to get through the store upright and home in one piece…and ignore idiots like me who he thinks are mocking him.

Do you remember George in The Seinfeld Show? How easy it was for him to "open mouth and insert foot"? Well, I was able to do much the same without ever making a sound. And once again, I got to experience just how easily our individual perceptions fashion our realities without even a single word being uttered to further confuse the "issue".

Sheepishly, my knee and I clanked out of the store.

Yesterday's Tomorrows

~~~~~~~~

Life is no dress rehearsal.

Do you often feel like too many days all seem the same? And even though some routine can be good and comforting, do you often find yourself thinking "Will my life *ever* be what I want it to be?"

When Alice was in Wonderland, she came to a fork in the road and asked the Cheshire Cat which way to take. He replied "That depends a good deal on where you want to get."

Her response? She wanted to get "somewhere".

Well, if getting somewhere and change is what you want, two things need to be recognized. First, *life is no dress rehearsal* and it's quite possible we'll run out of tomorrows while waiting for "things to change", be it ourselves, others or circumstances. (You know, the *"When I......."* syndrome.) The second thing is change for the "sake of change" without any direction or goal can literally be pointless. (Where are you pointing to?)

When traveling the road of transformation, at some point we have to accept that we are the "agents of change" in our own lives. And when it does occur, it is most often preceded by a "change of heart" as it is drawn to something that is Life giving.

So, how *do* we make moments more Life giving? Well, one way is to simply make them by changing the way we do things by adding a sense of purpose. And I don't mean waiting for Valentine's Day or an anniversary to do the expected card and flower thing - which often make it feel more like a chore than a desire. No, it's more like "Did I purposely do anything today to make it meaningful?"

Why do that? Because to a great extent life is a series of people, places and events that make the "Bookmarks" we call memories. I mean really, if things never happened, what would you have memories of? So...have you done anything lately that was worth remembering and would bookmark that relentless wave of time behind all of us?

Well, if you did, one thing is almost certain, *it involved others*. Why? Because the "food" of *everyday* life is found in interacting with others in a meaningful way on a regular basis.

For that simple reason we are not meant to be alone and unknown. But I've seen and experienced a lot of both, even in "committed relationships" with the irony being the one thing we *need* the most – the heart food that results from connecting with others - is often what we least pursue in any conscious manner.

When this is missing, the "easy" solution is to pretend a relationship is more than it really is and keep telling ourselves "It's not all that bad" when we *should* be asking "Is it all that good?" And the effect of this over time? Much like two polished, but hard river stones, day by day the people can wear each other down to a "Life-less" flat line like the tracings of a failing EKG.

It's at this point we may learn too late that while we can't live without dying, *we most certainly can die without Living.*

So why do we *really* want to be connected with another? As I said, it's our wiring that we are unavoidably relational and "interdependent". We *ALL* want to be loved and to belong. As people we simply desire to be needed and need to be desired.

But we have a choice to make. We can risk connecting with others knowing they absolutely *will* leave our life in some way...by decision or by dying. Or, we can limit our investment in them by the self-protective "strategies" we talked about. This means learning if what we're doing really helps make our life vibrant and alive – or predictable and guarded with each day an unsatisfying merry-go-round just to get through it so we can rush home to...*what?*

More crumbs? Not much heart food there.

In the "Midward" I mentioned folks married up to 60 years, which implies success. But not all would have agreed and quite a few had been unhappy for what seemed like endless years. Some too afraid to upset their "routine" had just gutted it out and sold passion for an unsatisfying complacency. Others, who often defined their spouse as a "good" person (meaning, it seemed, they weren't the love of their life) hoped the years invested would eventually "pay-off" But they didn't. And in the end? They had only deep regrets over not making the needed changes they so dearly wanted. Sadly, studies have shown that of the 50% of couples who *remain* married, only 25% *of them* describe themselves as "happy". From this I learned that while some marriages can be long and happy, far too many are just long.

S ometimes in life, however, there are decisions that *must* be made in order to move forward, literally. Like when you are trapped 100 feet underground in *The Gun Barrel.*

This very grim *extremely* tight crawl passage inside Knox Cave in upstate New York is notorious for 2 reasons: One: it's about 18 inches wide and 22 inches tall. (Think of crawling through your toilet.) Now imagine a 54 foot long toilet with you on your side, body completely encased by stone with one arm in front of you with headlamp in hand. Moving forward is done by flexing your ankles and pushing with your toes. Next, it is one-way in and out - if you get hurt in the far side cave, too bad.

Now, can we say beyond belief claustrophobic?

On four prior trips in 1970 I had been rightfully intimidated as I stared at the entrance hole and then turned away. My shoulders did not allow me to go in more than 5 feet and I was unable to breathe. I always thought this as discretion at its finest.

However, sometimes in life you have to go where it seems impossible and on the 5th trip, I did. After great effort, I was 25 feet in when just ahead of me bathed in the orange glow of the headlamp's flame, I saw a large denim butt and kicking feet attached to a portly young woman who was totally stuck at the choke point - and freaking out. As I was now likewise stuck "behind" her and unable to back out, my level of anxiety rose dramatically as well. Compounding the problem was she had hermetically sealed off the passage to the front, and I, to the rear. This left my face in a 5 foot long 18" stone tube of oxygen that was rapidly being used up by me and my burning headlamp.

They say "necessity is the mother of invention" and, as I truly needed to go forward, I started inventing. So, after making a thorough ass-essment of my situation and remembering that heated molecules want to move, I turned my headlamp to full flame, inched up to her derriere and liberally warmed the barrier before me. Well, this physics experiment worked much better than expected as within moments, and with a muffled cry, the quivering gelatinous mass before me begin to slowly creep forward like a great ship pulling from its berth. And as long as I kept up the heat, it kept moving until we both popped out the other end. At this point, I had had enough, turned around and went right back out the other way. She may still be there.

In hind-sight, and given the open flame, I truly believe it was the grace of God she did not have burritos for breakfast.

Life in 3-D

~~~~~~~~

Time to shoot the messenger.

It's well known that our parents pen more than just a few lines in our "book of behavior" and to be emotionally healthy as adults, it helps immensely to know we were wanted and "belonged" as a child. Childhood is also the time when dreams are formed for what our life will become as in our appropriate innocence, we build the frame and canvas for the adult picture we will later paint upon it.

But if we were not accepted and loved, then like water, a wounded heart will frequently seek its own level in the 3-D's.

Here's how...

Even though we think we make wise decisions, we often become a self-fulfilling prophecy by trying to find stability in our past. We begin this process by gravitating to a mate either similar to us ("They understand me!") or to the parent that hurt us believing if we can get *this* person to admit our worth, we'll heal the past injuries. But both of these are recipes for heartbreak because if we were brought up feeling we didn't *deserve* to be loved, we'll often choose someone that insures that legacy.

If we do achieve some level of union, we can doubt it will last and may quietly fear *desertion*, worried they will soon discover "I'm not good enough for them." Why? *Because that's the message we got as a child.* The outcome is we can actually fear success more than failure.

And even though our childhood messenger *was wrong,* if it became our personal truth, then our all too frequent solution is to *deprive* ourselves of having what we want so we won't have to fear losing it! But if we lure ourselves into believing "If I don't try I can't fail", then we've also failed to realize there's no future in our past...and Yesterday *is* Tomorrow.

The usual end result of Deserve, Desert and Deprive? Unfortunately, we often generate (and justify) the outcomes of the very things we dread while the years fly by and "The Book of Me" remains unopened and unread. But even though our past made us who we are, we are responsible for who we *become.* Maybe Einstein had the solution:

"Learn from yesterday, live for today, hope for tomorrow."

Phaser Fulfillment

~~~~~~~~

Set to "mutual fulfillment."

No, this is not the warm fuzzy you may have after vaporizing your spouse. (It's quite alright to use the "stun" setting, though.)

I think we can all be described as "phasers" in that we travel through life's stations in the guise of different phases. If you don't, that means you are stuck somewhere and haven't grown. Sorry. I also think these phases co-exist with the "Learning, Understanding and Application" I noted in the "Backward".

In childhood and our early years, our main phase is that of selfishness as we feel our way into an unknown world believing we have a right to have whatever we want in order to feel safe and satisfied. This is most evident in the child who naturally demands the world cater to them because they are entirely dependent on others.

In the adolescent, an "arrogant innocence" often causes them to have all the answers to all the questions they haven't even had time to consider, much less experience or understand. Couple this with incomplete brain development to project the future consequences of decisions and you have a dicey stage.

The young adult then moves out in the world and perhaps this next phase may be titled "acquisition" as they usually seek to identify themselves in the form of a "bigger and better" car, home and a million other *things*. Often the "success" of this phase is measured by what we have relative to what others do, or do not. In a sense, others can define us more than we do.

Hopefully, as we mature more into the adult phase, we realize three things about life: It's finite, it's not about things and it's definitely not entirely about me. (If it continues to be "all about me", that may indicate an unfulfilled childhood phase.) As adults, we begin to learn that not only do people *want* to matter, but that they actually do! It is this phase where relationships start to become more clearly defined and refined. And that it's not just the people that matter, but the time we spend with them as well.

Many older folks are quite clear on this time matters thing. I once sat next to a sweet, elderly Southern couple at lunch and

inquired of the wife how long they'd been married. After 20 minutes of leisurely installing her teeth, she replied
"Two months." I said that was one long engagement, no?

They went on to explain they had met each other only one time almost 50 years ago as a result of going on a double blind date. But each had been with a different person whom they eventually married and both of whom had passed. The man seeing in the newspaper she too was now a widow, wrote her a short note of condolence and here's the letters that followed over the next two weeks:

He: "Do you remember me?"
She: "Yes, I do."
He: "Would you like to get together some time?"
She: "Yes, I would."
He: "Would you mind if I also 'Court and Sparked' you?"
She: "No and if you want to marry me the answer is Yes."

So, here's the question: Was that an example of "Timing is everything", or, "Time is of the essence"? Maybe it was both? Or…was it the expression of our innate *need* for companionship?

Anyway, in the "Hope of Romance" we talked about the relation-"ship". If there is a relationship (and the folks are on the *same* ship), then by default, they need what I just mentioned: companion-"ship". Once that is there, we can then consider what defines a "successful" relationship and whether there is a simple and common premise that covers all of them.

I think there is - and it's so obvious as to often be invisible:

Mutual fulfillment.

Double Huh with a half twist.

That's all. It simply means the important desires and needs of both folks are met *on a regular basis*. And really, isn't that the reason for the relationship to exist in the first place? (We also always do better with folks who help us feel better about ourselves - which is how relationships *start*, no?) On the longer term basis, it's appropriate and reasonable to negotiate and define what's important to each. But a frequent problem is that "what's real may never get said and what *is* said may not be real". So unless both folks are accomplished psychics, then what the other *really* wants and needs is frequently a lifetime mystery.

So in the end, if the relationship doesn't work for both, then all both get is a lot of work. Worse yet is if one's efforts are not appreciated, which then makes it nothing more than a thankless job – and one without any payment in heart currency at all. And ungrateful people really can be a total bore, no? Finally, while it's a tragedy to not be where you want to be, it's just as tragic to be where you don't want to be.

But at some point, we need to decide if we are being fulfilled or not because, like any other problem in life, we can't fix what we're unwilling to identify and admit. This means we need to be 100% responsible for our 50% of the relationship. This brings us right back to being real with ourselves and realizing we do have a right to our thoughts and feelings. And, as our feelings require no apologies, we should have the freedom to discuss them. The "red flag" to watch for here? When others tell us *how* to feel, or worse, that we *shouldn't* feel the way we do.

Hopefully there is a mutual understanding that another's life is as important as ours. Also, when a regular supply of joy, smiles and laughter with the simplicities of life is coupled with a sense of physical and emotional security, you have lots of raw material to build wonderful relationships with. But if there is more boredom, sniping and no real desire to please and fulfill the other, then the "mix" is problematic. Life is hard enough under the best of circumstances, so why *spend* your time on those who make it even harder? (And yes, some *are* more work then they're worth.) And while all relationships have peaks and valleys, it's abnormal to *live* in the valley! If you are, its wisdom to know the cavalry is not out the window…but in the mirror.

Question: Is it enjoy-*able* doing things *together*? (Literally meaning are we *"able* to enjoy*"* being with them?)
Or ~ do we just tolerate them to have something to do?
In other words, do we thrive…or strive to simply survive?
Sometimes, under the latter circumstances, the dance between the two becomes one of not letting go too soon versus not holding on too long before it becomes too late. In that case, I'd say a good friendship is arguably better than a bad marriage.
So if it's more enjoyable to do things alone, then setting the Phaser about 2 stops *past* stun can work wonders. And quickly.
Bzzzzt…..

Pay Attention...I'm Trying To Sing

Something powerful meets something wonderful.

Every soul that has ever lived has written the same book on a subject they are the expert on: "The Book of Me". Each and every book has the picture and name of the author on the cover and, if it intrigues us, we pick it up and begin to look it over. But take caution: the one's titled "It's *All* About Me" usually have only two very brief chapters:

1) "How You Can Make My Life More Convenient"
2) "Compassion & Grace – No Comprende"

Unfortunately, after purchasing the book and reading the forward, many just check the Cliff Notes version every now and then fully expecting that's adequate to actually follow the story. Alas, after doing this for years they wonder why they "just don't understand" the contents, much less the author!

But this is a *living* book and new pages are *written every day* filled with vital new details and the writing does not pause or take a break. So whether it gets reads it or not, the book will still march to the other end of our life. As such, its only usefulness lies in being read in order to actually get to know the author. This brings us to that niggling proximity vs. togetherness again.

You see, one can "own" a book - but simply never read it.

As mentioned elsewhere, I believe our actions and behavior are always by choice. So, if it becomes obvious day after day that the "reader" of my Book of Me consistently chooses to be uninvolved or a token grunt is what passes for conversation, I might have to wonder how much attention I am "worth". Or even the reverse, if I do it to them!

In my early years, I was quite affected by Thoreau's observation of "Most men live lives of quiet desperation and go to the grave *with the song still in them.*" I still feel this holds much truth, but it needs to be updated. I now think many of us live lives of *"noisy desperation"*. Given the amount of time we "spend" at work, in traffic, reading email, using the Internet, cell phones, Blackberrys, Blackjacks, TV and I-Pods, much of our free time (what's "free" time?!) is quickly gone - with those who are supposedly important to us, getting what's left over.

223

But consider this: About the only thing our technology has accomplished is to try and "keep us together" by allowing us to *be apart*. We have "advanced" to where we believe the illusion we can maintain real relationships by simply pushing buttons.

We've read all the necessary manuals except the one on how to be us. We're plugged into everything - except each other and Tweet, Text, Space & Face as though that would actually satisfy a flesh and blood heart's need for human connection.

So how weird is that? Do we feel "safer" that way?

Call me un-evolved, but because 90% of communication is *nonverbal*, I still prefer the actual *presence* of someone so I can see their eyes and hear their voice. Besides, no has yet to beat the oldest and best IM's going: A simple hug, kiss or smile. ☺

So instead of all this diversionary stuff, how many of us would rather be nurtured by someone who cares and actually *wants* to pay attention to us? Someone who looks in our eyes instead of at some type of screen when they speak and wants to know our song? And that's important, because "togetherness" is the result of deliberate attention and no words, cry or song is *ever* heard…unless someone actually takes the time to listen. (Have you ever noticed when we care about someone, we might lie awake hours thinking about what they said? And if we don't care, we fall asleep before they're even done talking?!)

But let's be honest, every one of us has heard the soft inner cry of "Pay attention to me!" at some time, no? (After my 12th surgery, I remember actually saying it verbally…at 3 A.M.!) And that cry is normal when it occurs as the exception rather than the rule. But some have heard this inner voice so much, they no longer recognize the warning it represents. The result? Deafness to the pleading message they are sending themselves.

But for some, love is spelled T-I-M-E (see "Love Lingo") and there *really* are those who want to read your "Book of Me" to know what happened to shape the author and to *hope* and dream about what could be next. And even though some of the pages will be dry and fragile and others will stick together and give way unwillingly, there are those who will patiently unfold and comprehend what is written and provide a safe sanctuary for it in their heart. And why? So they could hear our song and perhaps bravely share theirs.

Out of this purposeful interest comes *knowing* one another. And out of that comes...*connection*...which is where and when *something powerful meets something wonderful.* And out of connection comes...*Synergy!* All of which leaves us with a well fed and cared for soul with a *satisfying* sense of belonging.

So, I guess the bottom line we encounter on an ongoing basis is: "Am I *worth it* for you to *spend* your time paying attention to me?" (My doggies clearly think it is!) I know that sounds entirely self-centered...but really, what other *healthy* reason would we bring another into our lives if not to acknowledge their presence? Why would they even need to *be there* if it wasn't for that?! I mean, if we invite them into our life because we *want* them to be there, is it not reasonable for them to expect to be paid attention to?

And in doing so, we confirm each others value and worth, and what's *not* good about that? I'd bet virtually every one of us was first drawn to someone because they made us feel *really* good about ourselves when we were around them. In our natural desire to be understood by those we care about, we knew we were needed and our efforts appreciated. And listen, it's OK to want and enjoy that! Remember "Conspire to inspire"?

So if that's changed, what happened? And why?

And this applies not only in the home, but to our friends as well. Maybe the measure of someone's worth to us is really very simple to determine: How much time are we willing to *spend* on them...and them on us? Likewise, those who value *you* will seek you out. And those that don't, well, they probably won't.

Ouch again. This was a hard lesson for me to learn - and even harder to accept. But there's wisdom if that acceptance ends useless strife with another. There is also wisdom in discovering how much you know of your partner's own Life and Love map. If it fits on a postage stamp, that's a problem.

And about "singing your song" to another? Never ever regret at least trying – someday someone may truly listen...and we can all use the practice!

Remember while the brave do not live forever, the cautious rarely live at all.

Answer to question on p. 195: Bashful!

Regrets

~~~~~~~~

"Well done is better than well said." Ben Franklin

Paul Tournier once wrote "People spend their entire life indefinitely *preparing* to live."…they just never get around to actually doing it. For some of us that simply means that after great thought, "We conclude that what we should do with our life is to figure out what we should do with our life."

But listen, life's *not* waiting around the corner. It's staring us in the face right now and at every moment it's the dynamic expression of who you are. So if you are still waiting to "live" your life, do you ever wonder if you'll regret the wait? I have.

I can tell you this: Time can temper the regrets we had for things we *did*, but it does not lessen the sting of the regrets over what we did *not* do…and wish we had. Because of this, the words "coulda, shoulda and woulda" don't compute all that well for me. But in truth, no one likes regrets, especially when it's too late. And most definitely when they've replaced their dreams.

Of the many who told me they did have regrets, it was never about work, where to live etc., but of the heart when it was not acknowledged or shared and when dreams were not pursued. *It was about not taking a chance when they had the chance.* Many now have the best of everything and deny themselves nothing in the material…and still find themselves empty inside and emotionally divorced from those "closest" to them. They are gorged on all they want, starved for what they need and unfulfilled for lack of real heart food. But this food also has to be available from whom you are with, it is not a one-way street - and though it is a *need* for everyone, some fear intimacy and others are so intensely private, they're incapable of giving it.

As I mentioned before, the greatest number of problems in life (including many health related) will involve some kind of relationship with other people. And while the problems can appear complicated, the solutions are often quite simple…and we usually know what they are, but are hesitant to act on them.

But if "The truth will set you free", won't error bind you? Sure will. And this error makes for a bad curve on the road to Heart Mountain where the same "accidents" always occur.

226

Why? Because if there's an ongoing problem in a relationship, then *there's always a "system" in place to support it.* And that's a fact...and ignoring the facts doesn't change the facts.

But instead of planning a better road, or taking a new one altogether, we often quietly just build more hospitals at the curve and check ourselves in until the emotional bruises fade again for a while. And then we head for the same old road once again.

Soren Kierkegaard's advice was to "Define life backwards and live it forwards". I see this as meaning to evaluate our strengths and weaknesses and then use or correct them as needed with a plan to move forward. Consider this: Is it not odd that none of us would even think about going on a two week vacation without some serious planning? Yet beyond the wedding, we frequently mortgage away our entire life to someone without any real plan whatsoever! And if we don't know what *we want our life to look and feel like*, how will we know what our destination is - or more importantly, how to move towards it?

So, in my eternally humble opinion, the best place to start is by being open with the person sitting across the table. Decide if we want to cherish or control them. Why? *Because we can't – or don't - love those we want to control.* If we want to control them, then by default we also judge them because we have decided we know what is best for them. At that point we no longer have a partner, but a parent-child relationship. So acknowledge what your heart really needs, admit what it's missing and communicate that part of you. If they ask you

"What's wrong?" and there *is* something wrong, don't say "I'm fine", "Nothing" or "It doesn't matter"– which are simply "lies of omission" and an attempt to convince yourself you're not really feeling what you're feeling. And like the box says on p. 166, what sense is there in bringing someone onto the stage of our lives "forever" and then only peeking out at them from behind the curtain - while hiding the truth of ourselves as though it had no value? But if the gift of our self and Life-*Time* goes to only one person, shouldn't it be to someone who *really* wants and appreciates it?! So while there's never a need to be "brutally honest", meaning we use "truth" to purposely hurt another - still:

You do have the right to be you!
And you *have* to be you.
Everyone else is taken!

Give your feelings a voice and tell others what they *need* to know and not what you think they want to hear. To do less is not honoring to you, to them or the relationship. And understand it's OK to ask for what you want and to say how you'd like to be treated. What's not OK is to expect others to be clairvoyant.

Nevertheless, if this sounds familiar, know we can *choose* to believe a better truth! Let's not discover too late there *really was* a wonderful mountain to climb but all we did was go around it but never up. Or that we only "prepared" for life, but never lived it. Remember, pleasure is not just the absence of pain but the addition of joy! So if you need to, start by being real with someone - you. Even if it begins with just an honest, but good healthy cry. Listen, none of us would buy a house to live in without first getting an honest appraisal of its value. Should we not do likewise for the life we live in? Think about it. *You've spent your entire life to be where and who you are right now.* Was it worth it? Have you had "The time of your life"? When your life is completed, will you have had a *complete* life?

If not, perhaps it's time to question your perceptions of the "facts" and start to live life like you mean it. Life is, after all, about choices...and maybe it's time for a new one, like Plan B?

In the classic book "A Room with a View" by E.M. Forster, a main character, Lucy, isolated her heart by denying her feelings and what she knew to be true. The end result?

"She gave up trying to understand herself, and joined the vast armies of the benighted, who follow neither the heart nor the brain, and march to their destiny by catch-words. The armies are full of pleasant and pious folk. But they have yielded to the only enemy that matters - the enemy within. They have sinned against passion and truth, and vain will be their strife after virtue."

So if you're in a relationship and don't find yourself inspired to be a "better version of you" and if you aren't the Prez of each other's fan club, frankly maybe it's time to ask yourself "Is this what I want?" And if not, see what you can do about it.

Yogi Berra once quipped "In theory, there is no difference between theory and practice. In practice, there is."

So except for the ones where you're naked in public, I take that to mean we should be willing to fight for our dreams...or stop being sad or angry about not having them.

This then brings us very nicely to the subject of loyalty for which I'll offer a profoundly trite analogy: Our hearts are like little ships sailing out there on the "Ocean of Life" looking for the security of a safe and loyal harbor to call home. In doing so, we might find a safe haven - or - we might just dock somewhere out of habit or *misplaced* loyalty. And that kind of port might not necessarily deserve our ship being there.

In doing so, some will dock without the proper skills, get everyone tangled in their ropes and leave them hanging helplessly in awkward positions. Others come in far too quickly, crash into the dock and damage it and the ship. And yet others will *temporarily* flee to any port in a storm just so they are not out on the ocean all alone.

And when the storm is gone? So are they.

So, why do we do it? I'll suggest it's sometimes less loyalty and strength and more pride and stubbornness to prevent us from feeling stupid. See, if we give our loyalty to someone who we know *really* doesn't deserve it, we also know that's not very smart. However, the longer this goes on, the more difficult it is to admit it *is* going on...even to ourselves. (This I know too well firsthand and it's *not* a good way to "spend" time!)

It's sort of like the gal who has long hair and wants to cut it, but only after she thinks about it. In doing so, it grows even longer which makes her want to think it about some more. And on it goes until it's so long she trips over it, it wraps around her neck, strangles her and she keels over bug-eyed. (You didn't know all of that would happen, did you?).

But the irony is that in our attempt to not *look* stupid, we *become* stupider as we martyr on hoping to see the Wiz at Oz who will make all our fantasies come true.

I also think in a relationship, it's foolish to be "loyal" to someone we don't respect. Respect is *the* cornerstone of love and if we don't respect them, then loving them is questionable, so who are we actually being loyal to?

So while loyalty can be a wonderful and comforting state of mind, maybe it's a good idea to never let it become synonymous with emotional and intellectual numbness. Remember, *trust is earned* and not all ports provide an equally safe haven.

And not all ships have safe captains.

Practical Affairs

~~~~~~~~~

Rut, grave or both?

Unfortunately, it's not all that uncommon that we can find ourselves in a relationship that provides little or none of the comfort and heart food we need and where even the small "thank you" is gone. When that happens, and because food *has* to come from somewhere, it's almost natural to try and use our job, things or other people as a substitute for fulfillment.

If our level of need has gotten to this point, it's a pretty good bet our primary relationship has become mostly a "Practical Affair" that runs more on inertia - and less on real desire or interest. We maintain separate parallel lives in the same home with little or no emotional connection.

(Is this where roommates get off the train and go to live?)

When this has become our situation, "devotion" to a relationship may actually be just a comfortable framework for us to be devoted to ourselves in our quest for fulfillment elsewhere. The domino effect that follows can lead us to value others in proportion to how well we think they can meet our needs. Eventually, all of this can evolve into just a "support system" for us to use in our "real" life outside the relationship.

We can often manifest this by expending a lot more energy and effort researching what car to buy or on home improvements than we do on each other. We become far more courageous and generous with our credit cards than we do with our hearts and words. Who knows, but maybe at this stage we need a new kind of "plastic surgery": Cutting up the credit cards to help us finally learn that the best things in life...are, well, not things!

And things should never replace people.

In any case, beware. What may appear to be a "comfy routine" may be just a rut in disguise and a rut can be a grave in disguise with the only difference being the length and the depth. Graves are *not for the living* and one stagnant day dissolving into another without distinction makes for few memories.

And very little heart food.

And without food, things die.

And dead things do belong in graves.

May I Serve You?

~~~~~~~

We are what we do.

Now, as opposed to having a dead roomie that needs burying, would we rather live for a love worth dying for? And is there a "One" more suitable for us than anyone else? You know, a singular "soul-mate" we're destined to be with?

Perhaps. But then, what's "destiny"? Is it simply the *result* of the selections we make in life? I'd like to think so because that makes it more choice than chance! If so, this would include who we put on, or push off, the stage of our lives.

But could The One simply be who we have the "3 Good C's" of *ongoing* Comfort, Chemistry and Commitment with? That we admire and look forward to *spending* time with even if it's doing nothing but hanging out? Is it whoever inspires us to be better and is a *catalyst* for lifting our heart and stimulating our mind? That we can be playful and flirt with? Someone we can *depend* on as a soft place to fall and whose life is as important as ours? And one we can live without…but don't want to?

All which lasts beyond the "Bait & Switch" dating scene?

If so, I'd say they *are* our hearts "always and forever"!

And if all of this is *not* present, why are the *people* involved present? So be wise, "think back and look forward" when choosing The One. Remember, your choice will also affect the destiny of others. (Newsflash: brain MRI's now prove "chemistry" *can last a lifetime!*)

But even if we are with the "right" One and even though the laundry and dishes still need to be done, the garbage taken out, leaves raked and a zillion other things, Life really can be more than just a series of "forgettable moments". Why? Because our thinking *actively* changes to "How can I make life better, more interesting, fun, safer and comfortable for this person? How can I move some of the stones out from their path?" And then *doing* just that because we *want* to as opposed to have to. Remember, love *is* "Show & Tell". Again, Duty vs. Desire.

And believe it or not, it's satisfying to do just that. When this heart change occurs from the inside out because we truly value and need another, even a trip to Target' can feel like a date.

But while one can give without loving, one cannot love without giving. It's axiomatic and will express itself not only in words, but in deeds. *That's its proof of existence*...and in doing so, it reminds *you* of *their* worth. Anything less is just that – less! And remember, words are cheap. We are what we *do* far more than who we say we are. Maybe Mae West said it best:

"An ounce of performance is worth pounds of promises." And it's rarely a matter of am I *able* to do it, but am I *willing* to?

So, if we desire the other person and *want* to make heart food, here are a few ideas - most of which cost only time ~

Men: Be a sight for sore eyes and not one that makes her eyes sore. Turn off your PC or TV and surprise her with a dinner you made yourself. (Even if it's crap, you'll have a good laugh and your efforts will still be appreciated!) Send a handmade card that thanks her for no reason and *talk of things that matter to the heart* instead of just things that need to be done. Have chocolate strawberries and champagne on a Tuesday, get a honeymoon suite for a weekend or spend a rainy Sunday afternoon in bed and catch up on each other's life. Camp out in the backyard, give her a 5 minute foot massage (hands and arms if she types all day!) Pull out chairs, help with her coat, open doors for her and now and then, be a Prince and kiss her hand so she feels like a Princess. Just do things that show her she has worth to you.

Like putting the toilet seat down.

Ladies: Hold his hand like you mean it, tell him about the things he does well, how much you appreciate his efforts and *why he is your hero*. (A man will move a mountain with a teaspoon for a woman who believes in him!) In a restaurant, butter his bread and if you have the mind to, play footsie under the table. Snuggle up to him *while* watching TV. If he has hair, run your fingers through it. Find a "signature scent" that reminds him of you no matter where he encounters it and you, too, will always be snifficant. Plan a date and give him a *real* kiss when he comes in the door. And remember – sometimes being a bit "bad" can be *really* good. ☺ (A guy with a woman like this doesn't get "lucky". He *is* lucky!)

Just make heart food...and *Bookmarks*...and do it often. Because if you don't...out of nothing, comes nothing.

Loving another is a type of illogical math whereby the catalyst of two people creates the formula of $1 + 1 = 3$. This is the synergistic concept of "The whole is greater than the sum of the parts" and when you combine them you get a result that neither is capable of individually: the creation of "Life" for both.

But truly, the point is simple: *If we say we value someone, then let's do things that prove it to them...and to us!*

Because if they're not worth "spending" the time and thought on, what does that say about how "special" they really are? Remember, love is something we *do* for another and not for our self. And like truth, it's an action word so that when all is said and done, there *should be less said and more done.*

So, am I saying we have to memorialize "Gold Moments" every day? Of course not. Sometimes just hanging out watching TV – or just being quiet - may be the perfect way to "spend" that moment. But I think the danger is when we "fall out of touch" on the daily basis and then - just assume we can make up for it with "special" times like vacations, anniversaries and birthdays.

But honestly, wouldn't a Bronze Moment maybe every few days be kinda nice? Would it *not* feel good if for no particular reason someone held you, looked into your eyes and simply said "I *really* appreciate you"? Or took the time to notice and praise something you did? That's all - a touch of implied trust, a simple word of encouragement. I mean, how hard is that? But out of it, we get what we all want: Heart Food! (Up for an experiment? Unplug all the TV's for one week. I promise you'll learn a lot about your relationship.)

Now while I'm easy to please, wouldn't these little niceties add sweetness to any relationship when done out of gratitude for another? If so, then make this the *new* "normal"!☺☺

Perhaps Springsteen summed up these last few pages very simply in five words: "*Everybody* has a hungry heart."

Truthfully, I can't help but feel to make life's journey without this, to not surrender and be "swept away" by someone's love, to not hear the song of another and to only feel "liked a lot" instead of deeply loved and cherished, is to not have lived.

So, if you're somewhere and your heart's not in it, why is your body? Because ultimately, "playing it safe" and saying none of this matters will provide none of the safety or satisfaction we so dearly desire and need. What it will give us is year after year of lost time in ritual mediocrity and living on crumbs while the nearby real banquet goes unnoticed and untouched. And once again, as Ben Franklin noted

"A house is not a home unless it contains food *and fire for the mind* as well as the body." Amen Brother Ben.

Love Lingo

~~~~~~~~

Becoming bi-lingual

It's been said there are five "Love Languages" by which we express - and are most likely to understand love. They are (in no order): Quality Time, Service, Touch, Affirmation and Gifts. Most of us will respond to several forms, but usually one will be primary. As an illustration, if your method of showing love is by "service", then you might work on someone's home or car or make a meal for them. If it is gifts, you will find buying them thoughtful things easy to do. (Don't confuse this with "buying off" someone as a substitute for time and attention!) If your manner is touch, then you will enjoy giving or getting a simple caress, massage or anything that would please them. (Concerning this "language", I also believe there can be deep connection and healing in the human touch. Perhaps that's why we intuitively hold another in love, place our hands over where we hurt and hug total strangers in a crisis. Maybe it's also why God made Chiropractors?)

But while it's useful to know *your* method of expression, it's just as important to be "bilingual" and know your partner's primary style. This is because that is the form they can most easily interpret and accept what you do as an act of love. As an example, if both peoples primary style is touch, then it's almost a virtual lock to be a great combination. This is because they will very naturally do what is most appreciated, fulfilling and easily understood by the other as loving. For these folks, the simple act of holding their hand, a backrub or being enfolded in each others arms means they are connected to the heart that is connected to the arms holding them.

I remember someone who, when we were driving, would turn just slightly in her seat to more directly face me, which was "affirmation". She'd then put one arm through mine and rest her other hand on it (touch). These tiny subtle gestures of desire and caring filled me up beyond words as she pulled me safely into our own little world. And at that point? We were "together".

So, is it time to learn a new language?

Better yet, learn two: Yours *and* Theirs.

I'm So Blue

R emember me saying we never know when our time will run out? Here's my latest reminder. Recently I went to the ER for the possible diagnosis of a kidney stone which truly came on like a bolt out of the blue.

That evening, in the span of 20 minutes I went from feeling fine to completely frenzied with pain. At the hospital they attempted to subdue the pain with morphine, which gave no relief. The subsequent CT scan for the suspect stone was negative but the pain definitely wasn't, so into my IV port went another shot of the stuff. Even so, I was still writhing in agony so they next gave me an injection of Dilaudid, which is much stronger than morphine. And then very quickly...helplessly and silently off to "sleep" I went. Moments later a napping Janie opened her eyes just as I was changing my color palette from autumn to winter during my very first up close and personal Code Blue.

What she saw made her gasp: Purple face, gray lips and no breathing which made her run out in the hall yelling

"He needs help!" which got very little response. I mean, everyone in the ER needs help, right? But changing her words to

"He's NOT breathing!!" was a different story and 3 doctors, 3 nurses and 2 EMTs came rushing in with a crash cart. The next thing she heard through the pulled curtain was

"I can't find a pulse!" Thankfully, an injection of Narcan and oxygen reversed the overdose and brought me back to the here and now where I awoke to 8 people loudly shouting my name, slapping my body and making a lot of commotion in general to my complete bewilderment. I had just been resurrected...and for only $5,009.90.

The nurse later confessed that as I was not on monitoring equipment and had I not asked for someone to be in the room with me, they simply would have found me dead in the bed.

Huh. The life-lesson learned? *Never* go to the ER alone!

And about the "Other Side"? Ask me sometime. (I will tell you there is no pain there.)

Now I ask myself, were all the "saving" events coincidental, or was it all simply the grace, or plan, of God? Again.

Luckily I had no dain bramage - but as I now have enough emergency room ID bands to wallpaper my bathroom, it makes me ponder two things:

How many "lives" *do* I have left?

And while I was "gone"...did I *spend* any of my "Life-*Time*"?

Dream On

~~~~~~~~~~

Time to wake up and smell the woohoo.

Because someone, somewhere has a voodoo doll of the body I live in with enough pins in it to resemble a porcupine, I hurt all the time. This unrelenting dark spot in my life has taught me a thing or two because like stars piercing the night sky, finding the contrasting bright places in life is now a full time adventure. The unexpected blessing of the pain is not only is it constant proof I'm still alive, but it makes me want to dwell my attention more on others and to think about what really "gets me through the day". Is it work, TV, food or best of all, "spending" my Life-*Time* on those I want to be with?

This is coupled with a profound gratitude for those who have truly touched my life and *spent* their time with, and on me. Some of us have literally risked our lives for one another. Others have shown me a breathtaking grace and beauty just by their presence and by *emotionally* risking themselves with me. In doing so, they added a wonderful richness and made it so very clear that it takes a *willing* union of two to make a bonding of souls. These folks also taught me that "things" are only an imitation of real life and that without regular heart food and an occasionally genuine "Woohoo!", life can be Life-less.

And yes, I know some will read this, yawn and move unmoved to the next "moment" of their life as they step back on the merry-go-round that stops at Friday.

And that's OK...for them.

But the poet Robert Browning wrote "A man's reach *should* exceed his grasp, or what is Heaven for?" The heart food and Synergy between people I have described *can be* a part of Heaven...right here on earth. Now, the question is, do we desire it badly enough that we'll reach for it and, accept it when found?

In the movie Shadowlands, when C.S. Lewis finally learned about love, he said "We love, so we know we are not alone." I would say "We love so as *to be known*." Loneliness is banished by belonging and we belong when we are known.

And we all know this - we really do. And isn't it what we truly want...and isn't it what our heart needs?

Within this paradigm I have discovered the two kinds of people in my life - those that are in my life...and those that *add Life* to my life. And that without the giving and getting of heart food, relationships can easily become just a "Practical Affair" that uses another as a crutch to get me through my Life-*Time*.

I also now know the only place we truly live is in the hearts of others - both while we're alive and after we are gone. And the only love we get to keep ~ is the love we give away. I've learned that every real Love begins with a smile, grows with a kiss, and always ends with a tear. Also there really is a difference in "loving" someone...and being *in love* with them. One takes little thought and effort while the other is an extraordinary place where fire in the heart lives side by side with peace of mind as we intentionally *choose* to be kind, gracious and generous to another. It's where our purpose includes having someone else's life benefit by our presence.

A profoundly simple instance of this was when someone did something very nice for me that took quite a bit of extra effort. When I responded

"Thank you! But you didn't *have* to do that." she replied

"That's *why* I did it." Enough said, no?

Let us learn to be demonstrably grateful to the kindness others show us and make amends where needed in our personal "You-niverse". It'll help us function better in the bigger one.

Now it's your turn to decide which path is more attractive, satisfying and has the most value to you. And choose wisely for the simple reason we all *hope* our dreams come true and we all *need* heart food to feed that hope.

And if you're already truly honestly content and happy – then I think that is simply wonderful. You are blessed.

But if you are not, it may be time to ask "Do I *like* my life?" If you don't, then understand *you* are the one in control of it and that *things won't change unless you change things* - which includes your thinking. So if you want to do that, don't wait too long because there's no guarantee whatsoever you'll be here 5 years or even 5 hours from now. My Code Blue was another very rude – *and entirely unexpected* - reminder of that. (Everyone wants to go to Heaven, but who wants to go right *now*?!) Remember...like it or not, life is an hourglass of time that's being spent constantly.

Tickety-tock and all that.

And while it's one thing when time is stolen from us, it's inexcusable if we let our dreams get stolen as well. But perhaps just as bad? Carrying an elephant around in our head until it ultimately sits on our headstone. And the worst saved for last? Having our final thoughts be "Is that all there is?"

Gus soldiered wearily like a silent apparition out of the driving snowstorm. With the face of a red wolf and the heart of a lion, he was soaking wet, shivering and starving. Abandoned by his owners two weeks before I spotted him, he had lung damage, heart and intestinal worms, a broken tooth, one ragged ear, was deaf and eyes dull with cataracts. He couldn't bark and his legs buckled from arthritis when he tried to walk. His thick matted coat had a stench so awful he seemed ashamed by it and his head was drooped in despair. We put him in the car and directly into a hot bath and began the process of healing and loving this severely neglected and broken 10 year old dog.

In taking up residence, he first sought refuge in a corner of the dining room, out of the way and to him, invisible. With a soft bed, healthy food and attention, he moved to where he could peek in the kitchen, and from there, one evening to the TV room where he lay with Hershey and Sophie. He was visibly changed after his professional grooming where, fresh and clean and no longer embarrassed by his odor, he sat like a Little King! Unable to play Frisbee, Sophie would bring him one as he lay in the grass and watched the other dogs run. After 2 months of being sheltered, held and loved, late one night he softly limped into the bedroom and lay at the foot of the bed, at last accepting his acceptance. His eyes had brightened, his tail was wagging.

Gus may have had heart worms, but he also wormed his way completely into our hearts without ever making a sound. With silent nuzzles, thankful eyes and a gentle nobility, he knew he was part of a family that loved and wouldn't betray him. His contentment lay in simply being near enough to watch others and having his special bedtime cookie. After $1,000 in vet bills over 3 months, it seemed his problems were under control when in the middle of the night he had to be rushed for care of abdominal bloat, a quickly lethal condition. After treatment, he experienced yet another event one week later where the new x-rays and a very high fever revealed a much worse problem. In great pain, and barely able to move, he looked up silently from the table.

Terribly weakened, his trusting eyes found mine and told me his lion heart could fight no longer - and seemed to whisper

"Please Dad, love me enough to do the hard thing."

And once again in my life, real love ended in tears.

As I write, I am still wet with sweat and early morning rain from digging. His grave is a fresh open and deeply aching wound across my heart. He had fought the good fight, but in the end, there was too much to fight against. And I'm sad for myself for not having him here any longer to love and hold. But I'm sadder yet that he is no longer here to feel loved. He so deserved more time. In coming from the worst he brought out our best and was a living example of the transforming power of Hope and Love. For a time that was all too brief, we had *given each other Life*.

In one way or another, we are all Gus. *We love to be loved.* Despite our station in life and imperfections, we all need others to help us make it through. And we all need the acceptance that makes it safe to invest our hearts and time in each other's life. Did Gus sense his Life-*Time* was near the end? I don't know. But he sure rolled in and soaked up every drop of love he got! And I was blessed to witness how deep and wonderful the change loving kindness can bring to a heart - even a lion's.

Likewise, human hearts also beg to be known and accepted. For this reason we should never let the gift of Life-*Time* pass us by because our heart is stuck somewhere it doesn't want to be. Much like a dog locked in a crate all day that never *gets* to be, *Hearts make terrible captives when held prisoner of bad choices.* Long ago Shakespeare said "To thine own self be true" and part of that truth is believing in the best we can be, that we have a right to be here and there's something important for all of us to do. To me, that means creating the kind of self you really want to be and then let others discover the wonder of you.

Because we were fashioned with the ability to dream and the need to connect on a level that matters, Life can, and should be, joyful and fulfilling. It's our choice to pursue that - or - to settle for less and perhaps live in a secret world where no one is truly allowed to know us. One of these will leave the legacy of our life in the hearts and lives that were changed because we touched them – while the other may be only a few pictures stuffed in a drawer somewhere never to be seen or remembered.

So, I ask, can we ever *really* be "too busy" for others?

If so - or if our life is not satisfying - and we *choose* to argue our limitations, understand they will be ours for a lifetime, and therefore, become our destiny.

Gus had no choice. *You do. I do.*

None of us can change our history, but we *can* determine if our habits will be cobwebs...or cables and if the time has come to consider a Plan B. And that's important because what we are doing right *now* is helping to form what tomorrow will be - and tomorrow is where your dreams live. And because that's where that river of time is taking you, it's where you're *going* to live! So I guess the question is, are we making our future hopes meaningful today by making *today* meaningful?

I am confident that none of us would ever tell those we care about not to follow their dreams. Shall we tell ourselves any less? If so, then kiss them goodbye. If not, then plan your life so it converges with your dreams and kiss them *Hello!*

And the way to make dreams come true?

Wake up and smell the...

But of course.

The Forward

~~~~~~~~

Life is not a wheel. And you're not a hamster.

So what's this thing called "Life-*Time*" all about? Well, I gave my best shot at defining part of it, but if none of this makes sense, well, my bad! But here's Twain's opinion:

"It's no wonder that truth is stranger than fiction. Fiction has to make sense."

And here's what I think: It's not just about me or enjoying myself as much as possible, having the "best of everything" or learning how to perfect my "persona". It's definitely not about just making it to another Friday so I can do it all over again next week and next year and keep telling myself "*Someday I'll.......*"

So what is it?

For me it distills down to this: Time and Relationships - and how I invest one into the other while I Bookmark life not with minutes, but with *Moments*. It's cultivating an awareness of how and with whom I spend my time and knowing the only thing better than a dream fulfilled, is sharing one. It means having something or someone in my life to be hopeful and passionate about and *allowing* myself to need others – even if it's just a hug. And it's trying to know who will leave me breathless, as opposed to speechless before I invite them into my heart. It's also about the endless possibilities to be found by diving deeper into life, myself and others and knowing the "finer things" should not replace the *finest* things, which come from meaningful connection with others and with God.

And I've learned we all need someone to believe in us. That we bless others not by thoughts, but by word and deed and by helping to bring out the best in them and offering a "place of grace", I bring out the best in myself. I also discovered that even with the best of intentions I can make the stupidest of decisions that can alter my entire life. Because of this, I need to be willing to evaluate things as they really are to see if my old decisions are obsolete and simply don't work anymore. And if I don't like the answers, realize I can choose to change them. Finally, it's realizing that just like this book, I really am the author of my own script and have the most to say as to how each day is written and what life-roads I'll take.

241

So, am I on a mission to change the world? Nah. Just me. Do I *really* believe all that stuff about passion and romance? Yes, I do – because I've seen it work. Do I do everything good I wrote about? No, but as a "passionate pragmatist", it's a goal - and I'm trying! And I think there's more honor in trying and failing...then not trying at all. Do I have all the answers? Again, a large "No." Truth is, I'm still wrestling with just *understanding* some of the questions.

But where I once defined life by my productivity, in a mid-life epiphany, I did something I simply never thought to do: *I defined what Love means to me.* And that was good.

In doing so, I had heard my own heart's song.

Some folks have inquired as to what I am up to these days having abandoned my earlier self-destructive tendencies. Well, I am truly a changed man. Life is leisurely. I read more in quiet corners with a hot cup of green tea in an ergonomically correct chair using CF lighting. My PC car of choice is a beige Prius and aviation has flown from my blood. I no longer seek bends in the river to look around, peaks to climb, canyons to descend or clouds to dance upon and have assimilated far more into the mainstream of guy stuff. I can even sit and watch endless hours of football and now know that Joe Klamath is the forward center on third base for the dolphin-free Miami Tuna's.

Do what?!

C'mon- you didn't expect me to change *that* much, did you?! OK, here's some of the deal: I remain in practice part time doing my best to take care of my extended "family" of truly wonderful people. Some Plastic Brain stuff is studying new surgeries and treatments for my Peer Review business, reading, writing, learning to type, designing an airplane and making cars handle better. Down the road may be building a 0-60 in 3.5 seconds Factory 5 GTM car. And yes, occasionally I still do stuff others would consider "risky", but without the compelling agenda I once had to fill an empty place. I now enjoy them as the experience they are without having to push myself to the brink of disaster and I can find *some* adventure just driving to the store. (I even enjoy riding the buggies through the lot when I get there.) As to my faith, it can still be an enigma, but I *know* God has His eye on me and as a result, a judgmentally dreadful seriousity has been retired for a more graciously joyful serenity.

Also, as a result of this book I've become much more of a "word watcher" and try to choose them carefully as opposed to just throwing something out there to make noise. And I listen more. But the root of the root is truly savoring the time *spent* being with those who are important to me while learning to leave my self-sufficiency behind. And when this is done with deliberate intention, I can be joyful with them, or if needed... share their difficult times. Finally, I deliberately seek the "abundant Life" of life to be found in life – and that's fun because now I'm more aware of where and with whom I find it.

And best of all? Just like Gus, I'm learning to roll in it.

This book began with the flashback of my heart being stopped in the Emory emergency room and then my Mom giving life to me. Decades later (and a life that could have easily been several seasons of "House" episodes) without a shred of control on my part, we have come full circle with my heart stopping again in a Code Blue and shortly after, my Mom's life ending.

It was not long ago I watched her hold her newborn great grandchild with a loving kindness and the entire cycle of life opened itself to me in an instant. Charlotte, the icon of innocence and totally devoid of any concept of time or worry, sparkled with smooth skin and bright eyes full of hope and promise. And I saw Mom, then at 90 and worn by the world and years, struggling with the fact of the all too few days she had left while she had the baby to live for. Time had recently become very dear to her and she did not know she had only a few short months left. In that moment, I realized we all fall somewhere on the spectrum of awareness as to how we value our Life-*Time*. From unconcerned - to counting days. As I drove away and saw her waving in the mirror, somehow I knew it was the last time I'd see her alive and finally comprehended Kierkegaard saying "Life can only be understood backward, but it must be lived forward." Indeed.

I now have The Ig's ring she wore the hour she went home.

And my name? It was not until the very last moment of editing that I discovered Gary is from the German word "Gar" for spear. This is derived from the Welsh name "Gareth"...who was considered one of the gentlest, yet finest fighters of King Arthur's Knights. I kinda like that. I bet he would have protected my 5th grade friend, too.

And yet another circle was completed.

Writing all of this has been a blessing for me as it has drawn together strings of my life I never even knew existed. But it was difficult as well and I find myself a bit embarrassed about time spent poorly in spite of all my compelling "lessons" and sad over some friendships lost along the way…I ask their forgiveness if I was the cause. And I still struggle with some messy parts of my own life as I consider what needs to be done. But *now* there's an urgency that before was somehow hidden in the noise of life. And it's an urgency that, lately, is hard to ignore because the song inside is singing louder than the noise outside.

And it's a song of Hope.

I will also confess its scary letting these pages go out into the world. But sometimes you just have to put yourself out there and let the decision be made by time and others. And then learn another lesson in trust, faith and quite possibly, humility.

What I *do* know is Life is a tapestry of threads that are both strong and enduring, faulty and weak and, if we're lucky, a few strands woven in that are *absolutely* Golden …all of which I have shared with you. I do hope you've gotten at least some enjoyment, a smile and perhaps even a mote of inspiration about Life-*Time* from my journey. But above all, let's never get so busy with Life that we forget to live it - because when all is said and done, it's not so much how life treats us, but how well we are treating our life. And a big part of that is finding comfort and heart food in what we can direct:

The Time we Spend with others ~

Thank you for *spending* some of your Life-*Time* with me.

Now, go find your Golden Threads that believe in you and thank them for their value in your life.

Then, go add another chapter to your own "Book of Me"!

Because truly, the richness of the human experience ~ *your Life* ~ is as deep and rewarding as you choose it to be and that seems to happen best when we are true to ourselves.

As for me, and 2 years after I began penning this odyssey, I'm still on that river of time taking me towards the horizon… and there's still that wide-eyed little boy wondering what's around the next bend. Where, just maybe, Gus will be sitting on the shore, waiting. Because ya' know…*there is always that.*

Huh.

Post Script

After 6 months of preparation and 2 weeks before departure, I went to bed feeling near perfect. I awoke at 4 A.M. barely able to move with a badly herniated disc in my lower back. I finally had what I joked to patients about for years: A Sleep Injury.

The trip that was planned – and then postponed for 5 more months - was one final and very difficult push into Grand Canyon via the Grandview Trail with the objective of exploring one of the Canyon's few "accessible" caves in Horseshoe Mesa. Upon arrival, we discovered the trail – or what's left of it – was extremely primitive and steep with some 4 foot wide sections consisting of logs and rocks jammed into the sheer canyon walls and 300 foot drops to the side. It was almost inconceivable, and brutally cruel, how mules were forced to haul heavy loads of copper ore out of the canyon on this crude and dangerous trail from the mines miles below.

But before descending, and while poised at the rim, I once again peered off into the mists of infinity. At my feet was that incomparable, indescribable and achingly beautiful gulf that forever overruns all my senses. It was at that moment I made peace that I will never fully comprehend its effect on me.

What I did understand was that standing there at the edge of the world was like standing at the edge of my Life. I had *chosen* the best views I could find which also meant risking the heat and the cliffs, wind and the cold, sun and the lightning. Like life, I could have tried to see it from behind the insulated and framed limitations of a window, through the tiny keyhole of a locked door or had other people tell me about it. It was all my choice.

After hours of daunting descent including over and around rock slides, we got to the point where we could see the cave opening one mile away in the huge curving westward arc of the sheer canyon wall. The problem, however, was that mile was line of sight and the actual walk was far longer time and distance wise. But we had agreed on a turnaround time no matter how close we were to our goal. And that time was now. Disappointed, back up the impossible 115 year old trail we went.

The next day's effort was curtailed by 50 mph winds sweeping through the canyon that had come up in the night. Walking on the trails was like moving through a sandblaster. Worse yet, the next morning, between the four of us we had a migraine, food poisoning and a heart arrhythmia – and the temperature had gone below 30 degrees during the night.

None of us had the energy or heart to try the trail again.

But in that quiet, still, freezing dawn, I could swear I almost heard the Canyon itself exhale a great breath and softly whisper to me

"It's OK. You can go home now. You know me...and now you know yourself."

And I did. I accepted I will not attain all of my dreams and goals. But even so, I found a peace and comfort knowing it really is alright to pursue what has worth to me. So what now? Well, I'm not completely sure - but I do think the last part of me to get old is going to be my Heart. And I *really* like that.

How about you?

About the guy above

Gary Polizzotto, D.C. received his B.A. in Literature from Bloomfield College in New Jersey. He then made a deliberate southbound exodus from Soprano-land to Atlanta where he graduated Life Chiropractic College in 1979. While in the South, he quickly realized this was where he was *supposed* to have been born and decided to stay to make up for lost time. (Elvis's "American Trilogy" still makes him misty.) In wanting to hear as many of Life's whispers as possible, he resolved to make his journey through the years not only with just "good intentions", but also with the least amount of regrets.

So instead of taking the fast, flat, featureless interstates of life, he chose the winding back roads of the heart and soul where he came too close to dying way too many times and met countless truly wonderful and interesting people. The result of this was to have a few observations on Life itself - one of which was that you don't have to just "live and learn".

You can learn to Live.

And that's what this book is all about.